PORTRAIT OF YORK

Also by Ronald Willis

THE LIVING PAST: YORK CASTLE MUSEUM

NONCONFORMIST CHAPELS OF YORK 1693–1840

YORKSHIRE'S HISTORIC BUILDINGS

YORK AS IT WAS

YORK PAST AND PRESENT (with Thelma Willis)

Portrait of
YORK

RONALD WILLIS

Photography by
THELMA WILLIS

ROBERT HALE · LONDON

© Ronald Willis 1972
First published in Great Britain 1972
Second edition 1977

ISBN 0 7091 5912 9

Robert Hale Limited
Clerkenwell House
Clerkenwell Green
London EC1R oHT

Printed in Great Britain by
Lowe and Brydone Printers Limited, Thetford, Norfolk

CONTENTS

ILLUSTRATIONS

ACKNOWLEDGEMENTS

Help and inspiration during not only the writing of this book but throughout many years of discovering the delights of the City of York, have come from individual sources, but I am especially indebted to: O. S. Tomlinson, F.L.A., Assistant County Librarian, York and Selby Division; Maurice Smith, A.L.A., Principal Reference Librarian, York and Selby Division, and his staff; Dr E. A. Gee, M.A., D.Phil., F.S.A., senior investigator, York Office, Royal Commission on Historical Monuments; and Robert Patterson, B.Sc., F.M.A., retired curator, York Castle Museum.

Above all, I should like to thank my wife Thelma for her unfailing encouragement and the skill with which she has illustrated my words.

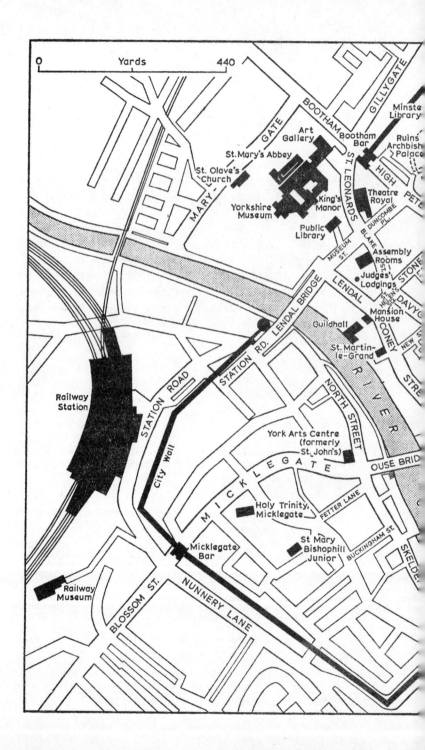

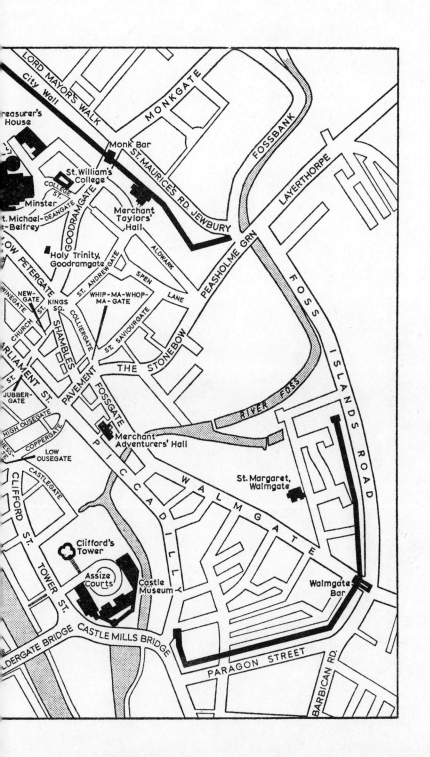

To THELMA
for everything

INTRODUCTION

To keep York Minster, one of the greatest Gothic buildings in Christendom, in repair for one minute costs 50p. In 1971, the year the city of York shared its 1900th birthday with the world, the cost was just 30p. Such are the inroads of inflation. Nevertheless, over the years, thousands of visitors have gladly contributed to the maintenance bill. At peak periods queues formed for the specially inscribed scrolls recording that 'time' had been bought.

Time, a commodity York has had plenty of in the past, is now running out. The city, the most medieval in feeling of all the country's historic centres, is under pressure from the twentieth century. It will take planning of the highest order, schemes of revitalization for 'twilight' areas and an imaginative conservation policy to bring it unscathed into the next century. A significant forward step was taken in the spring of 1976 with the opening of the £9,000,000 eastern by-pass, completed at Government expense without the demolition of a single property. Involving a new bridge over the river near Bishopthorpe, it is designed to siphon off coast-bound traffic before it reaches the city boundary.

Changes which seemed to threaten the city's ancient dignity and status came into force in April 1974 when, after years of talking, the nineteenth-century local government structure was dismantled. Yorkshire's three Ridings disappeared, together with York's county borough standing. The city found itself one of the eight districts making up the vast new county of North Yorkshire, extending over 2,000,000 acres. At the time, there were agonized discussions about the city's chances of becoming the centre of the new area. Though many felt that its indisputable air of being a regional capital would secure its position, the crown passed to Northallerton, a market town of some 8,000 people, formerly headquarters of the old North Riding County Council. The new county now maintains responsibility for education, youth employment, social services, consumer protection, strategic planning, national parks, libraries, highways, traffic and transport planning, buying and selling development land, road safety, police and fire services and, in conjunction with district councils, things like recreation parks and open spaces. Acceptance of an inferior role comes hard in York, with its university, art gallery, world-famous museums, a traffic-free shopping street which is among the most charming in Europe, a honey-coloured cathedral saved from collapse by a bold £2,000,000 scheme and, above all, nineteen centuries of 'history on the ground' at every turn. But at least the local authority was allowed to style itself York City Council.

In 1971, during the 1900th anniversary celebrations, York's visitors were conservatively estimated at 1,000,000 a year. This number was increased considerably in the following year, the 500th anniversary of the completion of the Minster as it stands today and the end of the five-year restoration scheme, an astonishing feat of civil engineering and architectural expertise. With the opening of the National Railway Museum in the autumn of 1975, the annual tourist influx is now estimated at more than 2,000,000.

For many years York passed its life quietly, the days punctuated by the Minster bells. Today with its tourism highly organized and its publicity pushed to the ends of the earth, it takes its place as the country's foremost historic city. By half past nine on a summer Sunday morning, foreign visitors may be seen tucking into ham and eggs in a restaurant only ten steps from the Minster's West Front, getting ready to savour the city's eccentricities—perhaps the sight of the peacocks that sometimes mingle with the traffic after escaping from the Museum Gardens; perhaps tea and toast in a 450-year-old café haunted by Marmaduke Buckle, an eighteenth-century ghost.

This book—neither a history nor a guide—seeks to show not only the gloss of tourism but the thread of continuity which makes York a place of infinite delight; a tangle of streets, court-yards, churches and guildhalls, all enclosed by the medieval wall. The day-tripper skims off the cream, but the resident comes to know the city in all its moods. Unravelling the secret of its appeal can be a way of life.

LIFE'S LITTLE DAY

ON SUMMER evenings the ivory fans flickered in the twilit rooms
of the town houses. The wines of Bordeaux were cooling. On the
west bank of the river, away from the great fortress, it was so quiet
that, between conversations, the icy tinkle of the street fountain
could be heard. The wickerwork chairs creaked comfortably.
Perhaps tomorrow would be hot too—a day for the silver-
mounted parasols. In the northern winter, when a snow-bearing
wind sighed through the bones of the forest, casting a skin over
the looping river, it was warming to glance into the corners of the
room at the sweet bird of spring, the hay-rake of summer and the
grapes of autumn. For these were among the mosaic symbols on
the floor of a Roman town house in York, perhaps sixteen
centuries ago. With at least five rooms and three decorative floors,
it was in the best part of the civil town—the *colonia*—raised to
that status by either Severus or Caracalla, and may have become a
treasured 'period' property in its time. To the successive families
who lived there, the authority of Rome and the paternalism of the
empire would have appeared as fixed as the stars. As they looked
out from this house, across the river to the white, red-banded
walls of the legionary fortress—Eboracum—the arrival of Roman
rule on this imperial frontier must have seemed a remote event at
the far end of the tunnel of time. Separation from Rome came in
AD 410. Looking back from that point to the year 71 when the new
governor, Quintus Petillius Cerialis, brought the Ninth Legion
north from Lincoln to subdue the rebellious Brigantes, was the
equivalent of our thinking today about the reign of Charles I.

The extension of provincial power created York, giving it in
time a fortress so splendid that no other fortification in the empire
surpassed it. But in AD 71 when Cerialis and his army pushed north
into the large kingdom of the Brigantes they found only a site of
the greatest strategic importance at the meeting place of a major

and a minor river. Cerialis, friend and relative of the Emperor
Vespasian, had an eye for the *opportunitates locorum*, realizing that
the morainic ridge on which the site stood supplied a natural
causeway across the swampy Vale of York to Calcaria (the
modern Tadcaster) and so to the West Riding and the south-
westward connection with the garrison on the far side of the
country. In addition, it was ideally sited for keeping watch over
the hinterland of East Yorkshire and Lincolnshire. It has been said
that York held the keys of Brigantia and has remained the military
centre of northern England ever since.

It is unlikely, however, that the decision to build the fortress
on this site was taken on the spot. Its advantages were probably
already known as Brigantia had been penetrated at least three
times, according to the historian Tacitus, in *c.* 48, *c.* 57 and 69,
and Roman military officers with their escorts had been through
the area on peaceful missions.

This new outpost of empire was spelt Eboracum by the geo-
grapher Ptolemy but the form Eburacum is found in the Antonine
Itinerary, a road-list of the early third century, and appears once
in an inscription. Students of language development accept
Eburacum as being akin to the Celtic word for 'yew'—the place
of the yews. Or perhaps it refers to a personal name and means
"the field of Eburos".

From the beginning, the fortress was legion-sized, that is, about
fifty acres covering a rectangle with rounded corners—shaped
rather like a huge playing card—and measuring 1,370 feet by
1,590 feet. The early rampart was made with whatever the men
could find near at hand, the foundation being springy boughs
lopped from the trees in the area. In lay-out it followed the
pattern of all Roman fortresses, the central place being occupied
by the *principia*, or headquarters building, and the main street, the
via principalis, running across its front. The other main street, the
via praetoria, formed a T-junction by joining it at right angles in
front of the headquarters. These streets were served by their own
gates, the *via principalis* running from the *porta principalis dextra* on
the north-west to the *porta principalis sinistra* on the south-east, and
the *via praetoria* being reached through the *porta praetoria* on the
river front. From behind the *principia* ran the *via decumana* to the
fourth gate, the *porta decumana*.

Two of the modern city's most attractive streets—Stonegate
and Petergate—closely follow the lines of the *via praetoria* and the

via principalis. A secluded lane, Chapter House Street, to the north of the Minster and running beside the Treasurer's House, represents the *via decumana.* In the cellars of the Treasurer's House, a National Trust property of various architectural styles, are a cobble pavement discovered in 1898 and a column base of yellow gritstone big enough to have supported an 18-inch diameter shaft. A second base was uncovered 15 feet away, showing that the pillars had stood parallel to the Roman street.

The site of the *principia* is now occupied, fittingly enough, by York's most important building, the Minster. During the recent £2,000,000 restoration scheme undertaken in the late 'sixties to prevent the collapse of what is one of the greatest Gothic buildings in Christendom, a substantial part of the Roman headquarters wall was uncovered.

Most of the building, found at a depth of 15 feet, was lying under the Norman foundations of the Minster and had been built of white magnesian limestone from the Tadcaster area, the same stone as that used to build the Minster. The Roman stone came, of course, from higher beds and was not of such good quality as that quarried by the medieval builders. Opportunities for archaeological digs in the heart of medieval cathedrals are rare, and the discovery caused widespread interest. In January 1969 the late Sir Mortimer Wheeler, then 78 years old and chairman of the Minster Archaeological Advisory Committee, balanced on a six-inch wide girder over the water-filled excavation to examine the *principia* wall. Later that year collapsed sections of a Roman column and its base were found in the south transept.

Paintings from a fourth-century room added to the Roman headquarters building were found under the east end of the nave. As dynasties rose and fell, and humanity reshaped itself on the long haul from barbarism to the moon-shot, they lay in darkness. The artist's pastel colours were preserved intact through the sixteen centuries which passed between the day they were applied to the plastered wall and the moment of their discovery. Four days and a lot of midnight oil later, all the fragments had been carefully lifted and given archaeological first aid treatment to ensure that the friable plaster would stand the handling necessary to transport it to a Wiltshire restorer. In the laboratory a pattern began to emerge; a scene more at home in Mediterranean lands than in the damp northern parts of an island off north-west Europe. Dove-like birds, painted pillars, panels in imitation of

2

York Minster: the South Door
York Minster: the East Window

marble, a theatrical mask of tragedy and an enigmatic robed figure gradually took their place on this gay fourth-century stage. Deep red, pink, green, lavender, white and yellow were the colours used. The paintings, together with not only the restorer's interpretation of the original arrangement, but the wall to which some of them were found still adhering, will form a major exhibit in the Minster's new undercroft museum.

It is generally accepted that the first occupying force was the Ninth Legion Hispana who had seen earlier service in Spain and had been commanded ten years previously by Cerialis, who brought them from Lincoln as the spearhead of his campaign. Between AD 71 and 74 the Ninth Legion built up the primary defences consisting of an earth bank with a turf-work front on a 'corduroy' foundation of green wood. Ten years later, when Agricola had been made provincial governor, it was decided to make the York fortress stronger and to hold it permanently. The Cerialis rampart was dismantled, a new oak foundation was put in and a clay mound with a turf front was raised. Some of the original timber towers were replaced by new ones, and an excavation in Davygate in 1957 revealed the oak stumps of four of the six timbers which had been used as supports. The tree from which they had been cut was more than 150 years old when it was felled so, as the archaeologist who made the discovery pointed out, it must have been growing nearby during Christ's lifetime. The stumps had survived for almost 1,900 years in the clay.

Under Trajan the gates and towers were built in stone. This was a great landmark in the life of the growing fortress and can be dated with accuracy. An inscription of AD 107-8 appears on a commemorative tablet in local magnesian limestone set up over the new *porta principalis sinistra* on the site of the modern King's Square. This fragmentary message to posterity is one of the most impressive items in the Roman collection of the city's Yorkshire Museum. The surviving centre section of the tablet has been imaginatively displayed so that the complete inscription is conjectured. It was found under King's Square in 1854 when a drain was dug along Goodramgate and Church Street.

It was then, for the first time, that stone was used for the buildings within the fortress wall. In its permanent form, the headquarters block, which was the administrative and spiritual heart of the fortress, was probably divided into three parts. Altars and saluting bases used in ceremonial parades were kept in a large open courtyard surrounded on three sides by ranges of colonnaded buildings, while beyond the courtyard was the large cross-hall echoing, in its architectural style, the nave and aisles of the great churches which were to be its successors. It is known that the cross-hall at Chester was about 240 feet long with a total width of 80 feet. With a bit of a squeeze the entire Legion could probably have been assembled there to hear addresses by visiting dignitaries, or to take part in the ceremonial which must have attended the opening of a campaign.

In adjoining rooms the administrative staff dealt with correspondence and accounts, their duties helping us to appreciate the deep sense of order and discipline which ran through the Roman army. The work involved in running a fortress of this size must have been great, much of the burden falling on the *signiferi*—the standard-bearers—and their assistants. One of the most notable military tombstones to be found in York was that of Lucius Duccius Rufinus, standard-bearer of the Ninth Legion. The monument, now in the Yorkshire Museum, shows him holding the standard in his right hand, and in his left what is thought to be a case of writing tablets. So we may picture this conscientious soldier and his counterparts in other units keeping company records and running a savings bank system for the men. Wisely, the Roman army issued only a small proportion of a soldier's pay in cash, the remainder being held to his credit in the books of the standard-bearer's clerks. In addition, any man could deposit money for safe-keeping.

Somewhere in the headquarters there must have been a safe place for the storage of the money, like the strong-room at Chesters, the Northumberland cavalry fort set between two milecastles on Hadrian's Wall. This sunken chamber, reached by a short stairway, lay below the main standard-bearer's office, is still covered by its third-century roof, and has a flagged floor. It was found accidentally in 1803 but was not excavated until 1840 when records show that the original door was found "in a sadly decayed state". Made to open inwards, it was of wood, sheathed with iron plates fastened with large, square iron nails.

Near the headquarters building, perhaps to the east, was the *praetorium*, or commandant's house, which may also have been used as an officers' mess. It would have been a courtyard house with heated rooms and a small bath suite. To the rear of the headquarters there may have been the hospital, for it was in a

similar position that excavators in 1898 found a building used for
this purpose at Housesteads fort on Hadrian's Wall. It had four
ranges of room with accommodation for medical stores and an
operating theatre as well as rooms for patients. An example found
on the Continent proved to be a long courtyard type of building
with small cubicles. There was a large reception hall and, at the far
end, a small operating theatre with running water and heating.

The remainder of the fortress area was taken up by barrack
blocks, granaries and the bath-house. In 1957 excavations in
Davygate revealed part of the barracks and the wash-room of the
quarters used by a centurion who often enjoyed non-standard
accommodation. In fact, refinements went as far as decorated wall
plaster; the centurions' quarters at Chester carried a floral pattern.
There was evidence in York that lead piping had served the
ablution room, linking it with a complex drainage system which
discharged into the river Ouse.

Granaries were vital buildings and usually solidly built with tile
or slate roofs often supported by external buttresses. The flagged
floors were raised on low sleeper-walls and there was plenty of
underfloor ventilation to keep the grain dry.

The presence of a large bath-house in the forepart of the fortress
at York is unusual, and today its remains form one of the few
visible links with the Roman past, as they are preserved in the
basement of a public house in St Sampson's Square. In 1971 the
brewers changed the name of the pub from the Mail Coach Inn
to The Roman Bath, cutting a circular viewing panel in the floor
of the lounge and illuminating the bath. Cleanliness and relaxation
were important in Roman military life, and regarded as part of
the daily routine of civilized men. The baths were a kind of social
club and organized on the principle of the Turkish bath in which
several interconnecting rooms were kept at varying temperatures.
An invigorating way of using the baths was to go straight from
the hot room into the cold plunge. Parts of both these rooms may
be seen under the York public house. The bath-house was built
early in the fourth century after the demolition of other military
buildings and so dates from the time when the south-west
defences of the fortress were extensively altered. But before this
was undertaken, a change of command took place, one which
followed the 'disappearance' of the Ninth Legion. Early in the
reign of Hadrian the Legion had been used in a campaign to
subdue the tribes of northern Britain. As York's last link with the

Ninth is the commemorative tablet from the *porta principalis sinistra*, it was popularly supposed that the Legion was annihilated during the northern campaign, but modern research does not support this rather romantic notion.

If the Legion had suffered heavy casualties in battle its numbers would have been made up by transfers from other parts of the empire or by fresh recruits. Annihilation is unlikely as the names of several survivors are known, but cashiering may have taken place after defeat involving a major disgrace—perhaps the loss of the Eagle. Whatever the Legion's fate, it was replaced by the Sixth Legion Victrix Pia Fidelis who came over from Germany and remained in York until the end of Roman occupation.

The final remodelling of the defences on the river frontage had what has been described as a "superlatively imposing" result. Crossing the river from the south-west the visitor would see facing him the great *porta praetoria*, flanked by six interval towers and two large corner towers, all with multangular forms. Through the limestone ran a dramatic red tile band. Today's visitor to the city does not have to imagine this for himself; a large part of the western angle tower, standing to a height of 19 feet above ground and capped by a medieval superstructure, is to be seen in the Museum Gardens together with a small interval tower and about twenty-five yards of the fourth-century wall. The tower's south angle counterpart was found in Feasegate in the heart of the city's shopping centre in 1832 and was later examined in 1852 and 1956. The plan is the same in outline as the west angle tower and the wall stands to a height of about nine feet under commercial premises. A tentative plan to make the tower available to the public was abandoned some years ago.

Though much remains to be found of the buildings within the fortress of this late period, there is little doubt that they were on a grand scale. One has only to look at the limestone head of a statue of Constantine I, found in Stonegate before 1823 and now in the Yorkshire Museum, to realize the impact this statue must have had.

Nearly twelve feet high and showing the emperor wearing an imperial oak wreath, it probably stood in the open in front of the headquarters building, a reminder of the high status of Eboracum where two emperors died—Severus on 4th February 211, and Constantius Chlorus in July 306—and where Constantine himself was proclaimed. The cremation of Severus was so splendid an event that a re-enactment of it was included in the programme for the 1900th anniversary celebrations held in the city throughout 1971. The solemn display of the full panoply of Rome on a winter's day far out on the north-western edge of the empire must have been a remarkable sight, and one that stayed in the memory for many generations. The body, in golden armour and wrapped in a purple cloak, was carried on a bier to the funeral pyre outside the city followed by his two sons, members of the court, military staff and legionaries. The ashes were taken to Rome where they were placed in the tomb of his predecessor, Marcus Aurelius.

As the fortress strengthened its hold on the surrounding district, a settlement known as Canabae ("the booths") began to hug the walls, mainly on the north-west and south-east sides, where trades-men and hangers-on lived and worked, at first in crude huts, later in stone buildings. Extensive river quays also sprang up to handle the heavy cargoes arriving by galley. Some legionaries specialized as river-pilots, and one of them, Marcus Minucius Mudenus (or Audens), set up a limestone altar "To the mother goddesses of Africa, Italy and Gaul". He described himself as a "Soldier of the Sixth Legion Victorious, pilot of the Sixth Legion" and added that he had "paid his vow joyfully, willingly and deservedly". The cargoes he handled may have come from the countries listed on the monument, found in Micklegate in 1752.

In the year 237 M. Aurelius Lunaris, a York merchant, perhaps trading in wine and olive oil, set up an altar in Bordeaux where it was discovered, carved with Eboracum's badge—a boar—in 1921. The altar was brought to York for exhibition in 1971. Lunaris described himself as "Sevir Augustales of the Colonies of York and Lincoln in the Province of Lower Britain" and added that he had been "ship-borne from York". As a Sevir Augustalis he was a member of a priestly college of six, concerned with emperor-worship in the *colonia*, the highest rank of chartered town. York had obviously reached this status by the early third century after the civil population, having found the land between the rivers a little cramping, had spread themselves in a ribbon development along the main road to Calcaria and the west. They must have used a bridge at a point directly behind the medieval York Guildhall and in line with the ancient Common Hall Lane which runs under the building.

The wine trade may also have attracted Marcus Verecundius

Diogenes, a native of the Bourges region of France, and his
Sardinian wife, Julia Fortunata, to Eboracum. He was also a Sevir
of the York *colonia*, and his coffin, discovered in 1579 about a
quarter of a mile west of the city walls, is now lost. It was last
seen and its inscription read in the eighteenth century at Hull
where it was used as a horse trough at the Coach and Horses Inn.
His wife's coffin was found in 1877 near the railway bridge which
carries the Scarborough line across the Ouse.

It is on the site of the *colonia*, at one time capital of Lower
Britain with a population of about 1,200, that the most personal
links with Roman York have been found. The town, with its
defensive wall, colonnaded buildings, baths, surviving street
fountain, elaborate tombs and extensive burial grounds outside
the inhabited areas, gave up many of the ghosts of its past during
the Victorian railway boom which led to the building of the
original station in 1839-40 and the present one in the 1870s.
Remains of a public bath with a furnace were found on the site
of the old station and yard in 1839 and were uncovered again just
a century later during excavation for a bomb shelter in the mound
of the medieval defences behind the old station. The baths were
extensive and included a *caldarium* that has been described as the
largest in Britain.

Only a few yards away, in Toft Green, apsed buildings and
remarkable mosaics—still to be seen in the Yorkshire Museum—
were found in the eighteenth and nineteenth centuries. The
religious dedication stone and foundations of one apsed building
were discovered in 1770 when a cellar was dug out under a house
in the street, and in 1840 a mosaic pavement set in a concrete floor
6 inches thick and the foundations of a second apsed building were
uncovered at a depth of 6 feet. The mosaic shows a lively picture
of a bull with a fish's tail. It was near here, in 1853, that the
beautiful mosaic of the four seasons—one of three floors found—
was excavated and preserved. Though the central head of Medusa
is badly damaged, the four female heads are seen against a simple
geometric background . . . a bird, a rake, a bunch of grapes and
a bare bough identify the seasons.

The presence of these charming mosaics is a reminder that
Roman occupation connected Britain to the mainstream of art
throughout the Empire, though results were not always as
pleasing as this particular pavement. The picture in the pattern
book was one thing; the end product in the hands of an

inexperienced workman was another. It is clear in the York pavement that the same skilful artist worked on all four of the heads, unlike the Four Seasons pavement at Cirencester where, of the three surviving, two are graceful and the third clumsy. Entire floors, based on originals of delicacy and fine design, could become travesties when tackled by local and over-ambitious enthusiasts, though today they are preserved no less carefully than the best products of the mosaicists, and often have a quaint appeal. Perhaps the best example is the Venus pavement from the Roman villa at Rudston in the East Riding which, with others on the site, was rolled up like a carpet and removed to a Hull museum in the early 1960s. Here, in a simple but effective room setting, very much as it must have appeared 1,600 years ago, the oddest caricature of Venus may be studied. At the opening ceremony guests were even allowed to walk on her—in their stockinged feet.

Of the 600 known or suspected villas in Britain, about a quarter of them had mosaic pavements. Each had at least one; Woodchester in Gloucestershire with twenty and Fishbourne in Sussex with more, are in a class by themselves. Pavements were obviously status symbols and it is probable that many towns had 'schools' of mosaicists. Perhaps one was based at York.

The town buildings also included a temple to the Egyptian god Serapis built, according to the dedication stone found in the eighteenth century, by the commanding officer of the Sixth Legion, Claudius Hieronymianus, a man who, at the turn of the second and third centuries, persecuted Christians after his wife's conversion to the faith.

About thirty deities are known to have been worshipped, from the unknown Celtic god with drooping moustache and wild Gorgon-like hair found on a gritstone plaque, to Mithras whose complex ritual was carved in crowded detail on a limestone altarpiece found in 1747 in Micklegate on a line parallel with the main road of the *colonia*. Mithras is seen with left knee bent and resting on the back of a bull which he is stabbing in the neck. A dog leaps up to catch the blood from the wound, and to left and right stand the torch-bearers, Cautes and Cautopates. The sun, moon and initiation scenes fill the rest of the carving. A statue of Arimanius, the Mithraic god of evil, was found during the cutting of a road archway through the medieval city wall in 1874.

A fragment of a gritstone altar was found to be dedicated to

"the Emperor's divinity and the Genius of York", and a relief
found near Bootham Bar in 1835 shows Neptune in his four-horse
sea-chariot. A limestone altar, found in Bishophill Senior—the
heart of the *colonia*—in 1638 and now in the Ashmolean Museum
at Oxford, was dedicated to "Jupiter, best and greatest, and to the
gods and goddesses of hospitality and home". It was set up by
Publius Aelius Marcianus, prefect of a cohort, to give thanks for
the continued health of himself and his family.

The levelling effect of time is seen in the way monumental relics
of this great Roman centre are today equated with small personal
possessions . . . the ivory handles of a folding fan; an octagonal
silver ring inscribed to the god Sucellus; a glass mirror; Julius
Alexander's soapstone stamp for marking cakes of his eye oint-
ment; ear-rings made from glass, gold or silver; parasol ribs with
traces of silver sheathing; a little bronze mouse. And, of course,
ornaments of jet, that rare material that is found on the coast
near Whitby.

As the province prospered, it began to export woollen goods
and corn, but there were one or two luxury lines in addition.
Tacitus knew all about British pearls (he thought they were of
poor quality) and they were still being sold in the fourth century.
Jet found a good market abroad, probably in the Rhineland, in
the shape of rings, pins, necklaces and portrait medallions made in
York. The railway excavations of 1873 provided evidence for the
jet industry with the discovery of several rough blocks and some
partially prepared pieces. On unrecorded sites in York three jet
pendants forming portrait medallions were found. One is of the
head and shoulders of a woman with hair arranged in a double
parting on either side of a chignon or cap; the second shows a
couple, perhaps husband and wife, facing each other; and in the
third a husband, wife and curly-haired boy are seen wearing
cloaks with brooches on their right shoulders.

Jet's popularity is accounted for by its comparative rarity, the
aura of magic which surrounded it (like amber, it becomes electrically charged when rubbed) and the more practical fact that it is
easily worked and polished.

The richer tombs of Roman York tell us a great deal about the
people of the town. The greatest number of burials and the best
sculptures come from the top of The Mount, a steady rise south-
west of Micklegate Bar on the road to Tadcaster and Leeds. One
house has the life-size head of a funerary statue built into the eaves,

while another stands over a Roman burial vault which was last entered in 1955. It was in this area, in 1861, that one of the most moving tombstones was found. The inscription has been translated as:

> To the spirits of the departed.
> Corellia Optata, 13 years old.
> Ye hidden spirits, that dwell in
> Pluto's Acherusian realms, whom
> the scanty ash and the shade,
> the body's image, seek after
> life's little day, I, the pitiable
> father of an innocent daughter,
> caught by cheating hope, lament
> her final end. Quintus Corellius
> Fortis, the father, had this made.

A little to the north-west of The Mount a coffin was found inscribed:

> To the spirits of the departed.
> For Simplicia Florentina, a most
> innocent soul, who lived 10
> months, Felicius Simplex, her
> father, of the Sixth Legion
> Victorious, made this memorial.

When found, the coffin had been re-used for the burial of a child older than the "innocent soul" for whom it had been made.

Family groups were often shown on tombstones, like the grit-stone memorial to 50-year-old Julia Velva, found in 1922 during the making of Albemarle Road which joins The Mount at right angles. Made by her heir, Aurelius Mercurialis, it shows Julia Velva as the central figure lying on a couch, her head propped on her left arm in that rather stiff way adopted for effigies of a much later age and which may be seen in many parish churches. In her right hand is a wine jar. The couch has a thick mattress and high sides. In a wickerwork chair in front of the couch sits a young girl holding what is probably a pet bird. Near her are a three-legged table with food, and a boy holding a jug. Aurelius Mercurialis is seen in front of a larger table with a scroll in his right hand.

Position of burial seems to have been tied to social standing. Soldiers of high rank may have been buried near Clifford's Tower, the medieval quatrefoil keep in the heart of the city's castle area. Well-placed citizens were found plots on The Mount, and the poor were buried in a rather haphazard fashion in the Trentholme Drive area, further out along the Tadcaster Road. Once past the summit of the hill, the country must have been considered quite wild, judging from one of the early roadside monuments associated with the *colonia*. A limestone altar, found in The Mount area in 1884, it had been set up by a Ninth Legion clerk, Lucius Celerinius Vitalis, to the honour of Silvanus, a god of hunting and the wild. "Let the gift, this gift, belong: I must beware of touching it," said the clerk in his inscription.

Trentholme Drive's Romano-British cemetery, excavated by Leslie P. Wenham, a leading archaeologist, and Head of the History Department of St John's College, York, gives a rather bleak picture of life for the average citizen. Analysis based on 280 examples showed that about one-tenth were children under fifteen and that more than three-quarters died before they were forty. Apparently it was rare to find survival beyond the age of fifty. On the other hand there was little evidence of mortal injury and no signs of diseases associated with malnutrition. The teeth were well formed and spaced and largely free from decay. Of 5,000 teeth examined, less than five per cent showed signs of caries. Fractures were fairly common and included those of thigh, shin, forearm, ribs and collar-bone; in most cases the healing was good.

But the scourge of the time was rheumatism in various forms; hard work in a damp climate was probably the cause.

The skeletons of what were probably legionary veterans showed evidence of old war wounds. One strongly built man of about forty had a large bony growth on the upper thigh bone and a number of healed breaks in his ribs and feet. The inference is that he received a heavy sword cut on the thigh, fell to the ground and was trampled on perhaps by enemy cavalry.

One of the vertebrae of a 45-year-old woman showed a remarkable variation in shape which would have given her unusual freedom of spinal movement. It was suggested that she might have been a professional acrobat or dancer.

Though strong, hardy and well muscled, the people of Roman York were of medium stature. The average height of 100 adult men was 5 feet 7 inches, and of 30 adult women 5 feet 1 inch.

Examination of the skulls gave a clear idea of the racial origins of the citizens. Most of the women were of one type—probably

local Celtic stock—but the men were much more varied. Five
male skulls were typical of the eastern end of the Mediterranean,
seven others may have been Scandinavian and a number were
probably Germans. One was described as "almost certainly a
negro", perhaps a slave.

On their arrival in Britain it was the Romans' custom to
cremate the dead and this continued until about AD 200 when
inhumation was introduced. For about seventy years the two
practices ran parallel, so it was not surprising to find evidence of
both intermingled at Trentholme Drive. The excavators found
skeletons in all kinds of postures—face downwards, crouched, on
the side. A couple were found in each other's arms and on the
back of the uppermost was the complete skeleton of a hen. In
seven cases coins were found inside the skulls, a practice borrowed
from the Greeks whose belief about the crossing of the river Styx
was well known.

Ashes from cremations found on this and other sites in York
were placed in urns, amphorae, glass jars, lead canisters, stone cists
and tiled tombs. The ashes of 13-year-old Corellia Optata were
found in a cylindrical green glass bottle originally sealed with
lead.

Perhaps the most surprising find was that made in 1875 on the
site of the present railway station booking hall and concourse.
In a lead-lined stone coffin which had held the body of an
adolescent girl was found her auburn hair, fastened in a bun by
two jet pins. It may be seen today in the Yorkshire Museum.

The urge to leave graffiti for later generations to read is strong,
and reaches its logical conclusion in the elaborate 'time capsules'
which are often sealed into the foundations of notable buildings
today. While the clay was still moist a workman in Roman York
wrote on a roof tile with his finger: "Pollio, to the guild, good
luck!" in much the same way as aircrew members flying from
airfields around York during the 1939-45 war cut their names
on the mirror of a famous bar in the city centre, a mirror which
is still preserved as a sort of secular memorial to those who did
not return.

On a mid-second-century flagon had been written "Pondo III"
and other examples of inscribed pottery left messages such as
"You relax", "Give me!", "Mix for me!", "Don't be thirsty!"
and "Long life to you!". And on a slip of bone found in the
breast of a skeleton in the railway station area was written: "Lord

Victor, may you have a lucky win!" . . . a pat on the back usually reserved for gladiators or charioteers.

Sometimes the inscribed objects are less casual and are made of precious metals, like the gold amulet, lightly engraved with two lines in Greek letters, found in 1839 during the cutting of an archway through the city wall. The first line is a meaningless jumble but the second has been interpreted as a transliteration of the Coptic "Lord of the Gods". Equally, it might be a variant of the Hebrew magic formula meaning "Bound by spells".

Two bronze votive tablets, originally covered in silver and meant to be hung from an altar, may be a link with Demetrius, a schoolmaster who, in about AD 84, thirteen years after the founding of Eboracum, told Plutarch of his visit to Britain on the instructions of the Emperor Domitian. These tablets, found in 1840, carried Greek inscriptions in punched dots. The larger reads: "To the gods of the governor's residence, Scrib[onius] Demetrius" and the smaller: "To Ocean and Tethys, Demetrius". Much has been made of this latter inscription, the suggestion being that this well-read man, having reached the far end of the western world on his fact-finding tour, aptly chose a dedication made by Alexander the Great on reaching the furthest point of his thrust to the east.

The major Roman remains are easily seen by starting at the Multangular Tower in the Museum Gardens, moving on to a short stretch of wall at the end of St Leonard's Place and then walking along the medieval wall from Bootham Bar to Monk Bar where the fortress wall reappears together with the remains of an interval tower and the north-east corner tower. The fourth-century bath-house is, of course, under the public house in St Sampson's Square. Roman relics removed from their original position are in the Yorkshire Museum and Hospitium, and there are a number of Roman items, including the street fountain from Bishophill, in the entrance to the ruined chapel of St Leonard's Hospital nearby.

Not far from Hadrian's Wall in Northumberland, the vivid figure of Mithras is to be seen sacrificing the life-giving bull; high in the woods of the Taunus region of West Germany the white walls of a Roman fort stand complete and four-square in the Rhine-Danube gap. Some hundreds of miles and seventy years separate these two outstanding experiments in an art which York might do well to cultivate. It is the art of drawing the visible remains of the Roman empire into the light of late-twentieth-century interest.

What is missing in York today is an example of colourful, tourist-attracting yet scholarly reconstruction of the kind to be seen in other parts of the United Kingdom and on the Continent. During the year-long celebrations to mark the 1,900th anniversary of the founding of Eboracum an imaginative plan to make public access to the defensive layers—Roman, Saxon, medieval—near the Multangular Tower was carried through, partly as a memorial to a dedicated young archaeologist killed in an accident on this site in the summer of 1970, but the city missed the opportunity to create something entirely new which would enable the visitor to identify with the settled, civilized, provincial life of Roman York as it was before the black tide of history swept away all the familiar landmarks.

This was done for the eighteenth and nineteenth centuries in a brilliant manner in 1938 when the Castle Museum opened its doors, though this bold step had its critics at the time. There were those who could not believe that the 'junk' of the past held the key to all its secrets. But today, undiminished by its many imitators, the Castle Museum has a regular annual attendance of more than 700,000.

The folk museum with its reconstructed rooms, houses and streets pointed the way clearly enough. Why didn't Roman York receive similar treatment? Visitors to the city often leave without realizing its immense importance in the Roman world, though they usually have a vivid picture of Georgian, Victorian and Edwardian life.

I approached the question as a member of the frustrated and potentially fee-paying public, struggling to catch a glimpse of the glory that was Rome in buildings inadequate for the purpose. Perhaps this prejudiced me in favour of display which is not only comfortable, modern, informative and well-lit but sometimes unashamedly theatrical. Coated in this way, the Roman pill is delicious. This was something I discovered in the reputedly hard-headed city of Newcastle-upon-Tyne, for it is to this city—as well as to West Germany—that we must turn to see how the Roman legacy may be most fruitfully invested.

In the quadrangle of the University of Newcastle is the Museum of Antiquities, established jointly by the University of Durham and the Society of Antiquaries of Newcastle-upon-Tyne.

The military and social history of the imperial frontier in the North of England is illustrated by more than 500 Roman inscriptions and sculptures. But the most dramatic feature of the museum lies beyond the double doors at the far end of the gallery. Once through them, the visitor finds himself in a short corridor. On his right is an illuminated showcase holding exhibits and photographs dealing with the excavation of the Carrawburgh Mithraeum on Hadrian's Wall. If he then presses two buttons, the art of presentation at its highest takes over as curtains which have been drawn across the glass wall on his left slide silently open, revealing a complete life-size reconstruction of the Temple of Mithras as it probably appeared in the fourth century. Simultaneously, a tape-recorded, eight-minute commentary provides background information.

The atmosphere of pagan mystery created by this somewhat unexpected revelation is remarkable. The lighting is subdued, picking out the coloured details of the three altars, the impressive reredos, the figures of the traditional torch-bearers and the benches on which worshippers sat. Under the slightly hypnotic effect of the disembodied voice, it begins to take on the form of an experience not easily forgotten.

Near Bad Homburg in West Germany, a large-scale experiment in reconstruction was undertaken between 1898 and 1907. Under the personal guidance of Kaiser Wilhelm II a complete Romer-kastell—Roman fort—was built on the crest of the wooded Taunus. The sentiments which prompted this grand and probably very expensive gesture reflected the Kaiser's self-conscious affinity with the Roman emperors. But today the result is a very popular tourist attraction. The camp, measuring 240 yards by 160 yards, was excavated in the 1850s and the road leading to it is fringed by Roman monuments and remains. By now, the rebuilt fort must have paid for itself many times over.

Suppose York began to think along reconstruction lines; began seriously to consider how it could embellish its Roman past in a way which would not only inform but delight the city's estimated one million annual visitors. Tinkering with the visible monuments—such as the Multangular Tower—is, of course, unthinkable, but there are other ways of underlining the attractions of the fortress and *colonia*.

The building of a full-size replica of a Romano-British villa, furnished, decorated, heated and landscaped, would be the most

attractive scheme, though obviously expensive to initiate. And if
the hypocaust was dependent on a discreet coke boiler, who but
the most ardent purist would object? The Trust responsible for
the excavation of Vindolanda on Hadrian's Wall proposed, late in
1971, that its site museum should be in the form of a fourth-
century villa.

Assuming this scheme fell down on purely financial grounds,
a scaled-down version might be possible—the setting of the floor
of the Four Seasons from the Toft Green Roman house in a
reconstructed, conjectural room. In this way its appeal would be
heightened beyond measure. With the introduction of murals,
hand-woven hangings and furniture, its true nature would emerge
for the first time since its discovery. However, as part of a large-
scale improvement scheme for the museum, some of the mosaics
have already been removed from the Hospitium, bonded with
modern resins and hung on the walls like tapestries.

The settled life of the town probably survived into the misty
years which followed the final withdrawal of Roman troops.
Little is known of events in the fifth and sixth centuries, but by
the first decade of the seventh century York lay within the
English kingdom of Deira, and was beginning to reappear as an
internationally recognized centre. In AD 627, as the Anglian city
of Eoforwic, it was the setting for the church built by Paulinus
on land granted to him by King Edwin of Deira. This building
was to be succeeded by the Minster. But it is the period between
AD 876 and 926 when York was a sovereign independent state
under the rule of Danish kings that should be uppermost in the
visitor's mind today, for the curious street names of the city—all
on impeccably lettered plaques—bear the unmistakable stamp of a
thorough Scandinavian occupation. The etymological by-ways
lying between Eboracum and York are complex, moving through
Eoforwic, Jork and Jorvik to the Middle English Yerk (to rhyme
with 'clerk'), the fourteenth-century Yhorke, the sixteenth-
century Yourke and the seventeenth-century Yarke. The form
York is not found in documents before the thirteenth century as
the use of the Latin name was almost universal.

The fact that many of the names are compounded with the
word 'gate' links them with the Old Scandinavian word for
street—gata—but the actual meaning of the whole name is not
always certain. The arguments about them are based on a lot of
scholarship, a bit of guesswork and just a pinch of romance. Some

St Mary's Abbey
Remains of former Archbishop's Palace

are self-evident and easily accepted. Spurriergate is obviously the street of the spur-makers, but Skeldergate, which some would have us believe, was occupied by shield-makers (Old Scandinavian *skjaldari*) may have a more prosaic background. This riverside street led to a public crane on the wharf where the operation of unloading vessels was known as the 'weigh'. 'Skell' is a North Country version of 'weigh' and the 'street leading to the skell' is a plausible explanation.

York's most photographed street name-plate and one which, like London's Carnaby Street, may be bought in the souvenir shops in facsimile, is attached to the city's shortest street. Whip-ma-whop-ma-gate is little more than a corner site between Colliergate and Pavement, and its name is of comparatively recent origin. In the sixteenth century it appears as Whipnam-Whap-namgate, Whipney-Whapneygate and Whitman-Whatmangate. This could have been the spot chosen for the local custom of dog-whipping on St Luke's Day, but the name is more likely to refer to the whipping post and pillory which stood nearby.

Aldwark—'the old fortifications'—runs parallel with the Roman wall and Bedern means 'the prayer house' being the site of the houses, hall and chapel of the vicars-choral. There is more to plain Blake Street than meets the eye, for its origin may be in the Danish word *bleg*, a place for bleaching. More than one Danish town has its Blegstraede. The apparently simple Blossom Street turns out, after much twisting and turning, to be the 'street of the ploughswains', while Colliergate has nothing to do with the far distant mining industry, but means the 'street of the charcoal dealers'.

Coney Street, one of the city's main commercial arteries, so familiar to Yorkists but understandably odd to visiting ears, is 'the king's street' and Coppergate is where the joiners lived. Feasegate means 'cow-house lane' from the Old Scandinavian *fe-hus* and Finkle Street is from the dialect word for a bend or corner. Gillygate led to St Giles's Church, destroyed centuries ago, which was used by the skinners' guild. Goodramgate, which runs to Monk Bar, appears as Gutherungate in the late twelfth century and is derived from a personal name. Danish finds were made there in 1878. Micklegate was the 'great street', its impor-tance lying in its approach to the only bridge in the city, and Nessgate, where a Roman temple to Hercules was discovered, led to the triangular headland between the rivers Ouse and Foss.

3

St Olave's Church
St Mary Bishophill Junior

The charmingly named Patrick Pool, at the east end of St Sampson's Church, once included the neighbouring Swinegate as well. In 1249 it was described as being "so deep and unused that no one can pass through it". Records exist of a law suit in 1564 in which a 50-year-old woman recalled that as a child her father sent her to gather herbs in Patrick Pool. It has been suggested that subsidence in this area was caused by the gradual collapse of the hypocaust system of the Roman bath discovered under the Mail Coach Inn in St Sampson's Square and which was found to extend under Swinegate.

Triangular Peasholme Green, near the Foss, has been identified as "the water meadow where pease was grown" and must have been shaded by mature trees in the Middle Ages according to a will which bequeathed "four of the best tymbre trees in Peiseholme grene".

Jubbergate, now cut into two by the Parliament Street of 1836, with its lower half renamed Market Street, may have been one of the first streets built outside the Roman fortress wall. In its earliest form it appears as Bretgate—'the street of the Britons'—and it has been said that these were Cumbrian Britons who accompanied the Irish Vikings to York and were segregated outside the wall. In the fourteenth century Jews, after their expulsion by Edward I, may have concentrated in the area to give the street its later name Jubretgate, but there is no evidence for this.

A little dog-leg passage leading from Stonegate to Grape Lane is today called Coffee Yard, though in the fifteenth century it was known as Langton Lane, after the family who owned property in the area. Its present name dates only from the eighteenth century when a coffee house called the Saracen's Head stood on the west side of the entrance from Stonegate. Now a gracious street of Georgian houses running north-westwards from Bootham Bar, Bootham may have been the site of merchants' booths in pre-Conquest days, and the short Spen Lane, leading from the old churchyard of St Andrew to St Saviourgate, may have been overgrown with aspens. The Shambles, of course, refers to the butchers' "flesh benches" set up in the open air.

A narrow lane overhung by half-timbering, running down the side of Sir Thomas Herbert's House in Pavement and emerging in Fossgate after a right-angle turn, Lady Peckitt's Yard once had two separate names—Bacusgail and Trichourgail—the suffix meaning a narrow passage between houses. Trichour is said to mean 'trickster'; perhaps this tight little corner was the haunt of the medieval equivalent of three-card-trick operators.

Knavesmire, the great common pasture which makes the approach to the city from Leeds so memorable, may originally have meant 'Knar's marsh' and the gradual use of the word 'knave' perhaps arose because the city gallows stood here, just opposite the end of Hob Moor Lane. A ditch which ran the length of Knavesmire from south-west to north-east was called the Tyburn, and appears on a map of 1625. Catholic martyrs who died at this provincial 'Tyburn' are commemorated by a plaque.

Stonegate, the first pedestrian 'foot street' in modern York and one of the most gracious shopping thoroughfares in Europe, leading from St Helen's Square to Minster Gates, received its name before the Conquest. So there would appear to be no foundation for the story that the name came from the fact that the stone used in building the Minster was hauled along this street. The Minister Fabric Rolls show that the stone, arriving by water from Tadcaster, was landed at St Leonard's Staith and taken along Lop Lane (the present Duncombe Place at the Minster's west front) to the mason's yard. Stonegate was the street where books could be bought, and in 1500 was the site of the earliest-known York press. Minster Gates was once known as Bookbinders' Alley, and today the beautifully preserved figure of Minerva, the goddess of wisdom, with her books and attendant owl, may be seen on the corner of the shop facing down Stonegate. John Foster, who had a bookshop here between 1580 and 1607, kept a stock of nearly 3,000 books—a good guide to the cultural climate of Elizabethan and Jacobean York.

Ogleforth, a quiet street running from Goodramgate to Chapter House Street, once housed the vanished church of St John del Pyke (perhaps because it had a steeple) and got its name, according to one authority, from Saxon words meaning simply 'high gate'. But I prefer the Old Scandinavian version . . . 'the owl-haunted ford'.

ALMOST A MIRACLE

IF, DURING the late 1960s, a medieval mason could have been conjured forward in time so that he could examine the east end of York Minster, would it have surprised him? I think not. He would have seen the great steel shores there merely as twentieth-century flying buttresses. His practical mind would have easily accepted them. But he would have been puzzled by the technical terms which buzzed around the tons of metal and concrete supporting the building he helped to create, and bewildered by the sheer size of the £2,000,000 rescue operation which began in 1967.

It was in April of this year that it was announced to the world that York Minster was on the move, that unless something was done immediately to bolster the foundations, the central tower weighing 25,000 tons—the weight of a fair-sized ship—had a life expectancy of fifteen years. "This is no ordinary appeal," said the Earl of Scarbrough, High Steward of the Minster. "A crisis hangs over the Minster. There is a real danger of collapse. Some may think that to talk of a collapse is an exaggeration, and as the days go by and the towers of the Minster still stand majestically there may come a natural feeling that all will somehow be well. We cannot afford such wishful thinking."

As if to back up Lord Scarbrough's urgent warning, three 'tell-tales'—slivers of glass fixed across ominous cracks—broke in the space of a month.

Large cracks were found in the two western towers and the east end was leaning outwards, 2 feet 11 inches out of plumb, creating a problem described as being seven times greater than that posed by the Forth Bridge. A mild earth tremor or piling work near the foundations of the 197-foot central tower could have brought it down.

The Surveyor of the Fabric, Mr Bernard Feilden, a brilliant,

cathedral-minded architect whose home is in the Norwich Close
and who was later to be involved in the restoration of Wren's
St Paul's, said the urgency of the repair work was dictated by the
fact that a point might soon be reached when the structure was
too delicate to survive the strain of the repair operation. In other
words, the patient was liable to die on the operating table. From
what he had seen it seemed almost a miracle that the foundations
had performed their task for so long. The condition of the fabric
was fully realized during Mr Feilden's two-year, stone-by-stone
examination resulting in a 500-page report to the Dean and
Chapter. In this painstaking work he was following the lead of
the archaeologist and antiquary John Browne who, in the mid-
nineteenth century, was so worried about the state of the Minster
that he explored a weakening cavity under a pier of the central
tower by candlelight, and felt strongly that the vibrations of the
mighty *tuba mirabilis* stop on the organ was threatening the
building's stability. There was a series of meetings in 1842 to
discuss repairs to the building, and the restoration work was
completed in July 1844 after subscriptions totalling £21,591 had
been amassed.

Though Mr Feilden's report made no specific complaint about
the heavy traffic which daily blunders along the south side of the
building along the ill-conceived Deangate, it is clear that this
hazard had played its part in the gradual deterioration of the
fabric. When I asked Mr Feilden about this aspect he said:
"As I was doing the inspection I felt the vibration of traffic
shaking the choir. When a heavy lorry went by, you could feel
it."

Deangate, an Edwardian short-sighted short cut, not only
destroyed the last vestige of the Minster Close on the south side,
but ensured that traffic would pass within feet of the walls and
windows. Few buildings of the Minster's size and fame are not
insulated from traffic by some kind of well-preserved precinct.
There have been worries about the cathedral at Lincoln, but traffic
there passes the building at a much greater distance.

"If you look at forty historic buildings which have traffic
running past them," Mr Feilden told me, "you will find they are
in a worse condition on the side on which that traffic is running.
This is as far as you can get in proving this point."

For an hour every day a young stonemason had the job of
inspecting the seventy-two tell-tales throughout the building,

while at ground level work began on raising 550 slabs covering the floor under the central tower. In June 1967 drilling operations to reach the Minster foundations made the scene like a miniature oil-field. The twenty horse-power drill, specially converted from diesel to electric power made three bore-holes at the rate of fifteen feet a day, one next to the nave pulpit, one in the crossing near the north-west pier and the third in the Lady Chapel. The first bore struck rock at eighty-two feet, but the general picture revealed by this work was that the lower limit of the building's foundations appeared to be 14 feet 6 inches beyond which lay virgin soil and brown or grey-brown plastic clay overlying the deep rock bed.

By 3rd July 1967, eight more tell-tales had broken; two were regarded as serious, and Mr Feilden warned of a danger at any time that one cracked stone might give way and set off a chain reaction leading to a collapse of the central tower. To test the tower piers water was poured in . . . it leaked out of the masonry joints as if from a sieve. In one hole in the west pier, twenty-five feet of hose disappeared. At that time the load on the piers was 46 tons per square foot, twelve times greater than would be allowed in a modern building.

In some of the remoter parts of the building no one had done any repairs for 500 years, since the completion of the Minster in its present form in 1472. Rain had poured in through cracks, doing untold damage by creating internal voids, just as caves form in limestone country. This emphasized the need for continuous care of the pointing and exposed masonry, washing the stone to preserve it from sulphates in the air and enabling defects to be spotted by the stoneyard masons whose job Mr Feilden described as "honourable but unending".

But for all the physical drama, the spiritual life of the Minster flowed on in its unhurried way; the choir on its route to the regular services dodged the polythene sheeting, the tubular scaffolding, the yawning holes, the snaking pipes, the tungsten and diamond-tipped drills. In the September of that first year, the Archbishop of York, in safety helmet and white coat, and carrying a battery-powered lamp, spent an hour touring the building, and work was held up for a memorable flower festival, ordinations and the harvest thanksgiving.

At the end of the year, a new priority made itself known. The east end of the Minster showed signs of active movement, and it was decided to shore the whole wall against possible collapse. The first of the five huge, 75-foot steel props arrived on site under police escort in February 1968. They were to stay in position until the spring of 1971. The anchor base of each shore had a built-in pressure cell linked to a hydraulic compensating pump so as to maintain a steady thrust. It was during the work of installing the first shore that, once again, the contractors showed their willingness to adjust their plans to suit local problems. The base hole had to be dug only a few paces from the junior school of the York College for Girls, and so as not to disturb the pupils with the noise from air compressors during examination time, the engineers put off the work until the start of the half-term holiday.

That spring and summer 4,000 gallons of grouting material were injected into the north-west tower to fill voids in the masonry, and an 'H'-type aerial sprouted in the park to the north of the Minster as key engineering workers, ranging over the great building, kept in touch through pocket radios and throat microphones. An exploratory tunnel, fifteen feet below floor level and nearly six feet high, was pushed towards the foundations of the Lady Chapel by men using the old pick and shovel methods, while above them the giant East Window, 76 feet high by 32 feet wide and containing more than 2,000 square feet of priceless medieval glass, was covered by reinforced plastic sheeting.

Meanwhile, in the central tower, an invisible stainless steel girdle of rods adding up to more than two-thirds of a mile in length, was drilled through at a height of about 120 feet to prevent the tower from 'bursting'. A start was also made on taking the 'lid' off the Minster, replacing the roof timbers of the central tower with lightweight pre-cast concrete slabs and stripping and re-casting the roof lead—a job which had not been tackled for at least a century. During this work the Minster wore a distinctive 'hat', a 58-foot square translucent canopy which not only protected the workmen from the weather, but acted as a support for the old oak beams as they were dismantled.

By February 1969, 10,000 tons of concrete had been poured into the Minster, and as the danger seemed to be receding, a note of optimism was sounded by the Dean of York, speaking that year at the annual reunion dinner of the York Minster Choir Old Boys' Association: "Fortunately the Minster survived into the age of technology. Now it should stand up against everything, except nuclear war."

York began to look forward to the service of thanksgiving planned for May 1972 to mark the completion of the scheme. A similar service celebrated the end of 250 years' work on 3rd May 1472.

A sure sign that the hard grind of the rescue operation had been successful was the search for new stone to replace weatherworn gargoyles, for what use are ornaments of this kind without walls and towers to support them? The search led inevitably to the quarries around Sherburn-in-Elmet which had supplied not only the builders of the Minster but of another well-loved building, King's College Chapel in Cambridge. Huddleston Quarry, the only one able to provide the right stone to blend with the fabric, was reopened. All round this area, and in the Stutton and Hazelwood districts, are ancient quarries which probably provided much of the building material for Roman York. Twelve centuries later the quarry in Thevesdale was granted to the Chapter of the Minster by William de Percy for the building of the south transept, and later in the thirteenth century Robert de Percy, of Bolton Percy, granted to Archbishop John Romeyn free passage for the transport of stone from the quarries. A right of free passage along an old cart road to the quarry was also granted to the Chapter by Robert de Vavasour about this time. River rather than road was the chief highway. The Fabric Rolls of the Minster show that stone was carried in wagons from the quarries to the river at Tadcaster and taken by boat to York . . . "*per navem a Tadcastre usque Ebor*".

The will of William Barker, dated 22nd October 1403, uses a quaint mixture of English and Latin to make a bequest to the Minster fabric for "carrying *unius* shypfull *petrarum per aquam*". In 1419 the large sum of £6 was paid for the transport by boat of 200 measures of stone from Tadcaster to York.

The money needed for the great engineering adventure came not only from York City Council (£20,000), the three Ridings and leading commercial firms but from the 'mites' sent in to the appeal office in High Petergate from all parts of the country. A pile of letters arrived daily, and staff never knew whether to expect £1,000 or 5p. Some letters were touching, some amusing; some brief, others running to three foolscap pages. A former chorister in his eighties recalled climbing the central tower steps . . . when he was only seventy. A couple in Kent decided to give a tithe of their ERNIE winnings; three little Buckinghamshire girls who spent their summer holidays in Yorkshire raised money singing songs at a garden party; a cheque for 1,000 Deutschmarks (about £100) was sent by the young people of Munster, York's twin town in West Germany; the Diocese of Sodor and Man, by far the smallest in the Province of York with only thirty parishes and 48,000 inhabitants, offered to raise at least £2,000, and a considerable sum was sent by personnel at Fylingdales, the RAF's ballistic missile early warning station on the North York Moors because "York Minster was a wonderful landmark for returning bomber crews during the 1939–45 war".

Sixty thousand people visited the Minster flower festival in September 1967, an event made possible by the voluntary work of 1,000 helpers. The result was nearly £8,000 for the fund. Donations were made by the Queen, the Duke of Edinburgh, Queen Elizabeth the Queen Mother, and the Duke and Duchess of Kent who had been married in the Minster in 1961. The great industrial cities of the West Riding promised many thousands of pounds, and £14,000 came from two companies, one American, the other Canadian, which at that time were prospecting for natural gas and potash on the North York Moors.

The Friends of York Minster arranged for the production of a Minster tea-towel, for sale to tourists, with the interior of the choir as the background of its design. An appeal for used postage stamps launched by the wife of the Dean of York brought in a million stamps and a number of private collections containing valuable specimens, including the rare penny black and tuppenny blue. Bits of the Minster—eroded parts of a pinnacle—were given to the Rotary Club at Beverley, thirty miles away in the East Riding, whose members sold the three tons of stone in tiny fragments to buyers in the USA. Each piece was mounted on a polished wooden plinth and backed by the slogan: "Buy a piece of history; save a piece of history".

One of the most dazzling events in aid of the Minster fund was the sale of works of art at Castle Howard, Vanbrugh's great mansion north-east of the city. The sale raised nearly £40,000. Pop singer Vince Hill paid £1,900 for a painting of the Minster by John Piper, and a reproduction was put on sale in the Minster bookshop. Bronzes were given by the late Barbara Hepworth and Henry Moore—both Yorkshire-born.

Orders from all over the world poured in for the York Minster special first-day cover, produced in connection with the GPO issue of commemorative stamps featuring British cathedrals in May 1969. Oak which had taken 500 years to grow and then spent another 500 as part of the central tower roof, was carved and sold on behalf of the fund by an 81-year-old man. A dinner-dance in the historic Yorktown Hotel in York, Pennsylvania, attended by the Dean and his wife, was held in aid of the fund, and the ten-year-old daughter of a rural councillor at Selby, fourteen miles away in the West Riding, raised money by turning her school grounds into a car park, despite the fact that her father had publicly described the West Riding County Council's phased grant of £200,000 as "mad hysteria at County Hall".

Built on the site of the Roman fortress headquarters, the Minster was like a slice of rich cake to the archaeologists whose interests did not conflict with those of the engineers who had to keep an urgent contract rolling at reasonable speed. At one time a whole section of Roman wall, weighing more than seven tons, was suspended in mid-air in the King's Own Yorkshire Light Infantry Chapel, just off the north transept. It was in the way of an expected wave of reinforced concrete, so the engineers used a diamond core drill to go underneath it and insert steel needles. The wall was encased in timber, then raised bodily more than twelve feet by block and tackle. When the concreting was completed it was returned to its original position. Pressed for time in the south transept, archaeologists called in a territorial army sergeant with his mine detector to help locate iron-bound wooden coffins of Saxon date. The detector, one of the latest models with transistorized search head and telescopic arm, was sent to York from Middlesbrough, and after only ten minutes' 'sweep' found twenty-one metal objects below the surface.

Few men are more familiar with the secret corners of the Minster than Dr Eric Gee, senior investigator in the York office of the Royal Commission on Historical Monuments who, with colleagues Tom French and John Bassham, the Commission's photographer, began a two-year close survey of the fabric in June, 1970. Dr Gee, who is President of the Yorkshire Archaeological Society, was in charge of the York office for twenty years and built it up to its present capacity. He has been fully seconded to work on the Minster which will form the subject of a volume to be published by the Commission. He has already completed his notes on the transepts and crossing, Chapter House and vestibule, and is now working on the nave aisles and western towers. For the first half of 1972 he was planning to study the building's eastern arm.

Much of his time was spent making a minute examination of the stonework and carving. "Only by looking at it in detail," he told me, "can one draw the proper conclusions. I have discovered that the south transept has had at least three 'builds' and that the north transept is earlier in date than we thought.* The Chapter House was built in three phases and again was begun much earlier than we realized."

The main practical difficulty of this specialized work is in-accessibility. "The tools of my trade", said Dr Gee, "are binoculars and a strong torch."

Bells for the thirteenth-century belfry of the thirty-second Archbishop, John Romanus, were actually cast in the Minster itself on the site of the fifteenth-century central tower. Excavators found broken bell metal and slag, and just under a medieval burial spot the stokehole and flue of the furnace were uncovered. The molten metal would have been poured into carefully prepared casts cut in the ground. Site casting was found to be practicable in days when the transport of heavy bells was difficult.

Only a few yards from this spot, in the north aisle of the nave, early sun cuts through the gloom to give back-lighting to a fourteenth-century window directly connected with bell-founding. The glass was given to the Minster by Richard Tunnoc —his name is derived from words meaning to strike a note—who had a bell foundry in Stonegate. A married man with two sons and a daughter, he was one of three bailiffs of the city in 1320–1 and represented the city in Parliament in 1327. He was buried in the Minster in 1330. Panels show how medieval bellfounders worked, and Richard himself with a bell decorating the flap of his satchel.

But the most dramatic discovery came in January 1968 during

* The converted King Edwin of Northumbria was baptised in a wooden church on the site of the Minster in AD 627. After Edwin's death in 633 the stone church he had begun to build fell into disrepair. This was largely rebuilt by St Wilfrid about 670, but was destroyed by fire during the Norman Conquest of 1066. The first Norman cathedral was built by Thomas of Bayeux, Archbishop from 1070 to 1100. The cathedral of Roger Pont L'Evêque, Arch-bishop from 1154 to 1181, had a Norman nave. A 250-year building programme was begun in about 1220 with the erection of the south transept by Walter de Grey, Archbishop from 1216 to 1255. The twin west towers were completed by 1472.

work quite unconnected with the Minster scheme when, through a private appeal, the tomb of Archbishop Walter de Grey was restored. His monument, with fittings made of Purbeck stone, stands in the south transept, a part of the Minster completed during his term as Archbishop. He died on 1st May 1255 and was buried before the altar of St Michael.

When Minster craftsmen lifted off the effigy and canopy they revealed a colour painting on the stone coffin lid almost as fresh as the day it was sealed. It had remained airtight for more than 700 years.

Colouring from the painting had been drawn into the mortar of the canopy foundation to give a 'fresco' transfer. It was thought that the painting had been covered within a year of De Grey's death and that the wet mortar had helped to preserve the seal. Shortly after the discovery I was able to admire the amazingly delicate colouring of the portrait as Mr James Williams, an artist-investigator with the Royal Commission on Historical Monuments, started several weeks' work on making an accurate reproduction behind the screens erected round the tomb.

On the night of 3rd May 1968 the tomb was opened in the presence of a select circle of experts, including the late Sir Mortimer Wheeler and the Earl of Stamford, a direct descendant of the De Greys. It was a scene similar to that on 17th May 1827 when the blue marble grave slab of St Cuthbert was lifted in Durham Cathedral.

Inside De Grey's coffin an ivory-topped crozier, a jewelled ring worth an estimated £20,000, a paten and a silver-gilt chalice were found beside the Archbishop's bones which were not disturbed. After the three-hour operation it was decided that these treasures and the painting should be on permanent display in the projected undercroft museum beneath the central tower.

Archbishop for nearly forty years, De Grey was responsible for his successors occupying the Palace at Bishopthorpe, three miles south of the city, as he bought this estate and gave it to the diocese in 1241, when it was known as the Manor of Thorpe St Andrew.

The city palace of the archbishops was built in the twelfth century on land to the north of the Minster, now the Dean's Park. Five hundred years later an archbishop was so greedy for the valuable lead on its roof that he had part of it pulled down. Today all that the public sees of the old palace is a fragment of cloister wall.

Sir Arthur Ingram of Temple Newsam, near Leeds, had the building adapted as a town house, and laid out the grounds with such taste that they were one of the sights of York in the early seventeenth century. A visitor in 1634 described them as a "second paradise" with their flower beds, shady walks lined with statuary, fishponds, bowling green and tennis courts. Little wonder that Charles I made his stay there a long one in 1642.

Time passed, manners changed and the day came when the old house was abandoned as one residence and was let out in sections. At the opening of the eighteenth century there was a dancing room at one end and a playhouse at the other. Some of the rooms were used for assemblies until the building of the Assembly Rooms in Blake Street by Lord Burlington. Thomas Keregan built a theatre in Lord Irwin's Yard and presented *Henry IV* there on 1st October 1734 but the establishment of a theatre in the Minster Close was unpopular with some people, and a petition was raised against it. Towards the end of the eighteenth century the great hall, 90 feet by 40 feet was used as a military riding school, except when the public flocked there to see panoramas like the one of the "British Fleet at Spithead" in 1791.

In 1817 the Dean and Chapter were allowed by Act of Parliament to buy the house and gardens from the Marquess of Hertford, who was the representative of the Ingrams and the Archbishop. The price paid was £2,200 and the old buildings, which had become little better than ruins, were gradually removed. The palace chapel of St Andrew was restored and converted into the Chapter Library. Before this improvement, the library had been in an outbuilding on the south side of the Minster.

A connoisseur of the close, that encircling sweep of velvety grass and gracious houses which protects many cathedrals from the clamour of the surrounding streets, the novelist Henry James usually tried to arrive in English cathedral cities at the day's end when the quiet Edwardian dusk added drama to the scene. Old stonework, he observed, was at its best "when the long June twilight turns at last to a deeper grey". English ruins, he found, seemed paler in the fading light, taking on a solemn and spectral air.

The close offers a world apart. Once you have stepped, for example, through the Erpingham Gate into the Norwich Close, leaving the traffic of Tombland behind, it is possible to walk to the superb watergate at Pull's Ferry through a sort of sanctuary. Apart from a few parked cars, this close is inviolate. At Salisbury, perhaps the most beautiful of English closes, the elegant houses, like the Mompesson House of 1701, stand in the enfolded peace that Henry James sought by twilight.

But York's close has become piecemeal, bisected—as I have pointed out—by the Deangate of 1903, a development which has done more to disperse the Minster's air of enclosure than any other project this century. There was a time when the street name, Minster Gates—a little pedestrian precinct opposite the South door and connected to it by a busy zebra crossing—meant just what it implied: one of the gates to the precinct. There were three more. One stood at the corner of Ogleforth and Chapter House Street on the north-east side of the Minster; one at the junction of High Petergate and Duncombe Place on the west; and one at the end of College Street, which is still to be seen, on the east. York's great local historian, Francis Drake, writing in 1736, said all four gates leading to the precinct were intact, the main one standing opposite the South Door of the Minster. "Anciently," he said, "these gates were closed in every night, but now they are constantly open."

Before 1814, when plans for tidying the precinct got under way, the area seems to have been heavily built upon. From the gate in Lop Lane (Duncombe Place's narrow predecessor) to the church of St Michael-le-Belfrey, a row of cottages masked the view of the Minster's West Front. St Michael's churchyard was removed in 1814 and the cottages and houses on the north side of Petergate went between 1824 and 1839. On the south and east sides of the Minster were the Old Deanery, the Old Residence and St William's College. On the north, the ruins of the Archbishop's Palace. In 1633 Charles I complained to the Chapter about houses built in and against the Minster on the west and south, including one said to be "within the very cross aisle". In an illustration of the mid-seventeenth century may be seen tenements and shops on either side of the South Door. A similar situation exists today in Richmond in the North Riding where Holy Trinity Church in the market-place has shops embedded in its fabric.

The Old Deanery stood across the present Deangate, near its junction with Minster Yard, and a passage ran from this building to Low Petergate. The so-called New Deanery, a stone house in the Gothic style built between 1827 and 1831, was taken down in 1940 when the present Deanery was built to the north of the site. In 1938 the maintenance of the New Deanery was described as "ruinously expensive". It was said that no Dean could live in it unless he was a very wealthy man. It had provided a home for six Deans ... Cockburn, Duncombe, Purey-Cust, Foxley Norris, Lionel Ford and H. N. Bate.

York's close had two prisons—Peter Prison and the Archbishop's Prison. Peter Prison lay just within the Lop Lane gate having been moved from Minster Gates, and lasted until about 1835. In 1832 it held a solitary prisoner, according to returns for that year, and earlier in the century the historian, William Hargrove, had drawn attention to the "wretched state of its accommodations".

There were two cells and two small 'day rooms' in the building, with quarters for the jailer and his family. Who knows why the lone prisoner found himself there? Had he been guilty of one of the offences frowned on by the magistrates of St Peter's Liberty? Like chewing tobacco in the Minster or wearing iron-shod pattens and clogs on its ringing flagstones?

The gradual drawing to a close of the five-year rescue operation in the Minster made access to the monuments and windows much easier. Not since the restoration of the north transept roof in the early 1950s (I recall touching the main beam, carved with the names of the men who worked on it, before the scaffolding came down) had the Minster interior been so difficult to appreciate. But as the tide of aluminium and polythene receded westwards, the choir was revealed as a soaring anthem in cream and gold. Soon afterwards, the glow spread to the interior of the central tower itself. Outside, the true honey colour of the magnesian limestone emerged after long and patient washing operations.

The Minster's stained glass, mostly six to seven centuries old, has for many years been cared for by craftsmen in the Minster workshops which, since 1966, have been incorporated within the structure of the York Glaziers' Trust, and reconstructed and equipped with the help of the Pilgrim Trust. Judged on size alone, the windows are impressive; judged on age and interest they are awe-inspiring. The great East Window measuring 76 feet 9 inches by 32 feet 10 inches was painted between 1405 and 1408 under the direction of John Thornton, a master glazier from Coventry. Mr Peter Gibson, superintendent of the Trust's glass workshop, has pointed out that only the east window of Gloucester Cathedral is larger, but the medieval stained glass there does not fill the entire window, so the claim that the York glass represents the largest area of medieval painted glass is valid. After removal for safety during the 1939–45 war, the window was entirely re-leaded, a task which took ten years to complete.

Five slim lancets, painted about 1260, form the Five Sisters Window, set in the north transept, and make up the largest thirteenth-century window in the world. Each light is 53 feet 6 inches high and 5 feet 1 inch wide, giving an overall area of 1,330 square feet. It was re-leaded in the early 1920s with metal from Rievaulx Abbey in the North Riding, which had been buried and lost in a roof fall at the time of the dissolution of the monasteries under Henry VIII.

The oldest glass in England, dating from about 1150, is to be seen in the north aisle of the nave in a panel set against a background of fourteenth-century glass. Measuring 2 feet 4 inches by 2 feet 6 inches, the twelfth-century panel may be identified by its rich blue background. A survivor from the Norman cathedral on this site, it shows a king seated on the branches of a tree, and until 1950 was very high up in a nave clerestory window. It was decided then to move it to a position where it could be better seen and the two sixteenth-century panels it displaced are now in the Chapter House.

Humour has its place in this incomparable collection of glass. Again in the north aisle of the nave, the early fourteenth-century panel known as The Monkey's Funeral offers the rich scene of a procession headed by a monkey ringing a handbell. He is followed by a cross-bearing monkey and the dead monkey, carried at shoulder height by four pall-bearers. In the right-hand corner a bereaved monkey is comforted by another, and a third has made a start on the wine at the funeral feast.

The Rose Window in the south transept was painted in the early part of the sixteenth century, though its central sunflower is the work of William Peckitt, a well-known York glass painter of the eighteenth century. The window was restored in 1970 as a memorial to the Earl of Scarbrough, the Minster's first High Steward, who died in 1969.

Monuments in the Minster vary from the modest little Tudor brass of Elizabeth Eynns, wife of a secretary to the Council in the North, to the elaborate memorials of the Stuart period, but

Treasurer's House
Hospitium and Watergate Arch

occasionally a romantic story is to be found behind the plainest of tablets.

The south choir aisle has a simple reminder of Frederick Vyner, murdered by Greek bandits in 1870. His mother, Lady Mary Vyner, also had a church—Christ the Consoler—built in the grounds of her home, Newby Hall, near Ripon, by the architect William Burges, responsible not only for the astonishingly rich church at Studley Royal, just a few miles distant, but for the riotous Cardiff Castle and the toytown towers of Castell Coch in its deep beech wood overlooking the River Taff.

It was on the morning of 11th April 1870, that a small party set off from Athens on a sight-seeing jaunt. The party included Lord and Lady Muncaster; a Mr Herbert, secretary to the English Legation; Count de Boyl, second secretary to the Italian Legation, with his servant; a Mr and Mrs Lloyd and their daughter; and Frederick Vyner.

That spring, bandits had crossed the border from Turkey, and were reported to be at large in the northern provinces of Greece. The party asked for protection on their trip, and two mounted policemen accompanied them. Because the road to Marathon was particularly desolate, the government ordered an infantry detachment to patrol the route in pairs, and the party's carriages were escorted into Marathon by sixteen armed men. It was in the evening, on their return, that a foolish decision was made. Keen to reach Athens as soon as possible, someone in the party urged the carriages to put on speed so that although the mounted police kept pace, the foot soldiers were soon left behind.

As the party reached Macro Narappos Bridge, shots were fired and the police fell wounded. The carriages were stopped and surrounded by bandits who took the passengers some distance from the road in spite of fire from the soldiers who had by then caught up with them . . . but too late to be of any use. Lady Muncaster's diamond brooch was taken and the others were robbed of purses and valuables. In an unexpectedly chivalrous mood, the bandits decided to send the women back to Athens in the carriages, and suggested that the men should draw lots to decide who should walk into Athens to arrange a £50,000 ransom. This duty fell to Frederick Vyner, who immediately handed it over to Lord Muncaster whose life, he said, was more valuable than his own. But the bandits wanted more than money. They also demanded an amnesty from the Greek government for

4

all the offences they had committed. Through an intermediary, the government argued with the bandits for several days. Even the king, said the government, had not the power to grant this amnesty. The bandits countered by advising a change in the constitutional law.

Told this would take too long, the bandits made an audacious suggestion that the British fleet should visit Piraeus, the port of Athens, and demand the immediate granting of the amnesty. Tiring of these manœuvres, the government said the bandits should be content with the £50,000 which would undoubtedly be paid, but by now money had ceased to carry much weight. Nothing would satisfy the bandits but the amnesty—money or no money.

In an attempt to persuade the bandits into a more reasonable frame of mind, it was decided to send a party of soldiers into the area with orders not to fire or use violence. But, as often happens in these situations, firing did break out, and the bandits moved the prisoners to a safer spot in the surrounding mountains.

Excitement, fatigue and the bad food they had eaten during the past ten days began to tell on the party. As they dropped one by one in the rough country they were crossing, the bandits shot them. Later their bodies were found and a funeral service was held in the cathedral church at Athens. Members of the gang who were afterwards captured, tried and executed, described the 23-year-old Vyner as "the youth" and said he was "the gentlest of them all".

Tucked away in a dark corner of the north choir aisle is the alabaster effigy of Queen Philippa's son, Prince William of Hatfield, who died in 1346. In the eighteenth century, this figure, probably made by the sculptor John Orchard, apparently had no fixed resting place. Horace Walpole, in a letter, complained that the prince's tomb was "tossed about without a yard of earth to call its own". After that, an empty Gothic shrine was found to fit.

Resting in the Lady Chapel "in the hopeful expectation of the last trumpet" is the curiously named Archbishop—Accepted Frewen, who died in 1664. Representations of books, shelved on either side of the inscription, are shown with the spines reversed, as they were in the old libraries.

An attractive small monument in the south choir aisle is to a remarkable Mrs Hodgson who died in 1636 at the age of 38. The epitaph says she was:

The best of wives, who, having blest her
husband with a numerous progeny of both
sexes, at last in her twenty-fourth
labour—she fell like a sentinel on
duty with the most perfect steadiness and
tranquility of mind, in so early a period
of life and such unfaded bloom of beauty
that she had the appearance rather of a
virgin than of the mother of so many children.

An Archbishop with a military background is also recalled in the
south choir aisle. The monument to John Dolben, who died in
1688, says he "Carried the royalist standard in the Battle of
Marston Moor and was dangerously wounded in the defence of
York . . ." This was in 1644 before he entered the Church.

Static, yet filled with arrested life; displaying their hopes for
the future; gazing sightlessly into the middle distance—all the
monuments seemed to underline the Minster's basic immutability
throughout the upheaval of the restoration as dust settled, drills
hummed, the tower hoist rattled upwards to places lost and
unvisited, lights penetrated corners where darkness had ruled for
five centuries. Changing yet unchanging, the great building was
an inspiration to local artists whether they worked in the traditional materials or in polyester resins.

Two of York's colony of artists live so close to the Minster that
its bulk fills the view from their windows and its bells drop deep
sound into the wells of their studios. So much Gothic stonework,
scoured by the wind blowing down the slow centuries,
fissured by the long cycle of frost and sun until the surface has
become as complex as a Bach fugue, is a rich textural feast. An
artist who draws astonishing beauty from pigmented and laminated polyester resins told me: "I walk past or through the
Minster every day. I feel the stone and its texture. I feel its monumental qualities and pattern. I see it in different lights. It changes
mood probably while I am walking round it. It is a structure
with ever-changing variations."

Seen from the north-east on dark winter mornings, the
Minster's working lights in the scaffolding labyrinth made a
strange pattern in the air. Like a medieval signal gantry, it was
alive with purpose, and inspired a second artist to explore its
spatial mysteries. His studies of the central tower rear up in
moonlit greys. Sometimes the Minster itself has been dissolved,

leaving behind the bristling scaffolding. In his early pictures there was no human life, but later figures began to appear.

As the restoration programme moved into top gear, the Surveyor of the Fabric told a meeting of schoolchildren that on completion of the major work there would be a scheme of long-term deferred repairs, and an annual £35,000 would be needed to keep the building in good condition. "That will be your job," he said. "The Minster is something that belongs to you—part of your collective memory and a symbol of the North. You cannot imagine Yorkshire without York Minster. I cannot imagine England without it. Is it worth it? You have to decide what you think about the Minster. Personally, if I ask myself whether we should have one more V=bomber or York Minster, I know the answer."

The 250-year building programme which ended in 1472 and gave the city the Minster as it is seen today, also saw the development of the walls, gates, posterns, hospitals, guildhall, merchants' halls, priories, friaries and St Mary's Abbey. It was York's architectural zenith. The shattered bone-white stones of the abbey are set, like an elaborate garden folly in the city's most attractive ten acres—the Museum Gardens—bounded by the river, the King's Manor, Marygate and Museum Street. A haven of rare and beautiful trees, it is also the home of the early-Victorian classical-style Yorkshire Museum and its medieval annexe, the Hospitium.

A Hungarian writer, visiting the city in the mid-1960s, visited the abbey after dark and found it "in a garden, lit by a pale green moonlight". It was, he said, as if some demented architectural anatomist had dissected a church by moonlight. He touched perceptively on its highly dramatic qualities which were first fully recognized in 1951 when, during the first of the city's triennial festivals, it formed the background for the revived Cycle of medieval Mystery Plays.

The original York Mystery Plays were acted by rough-and-ready medieval citizens on a fleet of two-deck wagons known as 'pageants'. Pageant Green, which was near the modern railway station, is where they were stored between performances. The day set aside for the day-long show was Corpus Christi, the first Thursday after Trinity Sunday which usually falls in early June. The Gilds which produced the plays were asked to provide "good players, well arrayed and well speaking" ready to move off about half past four in the morning. Each pageant in turn was taken to twelve or more 'stations' in the city, so anyone with sufficient stamina could stand at one of these vantage points and see the whole Cycle of forty-eight plays between dawn and dusk.

Mr E. Martin Browne, producer of the 1951 Cycle, realized that a modern production could not use this leisurely method (although in later years selected plays were given street performances on pageant wagons) and he was faced with the problem of compressing the Cycle into an evening. He combined the English and Continental systems of medieval stagecraft by choosing the ruined north wall of the nave of St Mary's Abbey as his background, using the window frames of the clerestory as 'Heaven' and a hill in the corner between the north and west walls as both the Garden of Eden and Gethsemane. Skilful cutting and dovetailing told the story of man from the Creation to the Last Judgement in a comparatively short time.

The production made use of an edited version of the Cycle by the late Dr J. S. Purvis, whose memorial plaque is to be seen in the timbered main room of St Anthony's Hall in Peasholme Green, now home of the Borthwick Institute of Historical Research, a York University department which he founded.

Though the York Cycle is not unique, Dr Purvis held that it was the finest and most complete body of Mystery Plays to be found connected with any English town or city. At one time it included fifty-seven plays, but the known version has forty-eight. The only complete text is that published by Miss Lucy Toulmin Smith in 1885 from a manuscript version in the British Museum, and Dr Purvis's version was the first text for acting issued since the plays had been last performed in about 1570. According to a list of 1417, the plays were performed at twelve fixed stations, though at times the number varied. The first station was outside the gate of Holy Trinity Priory in Micklegate, then the wagons moved downhill to the end of Skeldergate, across the river to Jubbergate, Coney Street, Stonegate, Minster Gates, Petergate and Pavement. It became so popular to arrange for the wagons to stop outside particular houses that the Corporation stepped in and demanded a high fee for the privilege.

Dr Purvis had an attractive theory about the origin of the plays, pointing out that the Cycle dated from about the middle of the fourteenth century and suggesting that there might have been a

general impulse to make these religious plays a form of thanksgiving for deliverance from the Black Death of 1349. During
preparation of the text he noticed that much of the language was
close to the dialect spoken in the North and East Ridings of
Yorkshire, and quoted an example from the Play of the Harrow-
ing of Hell, where Jesus orders the gates of Hell to open, first in
Latin, then in the local speech:

> JESUS (without): Attollite portas principes.
> Oppen uppe, ye princes...

But generally the words have a Homeric blend of simplicity
and nobility. Spoken as the summer twilight deepens, as the bats
explore and the birds head for home, they turn the ten acres of
the Museum Gardens, heady with the scent of crushed grass, into
a medieval dream.

St Mary's Abbey owes its origin to King William Rufus.
Twelve years before an arrow ended his reign on an August day
in the New Forest, he visited York to see how members of the
Benedictine order were managing in the pre-Conquest church of
St Olave. This church and four acres of land round it had come
into the possession of Alan, son of Eudo, Count of Brittany, and
in turn had been handed over to Stephen, a monk of Whitby, so
that he could found a Benedictine abbey. During his visit in 1088
the king found the premises inadequate and gave the monks
additional land nearby. The following year he laid the foundation
stone of the new house, dedicated to the Blessed Virgin. The
original St Mary's Abbey began to take shape. From the ruins left
by a disastrous fire which raged through the city in King
Stephen's reign—it was said to have "burnt down the cathedral
church, St Mary's Abbey, St Leonard's Hospital, with thirty-nine
parish churches in the city, and Trinity church in the suburbs"—a
new abbey began to rise in 1270 under the direction of Simon de
Warwick, the abbot. He laid the foundation stone and lived to see
the completion of the building twenty-two years later. This was
the abbey whose ruins rise today over the smooth sloping lawns
of the Museum Gardens.

Remains of some of the conventual buildings are preserved in
the lower storey of the Yorkshire Museum. They include some of
the wall foundations and column bases of the chapter house
vestibule, the entrance into the chapter house itself and the fireplace of the warming house.

The abbey grounds were enclosed by a wall with a circumference of nearly three-quarters of a mile, and the main entrance was in Marygate. Simon de Warwick's restored church was 350 feet long and the cloister lay on the south side of the nave. To the east of the cloister were the vestibule leading to the chapter house, the scriptorium and library, and the monks' sleeping quarters. On the west was the lay brothers' building and on the south the warming house and the monks' refectory. Beyond these ranges were the kitchen, novices' buildings, infirmary and a number of unidentified buildings. The hospitium (now an annexe to the Yorkshire Museum) was 100 yards south of the west front, and the abbot's house, later to become the King's Manor and now part of the University of York, lay north-east of the conventual buildings. Today stretches of the streets Bootham and Marygate are enhanced by the abbey wall and, at their junction, the attractive St Mary's Tower, round and with a conical roof.

A look at the duties of just two officers of a typical medieval abbey—the Fraterer and the Chamberlain—gives some idea of the life of the monks. The Fraterer's duties were in the refectory where he laid the tablecloths and had them washed, repaired and, when necessary, renewed. He poured the beer into jugs which were washed once a week. He washed the cups and spoons every day and kept count of them. He fetched bread from the cellars, and provided mats and rushes for the floor and the alleyways of the cloister. In summer he may have strewn flowers, mint and fennel to sweeten the air. In winter he supplied candles for the table.

The Chamberlain and his assistant provided straw for the monks' mattresses once a year. He prepared warm water for shaving, soap for washing the monks' heads and water for baths which were taken three or four times a year.

This may seem reasonably comfortable by medieval standards, but life must have been hard when the demands of regular worship turned the monks out of their beds in the early hours and into the freezing abbey church. However, it was too easy a life for some of the brethren and it was from here—five years before the fire damaged the abbey—that thirteen of the monks, including the prior and sub-prior, set out to found Fountains Abbey in the valley of the River Skell, not far from Ripon in the West Riding, in 1132. Today it is the country's most sublime ruin, lapped by an example of eighteenth-century landscape gardening unparalleled anywhere in the north of England. In the twelfth century the site was described as "A place remote from all the world, uninhabited, set with thorns and amongst the hollows of the mountains and prominent rocks, fit more, as it seemed, for the dens of wild beasts than for the uses of mankind." It suited the rebels. Benedictines lived among the townsfolk and worldliness was always at the gate. Life had become slack, and the splinter group longed for the more austere rule of the Cistercian Order whose members chose to live in isolated parts of the country.

The abbey's influence over the city and much of the north, which had lasted for nearly 500 years, was swept away on 29th November 1539 when it was surrendered under the terms of the dissolution of the monasteries. In 1541, during a royal progress through Yorkshire and other northern counties, Henry VIII, accompanied by Catherine Howard, stayed in York for twelve days. For their lodging a long, narrow building was erected on the south-west side of the deserted abbot's house; a vaulted cellar is all that remains today of this temporary royal 'palace'. During the visit the city streets were swept, sanded and gravelled. Henry's purpose in coming north was to receive the submission of those who had been implicated in the recent Pilgrimage of Grace, a rebellion against the king's first act of suppression.

In Jacobean times substantial remains of the abbey were still to be seen. The church walls and steeple were standing, though the roof had gone. The gatehouse was in good condition, but the courthouse it contained was in need of repair. It was during the eighteenth century that the city began to use the abbey as a convenient stone quarry. In 1701 stone was removed for the building of the York County Gaol; in 1705 material was used on St Olave's Church; between 1717 and 1720 stone was used to repair Beverley Minster in the East Riding; and about 1756 the abbey helped to build the landing-stage at Lendal Ferry. Writing in 1829, the Rev. Charles Wellbeloved, the York antiquary, said: "Within the memory of some now living a person was allowed to erect a kiln near the venerable pile and to burn its hallowed stones into lime."

The former abbot's house, now the King's Manor, occupies a site north-east of the abbey and forms one side of Exhibition Square, an open space of great potential overlooked by Bootham Bar and the city art gallery. Carved doorways, interlocking courtyards and gabled roofs combine to create one of the city's most romantic buildings. It is now occupied by a section of the University of York. For the first three centuries of its history it was the home of the abbot of St Mary's, and during the following century was the headquarters of the Council in the North.

Built in about 1270 for Simon de Warwick, abbot from 1258 to 1296, the first house on this site was probably three-sided, and may have had a stone ground floor with an upper storey of timber-framing. There was extensive remodelling in brick in the late fifteenth century. In charge of this work was Richard Cheryholme who was employed as master bricklayer in September 1483 by Abbot Thomas Boothe, and this work was continued under Abbot Sever (1485–1502).

The Council in the North was established in the Manor a month after the dissolution of St Mary's Abbey. Additional building began in 1560 and a north-west range was built in cut stone re-used from the abbey. New windows were put into the medieval house. A council chamber was created on the first floor by Henry Hastings, Earl of Huntingdon, who was President of the Council from 1572 to 1595. Here the frieze embodies his crest of a bull's head erased within a garter, and the device of the bear and ragged staff for his wife, Catherine Dudley. The last great building period was in the time of Thomas Wentworth, Earl of Strafford, who turned the large room known as the Banqueting Hall into a chapel and built a gallery between it and the Council Chamber.

After 1641 the Council in the North ceased to exist and the manor became involved in the Siege of York (1644) during the Civil War. Later it became the residence of the Governor of York, and parts of the building were legally used as a source of stone by local contractors. Weekly assemblies for dancing and card parties started in the reign of William and Mary and were held at first in the Manor's south-east wing every Monday evening. Later the assemblies moved to Lord Irwin's house in Minster Yard until, in 1731–2, Lord Burlington designed the Assembly Rooms in Blake Street, a building influenced by Palladio and Vitruvius. From 1712 to 1835 a girls' boarding school occupied part of the Manor, and in January 1813, the Manor National School was opened in the back court. The Yorkshire School for the Blind moved in in 1835, and it was for a principal of this school that, in 1900, a York architect designed the last addition to the building, on the north-west side of the forecourt. York Corporation bought the Manor for £30,000 in 1958, and the University took over after extensive renovations in 1963–4.

Set back from the narrow street called Aldwark and tucked under the north-east sector of the city wall, the Merchant Taylors' Hall belies its late-fourteenth-century date, for it was encased in brick in the late seventeenth and early eighteenth centuries. It was built by the Fraternity of St John the Baptist which was connected with the Taylors' Guild (often spelt 'Gild' in York). The tailors were responsible for the penultimate play in the Mystery Cycle, which deals with Christ's ascension.

The Hall was first mentioned in 1415 when the Corporation granted a portion of the city moat to four tailors and the Master of the Guild, and the earliest mention of the Guild is in the will of Peter de Barleburgh who, in 1390, left it the sum of 3s 4d. In 1446 a chapel was attached to the hall, and Mass was celebrated there. In 1489 a chantry priest, William Akers, who probably lodged at the chantry priests' house, left 6s 8d to the Master and brethren of the guild and also "all the glass and boards within his chamber". As late as 1606 at least one of the old customs was maintained. Thomas Gibson, a tailor, stated in his will of that year that he wished the Master and Searchers of the Company of Drapers and Taylors to be invited to his funeral. The Merchant Taylors' Company received its Royal Charter of Incorporation in 1661 as an amalgamation of three craft guilds—Taylors, Drapers and Hosiers, together with the original Fraternity of St John the Baptist.

The fine medieval roof of the hall covers the main 'double cube' room, measuring 60 feet long by 30 feet high and 30 feet wide. Charm is added by the fireplace and overmantel bearing the drapers' arms, and a small musicians' gallery of about 1800. The original main doorway and screens are still in position.

Two windows in the Counsel or Counting House which opens off the main hall are by the York glass painter, Henry Gyles (1645–1709). The larger window in the south wall is dated 1702 and includes in the top panel the head of Queen Anne (it was the year of her accession). A lower inscription says "This company had beene dignified in the yeare 1679 by haveing in their Fraternity eight Kings, eleven Dukes, thirty Earles and forty-four Lords." This must refer to the London Company of Taylors. Gyles's bill for this window was 10s. His second window shows the arms of the Company and carries his initials under the first word of the motto.

Famous for his sundials, Gyles was the last of a family of glass painters who lived in Micklegate, and must have been one of the first artist-craftsmen to use a trade card—a mezzotint portrait of himself done by his friend, Francis Place (1647–1728) who lived in the King's Manor. On the card, in flowing script, he offers "Glass painting for windows, as Armes, Sundyals, History, Landskipt &c. Done by Henry Gyles of the City of York." His oldest known work is a sundial at Nun Appleton Hall, near York, dated 1670, and illustrating the four seasons. He may also have painted a similar sundial over the front door of the Queen Anne Tong Hall, near Bradford.

All the organization involved in the export of cloth from Yorkshire in the fifteenth, sixteenth and seventeenth centuries was planned in the great hall of the Merchant Adventurers which has frontages on both busy Piccadilly—a street extended through to Pavement in 1910—and the quieter Fossgate. It is a superb example of a building which has come down to us virtually unchanged from the mid-fourteenth century.

The great hall, originally one room 89 feet long by 39½ feet wide, was not always as attractive as it is today. In the early eighteenth century it was divided into two rooms by a wooden partition and in the nineteenth century the oak roof was hidden by a ceiling, with the cross-beams boxed in deal cases.

It is easy to see how in one year alone—1358—a hundred standing trees were bought at Thorpe Underwood for its construction. They cost £21, over £200 in modern money, but the cost of felling, sawing and carting would have to be added. Out of the complexity of the timbering there emerges the feeling that one is standing in the heart of a great wooden ship; the hall, with its gently undulating floor, is rather like a more spacious version of the main gundeck of HMS *Victory*.

The land on which the building stands was granted on 6th December 1356 by Sir William Percy to three York citizens, John Freboys, John Crome and Robert Smeton. In the following year a royal licence was given for the founding of a guild or fraternity whose activities were mainly religious. Gifts of money came from London and from great Yorkshire families, like the Hothams, who included John de Hotham, Bishop of Ely.

The ground floor of the building is formed by the undercroft or hospital with its fireplace of about 1420, and an attached chapel displays the arms of Charles II, dated 1669. Though the royal licence to found the hospital for guild members who had fallen on hard times dates from 1371–2, wills of 1365 show that it was then a going concern. In that year Emma de Huntyngton left the hospital her feather bed.

A modern attraction in the main hall is the collection of twenty guild banners made for the city's historical pageant of 1909—an event not to be repeated until 1971 during the celebration of the 1900th anniversary of the arrival of the Romans. The banners show the heraldic devices adopted by the Merchant Adventurers, the Merchant Taylors and eighteen crafts. In many of them, obsolete tools of the trade are to be seen.

The arms of the Goldsmiths included a leopard's mask, a covered cup and two buckles, and the Cordwainers (shoemakers) displayed three goats' heads. Three alembics—an early form of smelting retort—appear on the Pewterers' banner, and the Tanners chose an oak tree, a bull's face and a fountain. Tree bark was used in the tanning process. The three leopards' heads of the Weavers carry shuttles in their mouths, and the Clothworkers are represented by two habicks—ancient instruments of the craft—and a teazle, used for raising the nap on cloth. Three doves, each holding an olive branch, formed the device of the Tallow Chandlers, and the Glaziers were identified by two grozing irons and four closing nails. The grozing iron was a craft tool with which panes of stained glass were shaped into curves and the nails were used to set out the design before being leaded. Nine aromatic cloves were the Grocers' symbol, and the Feltmakers placed a red right hand between two hat-bands and a black, conical hat. They had their shops in Fetter Lane, a corruption of Felter Lane. The Girdlers, makers of leather girdles, picked three gridirons as their punning device—they were commonly known as 'girdles'. The mill-peck, used for cutting grooves in millstones, appears on the Millers' arms, and three rope hooks signify the Ropers. Completing the list are the Vintners—three tuns; Curriers—craft tools; Masons—a pair of compasses; Dyers—three madder bags; Skinners—ermine and crowns.

In a house near the Minster two shades from the past face each other across the window recess in a room lined with seventeenth-century panelling. Sometimes the sun adds depth to the small features, lights up the gathers in the tarnished finery. A man and woman of fashion from Georgian England, they are modelled in miniature, in wax. For me these pale shadows of an elegant way of life have always epitomized the Treasurer's House in Minster Yard. From their corner of the Tapestry Dressing-Room they take the measure of time only from the passing seasons. A National Trust property since 1930, the house declares its pedigree through the preserved base of a Roman pillar deep in its capacious and rather mysterious cellars. If it is in its original position, now 12 feet below the existing floor level, it may have formed part of a colonnade lining the *Via Decumana*, represented today by the charming little Chapter House Street which runs past the side entrance to the house.

The great fire which swept through York in 1137 probably destroyed the first Treasurer's House on this site which dated from the end of the eleventh century. In the reign of Edward I there was a more imposing rebuilding, and thirteenth-century architectural evidence still remains in the undercroft of the north range. But the visible house today is an amalgam of seventeenth- and eighteenth-century styles, the main front being distinguished by pairs of Dutch ogee gables. In early prints and in a British Museum manuscript the gables are shown pointed. Their change in shape may have been the work of Robert Squire who took over the house in 1669 and whose elaborate tomb may be seen in the nearby church of St Michael-le-Belfrey.

Over the years famous names have been linked with the house. Matthew Robinson, father of Elizabeth Montagu, "Queen of the Blue Stockings", bought the house in 1721. In 1728 he divided the property, selling part to Edward Finch, a residentiary canon, and part to Bacon Morritt whose grandson was John Bacon Sawrey Morritt, a friend of Sir Walter Scott's. The novelist dedicated his long poem *Rokeby* to him. The other portion of the house was sold by Lord Winchelsea to Dr Jacques Sterne, precentor and canon residentiary of York. His nephew, the famous satirical novelist, Laurence Sterne, often stayed with him at Treasurer's House.

Seen from a window in the Treasurer's House, the central tower of the Minster slices across the sky. Through an artist's eye it is a hard-edged Gothic sketch, spare and dramatic; to the scientist it could have another meaning—as a fixed point of measurement. It is thought that from such a window the young deaf and dumb astronomer, John Goodricke, made invaluable observations in the late eighteenth century. Today he is commemorated by Goodricke College of York University, built in 1968.

It was said of Goodricke that "no other citizen of York has exercised so much influence upon the history of thought except Alcuin". He was born in Groningen, Holland, in 1764, the eldest child of Henry Goodricke of York and Levina Benjamina, daughter of Peter Sessler of Namur. On his father's death in July 1784 he became heir to his grandfather, Sir John Goodricke of Ribston Hall, Yorkshire, who, however, survived him.

He earned lasting distinction by his investigation of variable stars. At the age of 18 he discovered the period and law of the star Algol's changes. He first saw the star lose light on 12th November 1782, and observed it at York every fine night from 28th December to 12th May the following year.

The results were communicated to the Royal Society in a paper, and this won him the Copley Medal in 1783. The following year, between 10th September and 19th October, he discovered the variability of Beta Lyrae and Delta Cephei. In this way he laid the foundation of modern measurement of the universe. Fellowship of the Royal Society, the highest scientific honour, was conferred on him when he was only 21, but he died in York shortly afterwards, on 20th April 1786, and was buried in a new family vault at Hunsingore, above the winding River Nidd, in the West Riding.

Today something of York's special flavour is to be found in the social occasions at Treasurer's House, usually held in the Great Hall with its portrait of Charles I in the Van Dyck style, long oak table of 1600 and Carolean brass chandelier.

By a curious division, the northern wing now leads a separate existence as Gray's Court, occupied by the history department of St John's College. Here again, the superb Long Gallery is sometimes used socially and is a memorable setting, particularly on warm summer evenings when the doors are open into the garden, bounded by the most romantic stretch of the medieval city wall.

A few yards round the corner from Treasurer's House, not far from the Minster's east window, is a spot so unspoilt that it was chosen without hesitation by a television producer filming backgrounds for a dramatized life of Schumann. So St William's College became, for a while, a bit of old Leipzig.

The half-timbered frontage on to College Street (once known as Vicar Lane and Little Alice Lane) has been virtually unaltered since its erection in the 1460s. It masks an elegant courtyard with an early-seventeenth-century inner porch.

Built for the Minster's chantry priests, it passed through a number of hands after the Reformation and finally became tenements which were, as an old photograph shows, pretty far down the social scale. At the turn of this century, Francis Green, a Wakefield engineer, who had bought and restored the Treasurer's House between 1897 and 1900, became owner of the college. In 1906 he sold it, at no profit, to the Convocation of York as their meeting-place, and this was its main function until the amalgamation of the Convocations of Canterbury and York into the Synod of the Church of England. How many delegates to the parliament of the northern church, wearied by protracted discussion of Canon Law, must have found solace in their beautiful surroundings?

At the eastern end of College Street, where it joins Goodramgate, is a small half-timbered building which bridges the street. It is all that remains of a covered way which Richard II allowed the vicars-choral to build so that they could cross from their home in Bedern to the Minster Yard without being molested.

Bedern, a run-down commercial area ripe for redevelopment in the early 1970s, lies between Goodramgate and Aldwark. Once a courtyard 27 feet by 130 feet, Bedern sheltered the vicars-choral in the mid-thirteenth century. The vicars lived in thirty-six neat little houses rather like medieval bed-sitting rooms, and sharing the space with them were an orchard, garden, chapel and common hall. Fourteenth-century account rolls reveal the day-to-day expenses of life in this quiet retreat . . . five gallons of oil for the lamp in the chapel cost 5s 10d; wax-lights were 4d each; rushes for strewing on the chapel floor were 1d; 2d was the charge for washing vestments and the same sum bought a cord for the bell. Wood for the fire on the vigil of St John the Baptist was remarkably dear at 2s 4d, considering that a font cover could be had for 6d and book clasps for 3d.

Two men who created a herbarium in the garden earned 2s 4d and the vicars received similar pay for work on the ditches and the court. For four and a half days' work digging and planting seeds they were paid 1s 6d, and 2d was spent on drinks for them.

When it came to the acquisition of other church property, the treasurer really opened the purse strings. In the late fifteenth century the benefice of Nether Wallop came into the possession of the vicars and stayed in their keeping until the official dissolution of their college in 1936. Taking over this church meant that one of the vicars had to travel south in 1472, and the final bill for the journey and the legal costs came to £33 11s 6d, about £700 in modern money.

As late as 1971 the 600-year-old timbers of the vicars' common hall were still to be seen embedded in the fabric of commercial premises. It was in this high-roofed hall that on the evening of Boxing Day, 1419, two of the vicars-choral got into an argument as they sat over the fire. Robert Ripon thought John of Middleton was about to hit him with the poker, so he threw him on to the iron frame holding the kettle. Records show that Ripon was fined 3s 4d and Middleton 20d. So it was not all sweetness and light in a medieval religious community.

Tucked away behind walls which give no hint of its existence, chopped up both vertically and laterally, the hall was for many years used as the flour store of a bakery, but was empty and awaiting decisions when I visited it. The owner, a York businessman, offered the roof of the hall to anyone able to move and preserve it, perhaps as an object lesson in medieval timber construction. The timbers, with their unusual scissor construction, seemed in good heart, and carpenters' marks were still clearly visible in places.

The roll of John of Fulford, chamberlain for 1328-9, gives some indication of the date of the hall. Repairs are mentioned, so it would seem that it had been in use for a few years before this time. It also refers to the work of William of Ampleforth who "closed the wall of the great hall with stone". Two masons were paid 2s for repairing the entrance, and it cost 2d to have a window mended. Thick planks "bought for the principal seat in the hall" were 1s, four long boards of fir 8d, tiles from Beverley and brass 9d. When guests were entertained at the hall they were charged 2d for a one-course meal, 1d for breakfast or supper, and the same amount for drinks. Among the vicars Benedictine was a popular drink. In the winter it could be drunk once after dinner and, "after the washing of hands", once round the fire. After supper they could have three more drinks up to eight o'clock. It was on 27th June 1574 that the vicars stopped dining together in the hall, and in about 1772 it passed into lay hands when the lessee sold the building to Thomas Waud of York for £150.

From then on this quiet corner of the medieval city, where ripe

The Multangular Tower

DIEV · NOVS · DONNE · BONNE · ADVENTVRE

fruit lay in the long orchard grass and wax-lights burned steadily in the chapel, had a long downhill run into squalor. In 1844, the physician to the York Dispensary made a pilgrimage through the inner circles of the slums and found Bedern occupied by ninety-eight families. One entire building was let off in single rooms, and the staircase windows could not be opened. Sanitation was just a word. But even the slums have disappeared now, and in 1971 the Aldwark redevelopment scheme offered the chance of a bright future.

Between 1942 and 1958 no historic site in York was more dismal than the shell of the fire-bombed Guildhall, immediately to the north and lying a little behind the eighteenth-century Mansion House.

The great double-aisled timber roof had been ash on the wind since the Baedeker raid, and lines of temporary wooden hutments, used by a corporation department, filled the interior. Open to the sky, the walls took the brunt of sixteen winters until work began on the creation of a replica of the old hall, with the War Damage Commission meeting a large part of the bill. Two years later, in 1960, the restored Guildhall was opened by Queen Elizabeth the Queen Mother and has been an elegant addition to the city's attractions ever since.

The new timber roof came from Yorkshire estates and is supported on ten huge oak pillars each weighing $2\frac{1}{4}$ tons and each cut from a single tree. The 120 roof bosses are in the form of heraldic shields, and at the apex of the roof are the Royal Arms and the Arms of the city. One of the fittings to survive the fire was the plaque to the right of the dais, given by the city of New York in 1924. The wrought-iron balustrade to the left is the gift of the citizens of Munster, York's 'twin' in the province of North Rhine Westphalia. The opening of the Guildhall was attended by the *Oberburgermeister* and *Oberstadtsdirektor* of that city.

Though a charter of 1256 refers to a Guildhall in York there is no clue as to where it stood. But just over a century later, in 1378, an entry in the York Memorandum Book proves that there was a Civic Guildhall on the present site. A complaint was made of damage to the common lane which ran under the hall—a paved way to the river which may still be seen today. In 1446 this hall was found to be too small and plans were made for the building of a larger one through the joint efforts of the Mayor and Commonalty of the City of York and the Master, brethren and sisters

5

Coat-of-Arms: Merchant Adventurers' Hall
St Martin's Clock

of St Christopher's Guild. It was to have a chamber at the west end, a cellar under the east end, a pantry and a buttery.

First to be built were the Common Hall Gates, an arched passage with a small room above and battlemented walls, which stood a little to the south-east of the present Guildhall passage. Stone from Tadcaster and Cawood was used in its construction, but details of the building are sketchy as the earliest Chamberlain's Book of Accounts for 1446-7 has been badly damaged by flood water. On the front facing Coney Street were the Arms of the city and, from 1501, a figure of Ebrauc, the mythical founder of York. This image, sometimes known as Olde Yorke, had stood at the corner of St Saviourgate and Colliergate until in the seventeenth year of the reign of Henry VII (1501) it was taken down, renovated and set up in its new position. It stayed there until 1725 when the site was cleared for the building of the Mansion House, and was said in 1730 to be kept in the Guildhall Jury Room. Eight years later a restored figure of Ebrauc was ordered to be fixed in a niche on Bootham Bar and it probably stayed there for many years. A description of the Bar written in 1785 does not mention it.

A start on the building of the main hall can be dated to 1448-9 when the Chamberlain's Book recorded amounts spent on food and drink for the workmen driving foundation piles. Cords used to mark out the site cost 1d, and 66s 8d went on cut stone from the earlier Guildhall. The masons had a little thatched storehouse built for them as new stone from Newton quarry, near Tadcaster, arrived by road and river. Ten years later the roof was sufficiently complete for a council meeting to be held in the new building.

In Elizabethan York travelling companies of actors gave performances in the Guildhall, usually putting on two shows, one for the 'Establishment', the other for the citizens. But the townspeople, finding this kind of entertainment a little heady, enjoyed themselves too well. On 24th July 1592, it was said that doors, locks, keys, windows, boards, benches and other furnishings had been "broken, shaken, loosened and riven up" by the boisterous audience. So no more plays were to be performed in the Guildhall.

The elegant room which survives at the West end of the Guildhall today as Committee Room No 1 was known as the Inner Chamber or the Inner House, and was badly damaged in the Civil War in the mid-seventeenth century. In 1644 after the siege of York and again in 1645 it was described as "broken downe". Perhaps the floor had collapsed under the weight of arms and stores which had been kept there. However, it was back in use in January 1647, when it took eleven days to count the £200,000 due to the Scots army for helping the Parliamentary forces.

Early windows in the Guildhall were probably part glass, part wooden louvre, and there is no mention of stained glass until the late seventeenth century when Henry Gyles was paid £20 for a five-light window displaying the city arms. This was removed in the face of some opposition in 1863. An eighteenth-century panel by William Peckitt was destroyed in the air-raid of 1942.

But the glory of the Guildhall today is the west window of five lights, measuring 15 feet 6 inches by 11 feet 6 inches, created by the York glass painter, Mr Harry Harvey, who, following the example of the great glass painters of the past, has established his studio in Micklegate. High above the street, among the town houses of the eighteenth century, his patient work—which I have often watched—adds beauty to churches and cathedrals in all parts of the country. Unlike the windows of Piper and Reyntiens in Coventry and Liverpool, in which slabs of glass bonded by synthetic resins have been used to manipulate light, his windows are representational, but with an unmistakably twentieth-century stamp. Sometimes, where appropriate, his human figures display fashion trends datable to the period in which the window was made.

In sixteen main sections the window in the Guildhall covers events in the city's history from the arrival of the Romans to development of the railways, and provides a gallery of characters connected with York from Robinson Crusoe (supposedly born in the city in 1632) to Constantine the Great. At the foot of the second light the window's predecessor is seen engulfed by incendiary bombs.

On a commanding site at the corner of Aldwark and Peasholme Green, opposite the Black Swan inn, another guild hall, St Anthony's, now houses the Borthwick Institute of Historical Research, a department of the University of York. Founded in 1953 by the York Civic Trust, the Institute possesses a large collection of documents from the Diocesan and Probate Registries, opens its great hall to the public and mounts frequent documentary exhibitions. In its 500-year career it has served as workhouse, knitting school, a house of correction where every rogue was to be whipped and set to work, playhouse, hospital and, from 1705 to 1946, the Blue Coat charity school.

A little way up the Aldwark side of the hall there is the ghost of an elaborate doorway—a pattern of dressed stones set in the dark brick in-filling—which once led to the chapel. It was still in use in 1593 when the "poor folk" responded to a morning and evening bell.

3

UNDER STEEPLE AND TOWER

THE FORTY parish churches which rose over the tangled lanes of the medieval city in the early years of the fifteenth century have been whittled down by decay and demolition, the twin hammers which have changed the faces of our towns. Today about half are left. Under steeple and tower, in busy street or silent court, they continue to offer the stored peace of the passing centuries. They have been patient listeners to time's slow tick as the city grew, like the concentric rings of a tree, spreading from the Roman heart through the Saxon, Norman, Tudor, Georgian, Victorian and twentieth-century layers. For some, too many winter frosts have scribbled their signatures on the stone; the centuries weigh heavily, and closure has been reluctantly accepted. For others, there has been a change to secular use. In the summer of 1971 one of the city's most charming churches, with a complete and unrestored interior, closed its doors for a time because of danger to the many visitors it attracts. Though without a regular congregation, it still happily offers its stored peace among the uneven box pews.

A fifteen-member Working Party appointed by the Archbishop of York in 1961 to look into new roles for old churches, reported in 1964, after twenty-six meetings, that of all the buildings considered, only one—St Maurice's of 1878—should be demolished. The site, with its trees and neat gravestones, has now been landscaped. Though they felt that the exterior fabric of any church put to other uses should be properly maintained because a dilapidated church was a bad advertisement for the work of the Church, the committee was also concerned about the limitation of the number of churches preserved as national monuments or museums in case the impression was given that the Church in York was dead. Their report suggested that redundant churches might be used as a museum of ecclesiastical art; a *columbarium* (recessed vaults to house cinerary urns); a community centre with a chapel for deaf people; university purposes or for other educational schemes.

But more dramatic schemes were on the way, defended by some as "exciting", blasted by others as "fantastic nonsense". A group of professional men in the city, headed by a York University don and Heslington churchwarden, Dr Brian Morris, proposed the setting up of a controversial partnership in the autumn of 1968. It was to be between commercial developers and ecclesiastical authorities to preserve ten old churches inside the city walls by turning them into hotels, a restaurant and other secular public buildings. Dr Morris's group criticized the church authorities for lack of action in taking steps to preserve the churches and claimed that the Working Party's report had been "quietly shelved" while the condition of unused or only partially used old churches in the city worsened every year.

The group's report suggested the setting up of a private limited company to develop three churches as hotels. The largest-scale development was proposed for St Margaret's, Walmgate, which could, said the planners, provide accommodation for upwards of fifty people. They saw the church being used for dining-rooms and lounges, with a two-storey building standing on steel and concrete pillars in the church grounds and fronting Walmgate as the main hotel building. For St Martin-cum-Gregory the proposal was for a twenty-four-guest hotel with sixteen rooms built along the south side of the churchyard in a double tier with carports beneath, or with a car park at the west side of the church. St Saviour's was to be a hotel with more than twenty bedrooms with a possible bridge to the multi-storey car park nearby. St Michael's, Spurriergate, might be developed as a restaurant, and Holy Trinity, Goodramgate, might have the whole site developed as a shopping piazza and exhibition area, with a row of small, single-storey shops in the grounds selling tourist items and the church's early box pews adapted as display stands.

All Saints', North Street, said the group, could become a York Glass Museum containing an exhibition room for the York Glaziers' Trust, while St Michael-le-Belfrey, close to the Minster, would be a natural tourist centre. St Sampson's could be developed as a market centre, St Denys's as a student hostel and

St Cuthbert's as a centre for receiving and helping derelicts and delinquents. The group realized that some of the churches had faithful congregations, but felt it was not good for a building to be used only once a week. The problem was to balance the individual loyalties against the greater good of preserving the buildings.

Despite the fact that Dr Morris and his group were asked to submit detailed proposals for hotel schemes for St Saviour's and St Margaret's, the final report in May 1969 of the York Redundant Churches Commission was against the putting of the churches to commercial use. The commission was not convinced of the economic viability of the proposals and, using its 1967 report as a basis, came forward with a number of suggestions, some of which have been realized. Perhaps the most remarkable use of a redundant city church was the conversion of St Mary's Castlegate, into Britain's largest heritage centre. This £146,400 project was opened in September 1975 by the Countess of Dartmouth, chairman of the executive committee of the United Kingdom Council for European Architectural Heritage Year. The church was transformed to offer visitors a unique 'York experience', taking them through the centuries by means of slide shows, tableaux, models and art work to show the fascinating effect of 1,900 years of history on the city, its architecture and its people. The York Civic Trust took the church under its wing and paid for essential emergency work over the years. The heritage centre represents the culmination of twenty-five years' work by the Trust to ensure that one day this splendid fifteenth-century church would find a use worthy of it.

However, at the time of the commission's suggestions only one city church—St John's, Ouse Bridge—has been successfully converted to secular use as York University's Institute of Advanced Architectural Studies. Its skilful remodelling became an object lesson in the preservation and adaptation of ancient churches for the architects from many countries who attended courses there. In later years, after the Institute had moved to the King's Manor on the other side of the river, it became the York Arts Centre, scene of a number of avant-garde productions. So it is still possible to see the bones of this former church with its squat, timbered bell-tower which replaced the spire blown down in 1551. Street widening and bridge improvement works gradually ate away its churchyard, so that today the south door opens directly on to the busy street; this was the door used by a priest for nailing up a sermon against the supremacy of Henry VIII, a treasonable act which cost him his life.

Curiously, the church does not appear in Domesday Book, though in a charter of 1189–92 land is said to be between the cemetery of St John at Ouse Bridge end and the ground of William, brother of Warin. It was in the chancel of this church that a book given by Thomas Tubbac, called *Historia Scholastica*, was kept on an iron chain; it was here that in 1489, three years after Tubbac's gift, a local fletcher, Richard Croklyn asked to be buried "at the end of my stall". The goods of the church were kept in a chest known as the Red Ark.

While the music and drama of the last quarter of the twentieth century laps around the walls of St John's and keeps them standing, secular use of a sadder kind is to be seen on the edge of the great marsh which once covered a north-eastern sector of the city centre.

The name of The Marsh was given to the area between St Saviourgate and the River Foss, the tributary which joins the Ouse south of the castle, and the name stuck long after the swamp had been reclaimed. In the Middle Ages the marsh area was crossed by two streets, Hungate and Haver Lane, and there were three churches, St John the Baptist, All Hallows and—still there today—St Saviour's.

A quiet mixture of church, chapels, offices, flats and small shops, St Saviourgate runs parallel to the rather dull new artery, Stonebow, but not long ago it was a busy route to the eastern suburbs where double-deck buses fought for supremacy. St Saviour's Church is about half-way down on the south-east side, masked in summer by rank growth, its windows boarded, its doors locked to all but the staff of the museum which once used it as a store. During underpinning operations in 1840 several coffins were found at a depth of fourteen feet, below the Roman level of occupation. They were made of oak slabs two and a half inches thick fastened by wooden dowels. The skeletons were in a perfect state, but blackened by the marsh water. Another find at that time was a series of medieval frescoes between the arcade arches of the nave. No one knows what happened to these life-size figures of apostles; perhaps they are still there under the plaster.

Here in 1436 Thomas Bracebridge left money to maintain three candles in an iron candelabrum which he had made himself; and in 1513 William Schirburn, the rector, left, for his chaplains' use, two books, *Golden Legend* and *Marrow of Grammar*. They were to be chained near the chapel of the Virgin.

The day I visited St Saviour's I was on the trail of a story linking the church with Colonial America. Past the black, glass-sided hearse, beyond the hand-pumped fire engine, under the Edwardian prams and motor-cycles . . . somewhere in the chancel was the tomb of Roger and Mary Morris. The most colourful period of their lives was spent 3,000 miles from this deserted spot, in the New York of the second half of the eighteenth century. Roger was once a dashing lieutenant-colonel in the British Army; Mary was a member of the wealthy Philipse family and was said to have rejected George Washington's offer of marriage. During the reception which followed her marriage to Roger in 1758 a tall Indian wrapped in a scarlet blanket appeared at the door of the banqueting hall and prophesied: "Your possessions shall pass from you when the Eagle shall despoil the Lion of his mane". Later events proved the accuracy of this forecast, and this account of the wedding was often told by Angevine, son of the favourite coloured valet of the Philipse family, who was sexton of St John's Church, Yonkers, for forty-five years.

Roger Morris, born at Netherby, Yorkshire, on 28th January 1727, was appointed captain in Francis Ligonier's Regiment, the 48th Foot, which served in Flanders and at Falkirk and Culloden. He went with the regiment to America in 1755 and was aide-de-camp to Major-General Edward Braddock in the expedition against Fort Duquesne, where he was wounded. After service at the siege of Louisburg and against the Indians on the frontier of Nova Scotia, he was promoted major in the 35th Foot in 1758— the year of his marriage.

The following year he was wounded while with Wolfe at Quebec, and in 1764 he sold out of the Army, settling in New York where he became a member of the city executive council in the December of the same year. For the next ten years he and Mary lived either in the town house on Stone Street, the impressive Morris mansion on the Hudson River, or, for two months of the year only, in a comfortable log-house. Life was good until 1776 when all their property was confiscated in the American War of Independence. Their plate and furniture were sold by auction, and the mansion was used for a time as Washington's headquarters. Roger, a loyalist to the British cause, took Mary back to England in 1783 and died at York on 13th September 1794.

Mary was born in 1730 at the Philipse manor house on the Hudson. She was described as a "handsome, rather imperious brunette". In 1756, when on a visit to her brother-in-law, Beverley Robinson, in New York, she met George Washington who was a guest in the house. Family tradition says she refused his offer of marriage during this visit. She inherited a large estate, part of which was in Putnam County, New York, including Lake Mahopac. Every half-year, until the property was confiscated, she would visit her tenants to instruct them in household and religious duties. She outlived Roger by more than thirty years, dying at her home in Minster Yard, York, in 1825 at the age of ninety-five.

The Morris family eventually received as compensation from the British Government a fourth of the value of their American estates, and Roger's heirs sold their claims to John Jacob Astor in 1809 for £20,000. The Morris's younger son, Henry Gage Morris, was a rear-admiral. He lived at York and Beverley and died on 24th November 1851. Their great-grandson, the Rev. M. C. F. Morris, was rector of Nunburnholme in the 1890s.

Once suggested as a university debating chamber and sometimes used as an exhibition hall during the city's triennial Festival of the Arts, the Church of St Martin-cum-Gregory, half way up Micklegate—the 'great street' south-west of the river—is another redundant church hovering in the kind of limbo which seems to be reserved for these buildings. Nevertheless, it is, in the words of the Archbishop's working party, "a fine church and in good repair". Though the interior has been stripped of its fittings and rather severely whitewashed, it has good architectural qualities.

Built in 1175, it was a church favoured by rich medieval merchants and after All Saints', Pavement, and the now demolished St Crux, it has buried in it the largest number of Mayors of York.

In 1435 Thomas Pynchbek, a chaplain, asked to be buried in front of the porch, and in 1480 Nicholas Pereson, a dyer, gave 3s 4d towards the making of two silver candelabra. The threat of demolition hung over the church at the time of the Reformation and all the lead was removed in 1548. The tiles which replaced the lead were still in use at the turn of this century.

William Peckitt, a well-known glass painter in eighteenth-century York, was buried here in 1795 only a few years after he had placed one of his own windows in the church as a memorial to two of his daughters who had died young. His obituary in a York newspaper said "he had the felicity of reviving this favourite art, which was almost entirely lost, with the merit of an inventor, for he had no assistance whatever from any other artist in the many curious discoveries he made".

Further up the hill, in an area where Trinity Lane and Priory Street run off Micklegate to the south-east, may be seen a fragment of a great Benedictine Priory. Today it bears the name of Holy Trinity, Micklegate. A curiosity which catches the visitor's eye even before he has stepped inside the church, is the statement on the notice-board that the building was haunted in the nineteenth century. The Yorkshire historian Baring Gould, in his *Yorkshire Oddities*, recorded accounts from eye-witnesses who claimed to have seen a woman, sometimes accompanied by a second woman and a child, crossing the east window during daytime services. Movement of trees in the churchyard was thought to be causing the illusion, and they were cut down. The woman still appeared. However, since the chancel was built in 1886 there have been no further reports.

The churchyard also offers a strange set of stocks—with five holes. I did hear that there was a photograph in existence which showed the stocks occupied by twentieth-century stand-ins, but on inquiry it turned out that they had taken the easy path . . . the third man had only one leg fastened. There appears to be no solution on record. The five holes could have been cut to accommodate two whole offenders and a recalcitrant one-legged sailor, but a more likely explanation is that at some time in the now unremembered past the old stocks were in process of being sawn up for firewood. A public-spirited antiquarian stopped the desecration, but not before one end—the end containing the sixth hole—had been lopped off. The stocks, of course, were a type of pillory, an instrument not used in Britain since 1837. In the seventeenth century it was in common use as a punishment for those who published books without a licence, and in time it became a popular way of punishing libellers of the Government. A number of eminent men were pilloried in their time, including Daniel Defoe whose hero Robinson Crusoe was York-born.

Scouring wind and frost are no respecters of some of the minor curiosities to be found in York. Gravestones are particularly vulnerable to the changes brought by the passing seasons, so that many interesting inscriptions now survive only in the photographic negative. Letter by letter, the originals have decayed into illegibility. A small monument, rapidly becoming defaced through natural causes, is tucked away near the vestry door of Holy Trinity, Micklegate. From the fragmentary words still left, the casual visitor could never piece together the story in the stone. It started between eight and nine o'clock on the evening of Saturday, 15th October 1768, when the London to York stage-coach was trundling along The Mount towards Micklegate Bar. Readers of the *York Courant*, one of the local newspapers, were told a few days later that the coach was "overturned within a quarter of a mile of this city by the driver's endeavouring to pass the Fly, whereby the coachman had his left leg broken and shattered in such a manner that it was obliged to be immediately cut off, and a young man, who was on the box with him, was killed. There were in the coach one man, four women and a young child, who received little hurt". The young man—he was only nineteen—came from Morpeth in Northumberland and was buried at Holy Trinity.

The twelfth-century nave pillars of the church belonged to a conventual church which was half as long again and much higher than the present one. Records mention a chapter house and cloisters. Dormitories, refectory, infirmary, brew house, stables and all the other domestic buildings must have stood on land now covered by modern buildings to the south and west. The gate-house, which fronted on to Micklegate, with an attractive archway, was destroyed as late as 1855 for the building of Priory Street. It was at this gate that the medieval gilds of York staged the opening performances of their Mystery Plays, now revived and performed at three-yearly intervals with the shattered walls of St Mary's Abbey in the Museum Gardens as a superb backcloth.

The priory, valued at just under £200 a year, was surrendered during the Dissolution in December 1538, and for the next couple of generations the site was robbed of its valuable dressed stone. The turning of the priory church into a handy quarry was helped by the collapse of the central tower during a storm on 5th February 1551 and in the following year permission was given to remove "leade, tymber, bells, glass, stone and other thinges" from the place. The church was evidently demolished in stages, and the choir was still intact in 1569 when Isabel Ward, the last prioress of St Clement's Nunnery, asked to be buried at Holy Trinity choir "neare besyde my stawle". Stones from the ruins were still being carted away in the seventeenth century and the Norman doorway now in the centre of Sir Arthur Ingram's almshouses in Bootham—the elegant street running north-westwards from Bootham Bar—was bought and installed there for 13s 4d. The almshouses have now been converted into flats.

Two points of interest about the present-day church and its grounds are a wall monument to Dr John Burton, who died in 1771, and a charming half-timbered house, Jacob's Well, on the north side of the churchyard.

Referred to in Laurence Sterne's *Tristram Shandy* as Dr Slop, Dr Burton was a Jacobite antiquary imprisoned after the 1745 Rebellion. He remained a close friend of Flora Macdonald.

As deep as Jacob's Well. That was probably the landlord's boast about his barrels in the days when the timbered medieval house in Trinity Lane did service as a public house of that name. But apart from that brief nineteenth-century excursion into secular life, this house has always been connected with the religious life of the city.

It was closely associated with St Clement's Nunnery, the first institution in York to be done away with under the Suppression Act of 1536 at a time when it had been established for 400 years. Isabel Ward, who lived in the nunnery with eight nuns and eight servants, handed it over on the last day of August 1536. Granted a pension of £6 13s 4d, she retired to the house in Trinity Lane and died there thirty-three years later. In 1905 the house was converted into a church hall for the parish of Holy Trinity.

Not far from Holy Trinity, in the heart of the old Roman *colonia*, two churches dedicated to St Mary—Bishophill Senior and Bishophill Junior—once complemented each other. Now only Bishophill Junior remains, though its title is misleading, as its tower is the earliest piece of parochial church architecture of any size left in the city. It may be of the early eleventh century on earlier foundations. It is 26 feet square and for part of its height has walls 3 feet thick, pierced by narrow slits. The battlements and pinnacles are much later additions. The earliest associations with Christianity in York are at Bishophill. Eight years after leaving York on being proclaimed emperor in AD 306, Constantine the Great called together a Church Council at Arles at which

Eborius, Bishop of York, was present. Can there be much doubt that the Bishop had his church and residence on Bishophill?

Although the present building would be suitably dated as either very late Saxon or very early Norman, Saxon characteristics predominate, particularly in the tower. The Saxons often made use of Roman materials and much of St Mary's tower is built of small Roman limestone blocks. The herring-bone courses in the tower are of similar type to the early stonework in the Minster crypt. At the west end of the nave, by the tower wall, are the fragments of an old Saxon cross of the Northumbrian type.

Judging from medieval tax returns, this was a poor parish. In 1387 St Mary's Junior was taxed 25s against £7 10s for St Mary's Senior. The Dean and Chapter Visitation Book for 1481 reveals a sad little church in need of devoted parishioners and much repair work. There was not one good altar cloth, the bells had no ropes and the stairs to the tower were broken. Smashed windows let in the birds, and the churchwardens washed the vestments "scarcely once a year". The rain came in at several places, especially near the choir, and services were poorly attended. But those who did attend were criticized for their "much jangling and walking". Ironically, this building has survived its richer neighbour and the city has no snugger or better maintained medieval church.

Standing at the head of the steep, cobbled Carr's Lane, an alley running up to Bishophill from the riverside Skeldergate, St Mary's Senior had one of the most commanding sites in the city. Nothing is left now but a few leaning headstones and the scars of archaeological digs, though parts of the old church's fabric were built into a new suburban church. A generation ago, a visitor to the church recorded: "the arcade stands firm, and the rough-hewn timbers of the roof look good enough to last for years." In those days it was still possible to see details like the old piscina niche and the eighteenth-century bread shelf in this church where the sculptor, John Flaxman, was baptized. The brick tower of 1659 replaced a stone one which had been damaged during a heavy thunderstorm on 13th April 1378. The wind was so strong that night that the posts of the porch were carried 200 feet outside the graveyard.

The churchyard of St Mary's Senior has a little-known connection with one of the best-loved of all Charles Dickens's characters. Wilkins Micawber, still waiting for something to turn up, died in the workhouse at York on 22nd January 1866. But the name entered in the record of his pauper's grave was Richard Chicken, a richly eccentric man who had played many parts . . . law-clerk, professional actor, elocution teacher, railway clerk. There is little doubt that he provided the basic material of the character Micawber in Dickens's favourite novel, *David Copperfield*. For years Chicken was closely associated with the novelist's younger brother, Alfred Lamert Dickens, who worked for a civil engineer with offices in Micklegate and later in Railway Street, York. Until the demolition of St Mary's Senior and the clearing of the churchyard, there was to be seen, on the east side of the porch, close to the footpath, a gravestone erected to the memory of five of his children, three of whom all died on 13th June 1845 "of pestilential fever".

Charles Dickens often visited his brother and sister-in-law Helen, and it is reasonable to assume that he knew all about Chicken. Proof of this probably lay in the many letters Alfred must have written, though hope of finding it disappeared in the smoke of the bonfire which the novelist made of all his papers and private correspondence in the paddock of his home at Gad's Hill in Kent. But there is still the evidence of Chicken's characteristic letters, full of a wonderful circumlocution which fits the Micawber image. Chicken was described in his day as possessing an "indescribable character of faded gentility", and it was often said by his contemporaries in York that he was the *alter ego* of Micawber.

Chicken was born in Low Ousegate, York, where his father was a wine merchant, and baptized in St Michael's, Spurriergate, on 14th August 1799. He left Bingley Grammar School in the West Riding for a career on the stage, and first appeared at the York Theatre Royal on 1st April 1823, in the appropriately titled play, *The Poor Gentleman*. When in financial difficulties, it was Chicken's habit to write extraordinary begging letters. One, to the Lord Mayor of York, has been described as "a Micawber gem of the first water".

"Sabbath as it is," runs this strange, emotional letter, "I must devote a few moments of it to address you. In an emergency it is lawful to take the shewbread; works of necessity and mercy may be performed on a Sunday; the priests defiled the temple on the Sunday and were blameless. The night is far spent, the day is at hand. I have frustrated as long as I can my landlord's intentions, who will tarry no longer. . . ."

And so he rambles on, finally asking for money and employment. In a postscript he even suggests to the Lord Mayor that a coat or a pair of trousers would be welcomed. Reams of Chicken's letters addressed to various influential citizens and firms, were still preserved about the turn of this century. One batch in a solicitor's office was neatly filed and docketed "Curious letters from Mr Chicken".

In another letter he is worried about his personal appearance: "I take this favourable opportunity of enquiring if you have the matter of half a dozen pairs of despised gloves a little worse for wear." And his postscript runs: "If I may be allowed to express a choice, those coloured brown would be preferred."

Chicken's predicaments and those of Micawber were identical, even to the pawning of a pair of spectacles, but their careers did not end in the same way. Micawber was shipped off to Australia; Chicken stepped through the workhouse door. There he indulged his passion for letter writing. From the back of an old book he tore the yellow fly-leaf and wrote on it a last pathetic appeal: "You have perhaps heard that I am in the workhouse and in a bad condition of health. I don't expect to come out alive. The confinement and the society will kill me. I desire my respects to the clerks in the office, and hope that they will have the humanity to raise me a trifle to procure a morsel of coffee and sugar, with a little tobacco to console and refresh me. Anything left at the lodge of the workhouse will reach its destination." Once again, his best line is in the postscript: "The society of idiots, the ignorant and the profane is not adapted to me—poor Chicken!"

North-eastwards from Bishophill, across the river in Goodramgate, the street that winds from King's Square, the site of the Roman *porta principalis sinistra*, to Monk Bar, there stands a church which relied very much on the donations from summer visitors until its closure in the summer of 1971. Holy Trinity, Goodramgate, stands in a quiet churchyard, screened from the street by a row of houses said to be among the oldest in England. Built in the early fourteenth century under the name of Our Lady's Row, they are certainly the oldest in York still more or less in their original condition. In 1316 the parishioners agreed to the building of the houses so that a chantry of the Blessed Virgin might be founded on the rents.

I remember some years ago, while investigating the discovery of an unsuspected room in the roof of a medieval house only a

The Shambles

few yards from this spot, holding a Tudor child's shoe, still tied with a brown silk ribbon, which had been found there.

At the western end of the row there is a rosy brick arch of 1766 hung with iron gates made in the year of Waterloo. Once through them and into Holy Trinity's small churchyard, the press of traffic seems far away. This grassy plot, seen from the air, must seem like a bright green hole punched in a sea of city roofs; and in the centre a fifteenth-century church with a quite unspoiled eighteenth-century interior. It suffered no major restoration in the last century, and its high-sided, draught-proof pews add much to the charm of the building.

The alarm bell was sounded in this quiet spot in February 1971, when the Friends of Holy Trinity were told that structural collapse was imminent. Work had to be done immediately on the roof and ceilings. Closure and the consequent loss of the support of summer visitors followed. But this much-loved church, I found, did not stand empty in the bleaker months, for when I visited it that February I found it alive with foreign girl students, and a glance at the visitors' book showed that in the first three weeks of that unfashionable month tourists from Hungary, Sweden, Turkey, Australia and the USA had left their signatures behind. Visitors from nearer home had left comments too. From Stockport, Cheshire: "The most beautiful, quiet and peaceful place ever. Restoration that would change its character seems to me out of the question." And from Leeds: "The pews are of enormous interest and should not be modernised." The church was re-opened at Easter 1972.

Holy Trinity was first mentioned in charters of 1082 and 1093 as part of the foundation grant of Durham Cathedral Priory. Experts think both the charters may be forgeries, but do not deny that the church had an early foundation.

The lay-out comprises a nave with north and south aisles, a south chapel, porch, vestry and a tower with a pack-saddle roof. An intriguing glimpse of the church may be had down the narrow Hornpot Lane, running out of nearby Low Petergate. The name does not appear on today's maps, but this is where the horners of medieval York may have lived and worked. In those days books were protected by horn coverings, cups and pots of the poorer people were made of horn, and in the York Mystery Plays one of the shepherds gives Christ a horn spoon.

Projecting from the south aisle, west of the door, is the chapel

6

High Petergate

of the Holme chantry which would have been separated from the rest of the church by a wooden screen. During the ordinary parish services the founder's family used it as their pew with a slot—or squint—in the wall to enable them to follow the service at the main altar. The glass in the east window is dated about 1472 and there is' some old glass in the east windows of the north and south aisles, but most of the other glass is modern. The two-tier pulpit is of 1785, the altar piece 1721 and the handsome communion rails are seventeenth century.

It is known from a study of wills that in 1324 the church held an ivory image of the Virgin, and in 1437 John Tanfield left a silver girdle for this image. And in the same year Thomas de Alta Ripa, clerk, willed "that my book, called *Pupilla Oculi*, be securely fastened with an iron chain to the stall where I was wont to sit, for the benefit of all chaplains".

More than 150 years ago the fabric of this church was causing some concern, for the churchwardens' accounts record that in 1819 the north wall was out of the perpendicular. The rector promised £20 towards its rebuilding if it was done during his incumbency.

These accounts begin in 1557 when the Easter sepulchre and stalls are mentioned together with charcoal for the "hallowed fire" and oil for the lamps. The following year—that of Elizabeth's accession—the surplices were mended for 2d and the making of a wax candle for the rood loft cost 12d. In 1586 the church goods included a bow with fourteen arrows, and in 1600 the Lady Choir floor was paved with bricks from Clementhorpe, a riverside village, now well within the city, where plague lodges were built in 1604. Pikes were counted and found to total twenty-nine.

Bells were rung when James I came to York on 16th April 1603, and in the following year the parish raised 26s 8d for the relief of plague victims. A "cobweb brush" cost the parish 2d during Charles I's reign and when the king visited the city on 14th May 1633, the bell-ringers were paid 2s 8d. In 1650, a year after Charles's execution, the church roof was repaired with 300 tiles. It was during the Commonwealth that, in an excess of discretion, 6d was paid for "washing out the king's arms by my Lord Mayor's command".

Half a crown was spent on bell-ringing when Charles II was proclaimed and a shilling was paid out to the widow of a minister killed by a thunderbolt. Records during the reign of James II reflect the general unrest in the city where the garrison was surprised and disarmed by the Earl of Danby, who was largely instrumental in driving James II out of the country and bringing in William of Orange.

William and Mary brought quieter times. In honour of Tobias Jenkins, Lord Mayor and MP in 1700, a painted board for the sword and mace was erected in the church and a green cloth put in the Lord Mayor's pew.

In the time of Queen Anne two new flagons were bought for £1 4s and the bells were rung on 1st May 1707 to celebrate the union of the parliaments of England and Scotland. During the last quarter of the eighteenth century the church was predominantly two colours . . . whitewash for the walls and green paint for the box pews.

As the visitor enters the church of St Michael-le-Belfrey, on the south side of the Minster, one of the first items to catch his eye is an enlarged photograph of a page from the registers which begin in 1565. Dated 16th April 1570, it records the baptism of Guy Fawkes whose family lived close by. An hotel opposite the church's south wall claims to be Fawkes's birthplace, but the subject is controversial.

The painting in the reredos, a copy of a seventeenth-century picture, *The Adoration of the Shepherds*, at present in the National Gallery, was seen all over the world at Christmas 1967 when it was used by the GPO for threepenny stamps in the Christmas issue. The copy has formed part of the reredos since 1926. Part of the collection of Don Miguel de Espina Maldonado Saavedra, Conde del Aguila of Seville in 1798, the picture was bought from his heir by Baron Taylor for King Louis Philippe in 1832 or 1833. At the Louis Philippe sale in London in May 1853, it was bought for the National Gallery. The copy was commissioned by the St Michael-le-Belfrey parochial church council in February 1926, the artist chosen being Mr Peter Brooker of London. The unveiling and dedication ceremony was performed on Michaelmas Eve, 28th September 1926, by the Archdeacon of York. The painting and installation of this picture completed two years' work on the beautifying of the reredos which dates from 1708.

The register of burials is a varied cross-section of society in the neighbourhood, and includes a Dutchman killed in a fight in

1579 in Lop Lane, the narrow street which was the forerunner of the present Duncombe Place at the west end of the Minster; the parish bellman in 1580; a man executed at the local 'Tyburn' on Knavesmire where York's race meetings have been held since 1731; and the Secretary to the Council of the North. Marriage records show that two couples were married at 5 am.

In the vestry are preserved two pieces of the parish armour—a breastplate and helmet—reminders of the days when defence was a local rather than a national responsibility.

The present church dates from 1525 and took about ten years to build after the foundation stone had been laid by John Coltman, sub-treasurer of the Minster. So this is the only York church to date from the sixteenth century, replacing a ruinous church of unknown date. In 1470 Isabell Saxton of Petergate gave "a bed of arras" embroidered with an image of the Virgin Mary to be hung in the high chancel on St Michael's Day every year, and even in her day the church was in a bad state of repair. It was said that rain was leaking into the nave and that windy weather prevented the congregation hearing the services. Window glass in the choir was so dark that candles were needed to see the books.

Stepping from the darkness of his black, curtained niche, Archbishop Lamplugh is an arresting figure. It is the most remarkable of the memorials which punctuate the Minster's south choir aisle, and has been described as one of the most impressive monuments of the age. It has been there since 1691. The connection between this memorial and St Michael's Queen Anne reredos takes us back 300 years to the time when a 19-year-old Rotterdam-born Englishman came to work in York and was shown round the city by one of its most respected craftsmen. Did Grinling Gibbons, carver of the Lamplugh monument, and John Etty, who made the Belfrey reredos for £68, work together?

The best bit of evidence would appear to be a record made by Ralph Thoresby in 1702. This Leeds antiquary and topographer who had learned Dutch and French in Rotterdam in his youth, recalled one summer evening in that year when he "sat up too late with a parcel of artists I had got on my hands; Mr Gyles, the famousest painter of glass perhaps in the world, and his nephew, Mr Smith, the bell-founder . . . Mr Carpenter, the statuary, and Mr Etty, the painter, with whose father, Mr Etty, sen., the architect, the most celebrated Grinlin Gibbons wrought at York, but whether apprenticed with him or not I remember not well. Sat up full late with them."

There is really nothing more than this chatty note to substantiate the story that Gibbons worked in the city as a young man. George Vertue, an engraver who became a member of the Society of Antiquaries on its revival in 1717, records only that the great carver came to England when he was about nineteen and that he was first employed in Yorkshire. However, Gibbons' biographer, David Green, firmly attributes the Lamplugh monument to him, and adds that it was made for £100 under contract to the Archbishop's son, long after Gibbons had made his name in London, of course.

He also contends that Gibbons, who spoke Dutch and Flemish at school and at work in his teens, was all but illiterate when writing in English. His letters bear Dutch characteristics and end with ". . . Youer ombell obegent Sarvant".

A little more is known about his master John Etty. The cartouche recording his burial at All Saints', North Street, York, in 1709, says that "By the strength of his own genius and application [he] had acquired great knowledge of mathematics especially geometry and architecture in all its parts far beyond any of his contemporaries in this City." He is thought to be the Etty who was building for the Duke of Buckingham at Helmsley in the North Riding in 1665-6. His son William (not to be confused with the Royal Academician of the next century whose statue stands outside the York City Art Gallery) became Vanbrugh's clerk of works at Seaton Delaval and Castle Howard, and in 1724 he was working at the York Mansion House.

Though at one time apparently heading for redundancy and closure, St Michael-le-Belfrey is well supported by an enthusiastic congregation and its future seems assured.

Soaring over the southern end of the wide Parliament Street created in the 1830s, the graceful octagonal lantern tower of All Saints', Pavement, is a prominent landmark. In medieval times a lamp was hung there to act as a beacon for travellers in the dense Forest of Galtres to the north of the city. A light still burns there nightly as a memorial to the men and women who died in two world wars. On the south wall inside, near the vestry, are two seven-inch hemispheres of moulded glass, pitted and dulled by time. Mounted in a wooden frame with an elaborately lettered inscription on brass, they are almost certainly lenses from the original lantern.

In 1736 the York historian, Francis Drake, wrote: "The steeple at the top is finished lanthorn-wise; and tradition tells us that antiently a large lamp hung in it, which was lighted in the night time as a mark for travellers to aim at in their passage over the immense Forest of Galtres to the city. There is still the hook or pulley on which the lamp hung in the steeple." Drake's idea of "antiently" was probably not more than a century before his time, for parish accounts show that in 1631 a lantern was bought for 15s and that it cost 7s 6d to provide a light for two years. As late as 1913 it was said the hook that Drake had noticed still remained in the tower.

But the most remarkable feature of the church is the curious ringed head attached to the north door. Within inches of every passer-by and miraculously ignored by vandals, it is a 'Doom' knocker possibly dating from the late twelfth century and similar to others at Adel near Leeds and at St Gregory's Church, Norwich. It is a little 'Mouth of Hell' taken from one of the plays in the medieval Mystery Cycle in the form of an open-mouthed dragon swallowing souls. Inside the mouth there is the face of a woman.

Long connected with the municipal and gild life of the city, All Saints' is said to be the resting place of thirty-nine mayors. The church was from time to time in the fifteenth century used for council meetings. The chancel was removed in 1782 to enlarge the market place in Pavement, while the northern and southern parts of the churchyard were removed in the seventeenth century for street widening. Only a small part now remains on the west, with a tongue of cobbles parting the traffic flow on the east. The pulpit, with sounding board, is dated 1634 and the lectern, from the demolished St Crux church which stood at the Pavement end of Shambles—the only York street to find a place in Domesday Book—is a fine example of fifteenth-century woodwork. About 1386 the charger on which the head of John the Baptist had lain was said to be in the church, but was then surrendered to the "king's chapel"—probably the chapel in the castle.

For many years St Margaret's Church in Walmgate, which has one of the largest churchyards in the city, was hidden behind drab houses. These have been cleared away and the church now stands, surrounded by mature trees, across a wide stretch of grass. This is part of the gradual improvement of the street which leads to Walmgate Bar with its unique projecting barbican, and eventually to the Hull road.

Here, in the porch, may be seen the richest and most beautiful example of pure Norman craftsmanship in the city, though the doorway, said to date from about 1160, is a bit of borrowed finery and may have come from the old church of St Nicholas, damaged beyond repair during the Siege of York of 1644.

In 1827, probably in an attempt to scotch rather wild claims that the carving was Roman and somehow connected with Mithras, the artist John Browne published his opinions. He worked out that there were thirteen signs of the zodiac in the doorway and explained this by the insertion of the Anglo-Saxon month of *Trilidi*. Associated with this extra summer month he found a mutilated carving which might have been of a sheep and which he took to represent a sheep-shearing month. He also identified another figure, half human, half mermaid, in a fighting attitude. In its right hand it holds a battleaxe and in the other a circular shield. It represented, said Browne, "a roving Dane".

In the winter of 1675–6 St Margaret's lost its old tower when a large part of the steeple with the bells was blown down. The roof of the church was destroyed and repairs did not begin until 1684. The church was almost entirely rebuilt in 1852.

Churches dedicated to St Denys, the patron saint of France, and to England's St George were close neighbours in medieval York, but today only St Denys's church remains on its Walmgate site. A mixture of thirteenth-, fourteenth- and fifteenth-century styles, it could be called the Fishmongers' church, as the fish market was nearby and a number of fishmongers are buried there. One of them, Richard Parke, gave 10s to the fabric of the Holy Cross in 1480, and in 1505 another, John Sanderson, asked to be buried "before the old rood".

The church we see today is only part of the original building which, according to the historian Drake, writing in 1736, was "a handsome pile of buildings with a neat spire". But in 1644, during the Siege of York in the Civil War, the 116-foot spire was shot through by a cannon ball and the main part of the church was also damaged. Storm damage and unwise drainage work in the eighteenth century resulted in the dismantling of the spire and the west end in 1846.

It was during this work that a Roman altar to a previously

unknown local god, Arciaco, was found in the rubble foundation, and in 1940, during the building of the Labour Exchange on the church's south side, traces of a Roman building were discovered. The Roman road which left the fortress through the south-east gate on the site of the present King's Square must have run near these sites. The gritstone altar was dedicated not only to Arciaco but to the Emperor's divinity by the centurion M. Vitalis who "paid his vow willingly and deservedly".

St Denys's Church had a close connection with the Earls of Northumberland, as the York house of this family—the Percys—stood on the opposite side of Walmgate, near to Foss Bridge. The Earl of Northumberland who was killed at the battle of Towton on Palm Sunday, 1461, during the Wars of the Roses, was buried in the Percy vault under the church. In the early years of this century two clergymen explored the vaults and at the end of an empty passage found a sealed door carrying the arms of the Earls of Northumberland.

Medallions of glass believed to date from the eleventh or twelfth centuries are to be seen in the north aisle, where there are also twenty panels of a fourteenth-century Tree of Jesse. St Denys is seen in the fifteenth-century east window. One fourteenth-century window shows the donor offering his gift, robed and kneeling against a background of flowers, stars and giant butterflies.

The site of St George's Church, just inside the city walls, near Fishergate Postern, is now a rest garden. Though off the normal tourist track, this former churchyard was the burial place of the highwayman whose name has been linked with York for nearly two and a half centuries . . . John Palmer, otherwise Richard Turpin.

The church was not pulled down, but was allowed to fall into ruin not long after the parson, Bryan Bywater, was accused in 1552 of being too fond of playing cards and of failing to teach the catechism to children and servants of the families in the parish. In the late seventeenth century the Archbishop received complaints that the ruins were an eyesore, but a writer in 1730 said "the walls on a rising hill, facing the river Foss, in a melancholy yet delightful situation, now remain." Every trace had gone by 1818.

Turpin now holds the stage in this little visited quarter of the city, and is a reminder that the term 'Topsman', though it has a curiously modern ring, was, in fact, an eighteenth-century euphemism for 'hangman'. Use of it is made in a contemporary newspaper report of Turpin's execution at the York 'Tyburn' on Saturday 7th April 1739 when—with horse stealer John Stead—he stepped off the ladder into space and behaved "with the greatest assurance to the very last".

"It was very remarkable", commented the *York Courant* for 10th April, "that as he mounted the ladder his right leg trembled; on which he stampt it down with an air, and with undaunted courage look'd round about him, and after speaking a few words to the Topsman, he threw himself off the ladder and expired in about five minutes. Before his death he declared himself to be the notorious highwayman, Turpin, and confessed to the Topsman a great number of robberies which he had committed."

A full report of the trial was published on Tuesday 17th April. Its basis was the note taken by Mr Thomas Kyll, "professor of shorthand", who was in court when Turpin appeared before Sir William Chapple on 22nd March. Printed by Ward and Chandler and sold at 6d in their shop near Temple Bar, London, and in Coney Street, York, the report included a letter Turpin received from his father while under sentence of death in the condemned cell, still to be seen in the east wing of the former York Debtors' Prison, now part of the Castle Museum.

Turpin's popularity with the mob was demonstrated after the execution. The body was taken to the Blue Boar, an inn in Castlegate, and next morning was buried in St George's churchyard. The following day 'resurrection men' took up the corpse and hid it in the garden of a York surgeon's house. Determined that the highwayman's body should not be used for dissection, the mob discovered it, carried it through the streets, replaced it in the coffin, covered it with unslaked lime and reburied it in the grave. Today the site is marked by a modern inscribed headstone.

One of the city's liveliest parishes is centred on St Cuthbert's Church in Peasholme Green where overspill congregations are served by closed-circuit television. Though dedicated to the man who was consecrated Bishop of Lindisfarne in York Minster on Easter Day AD 685, it has been more popularly known as "The Cradle of Canada". In an area of the city overshadowed by a huge cooling tower on the bank of the industrialized Foss, St Cuthbert's is one of a trio of attractive buildings—the others are St Anthony's Hall and the Black Swan Inn—forming a valuable historic enclave. The inn—now famous for its regular 'medieval banquets' and its vast open fireplace—was the old home of the Bowes family. Later it passed into the hands of the Thompsons, and one of the daughters married a Colonel Wolfe. On 2nd January 1727 she gave birth to a son, James, who was to be the hero of Quebec, winning Canada for Britain. His mother was a regular worshipper at the church, and it is possible that she took her son there during visits to York.

It is a romantic thought that this church may have been built in the year of Cuthbert's death, AD 687, or that it may mark a spot where the saint's body rested for a while on its journeys, but documentary evidence suggests that this is unlikely. And the use of Roman material in its building is no clue to its date, as probably well into the eleventh century there was plenty of dressed stone from the fortress available to masons.

The eleventh-century St Olave's Church in its Marygate setting, backing on to the Museum Gardens, is the oldest of the country's twelve surviving medieval churches with this dedication to Olaf, Norway's patron saint. According to *The Anglo-Saxon Chronicle*, the founder of the church was Siward, Earl of Northumbria, buried there in 1055. It was given before 1086 by Alan, Earl of Brittany, to Stephen, a monk from Whitby, as a foundation grant for what was later to become St Mary's Abbey, now the central attraction of the adjoining Museum Gardens. In 1089 William Rufus gave Stephen four acres to the north in order to build the larger abbey and church. When the abbey was destroyed in 1539 the importance of St Olave's as a parish church increased, and while the King's Manor was the residence of the President of the Council of the North, it was his parish church. Lord President Huntingdon was buried there in 1591. In the Civil War of 1642–46, St Olave's tower was used as a gun platform, and damage was done to the building during the Siege of York in 1644. The church was rebuilt in 1721–22. The registers start in 1558 and, apart from the Commonwealth period, are complete. The first volume of 1558–1600 is made of paper, despite the order of Thomas Cromwell that they should be written on parchment.

High Sheriff's trumpeter . . . commercial cupid . . . puppet showman . . . Harry Rowe was all these in his lifetime, and it was his friend, the sexton of St Olave's, who dug his grave after his death in his seventy-fourth year on 2nd October 1800. The sexton also acted as chief mourner, for this great York character had died in the Marygate workhouse, a poor end for such a versatile man. It was said that "the evening of his life was dark as the consequence of his open hand . . ."

"A gentleman may be fitted with a wife as soon as his tailor can take his measure for a suit of clothes; and a lady may have a husband as soon as her maid can pin her handkerchief." This was the kind of advertisement Harry Rowe inserted in eighteenth-century newspapers when he was running his marriage bureau, known in those days as a matrimonial office, or even a 'wedding shop'. His picaresque life began in Nottingham in 1726. After spells as an usher in his father's school and as an apprentice stocking weaver, he enlisted in the Duke of Kingston's Light Horse, a regiment raised to check the career of Charles Edward Stuart. The Scots army was routed after an hour's fighting at Culloden and Rowe was said to have displayed "both bravery and gallantry", coming out of the fight little the worse for the encounter.

Penniless in London, he fell in with Orator Henley, a well-known quack doctor, acting as the 'groaner' who gathered up customers and convinced them of his master's skill. Later he built up the reputation of a Dr Wax, but feeling the hot breath of the law on his neck again, he left the neighbourhood.

Turning his attention to the 'wedding shop' business, he felt he ought to be married. Without the aid of a 'shop', he found a young milliner in his native town, married her, converted her stock into £40 cash and took a furnished house in Coventry as the headquarters of his new project. Letters poured in. From Bridlington a client wrote: "I have buried two wives. My apothecary recommends me to make trial of an old maid for my next wife, as he says that old maids are tough and can stand weather. I care little for her temper as I am as deaf as a stone."

But it was too good to last. His wife died and the business flagged. He became assistant to a widow who owned a puppet show and, choosing York as a centre, toured the surrounding market towns.

Hiring a room in the town, he would fit up his stage, footlights and drop curtain. His portable lighting system consisted of tin candlesticks made to hang on nails, and at the door he hung a large oil lamp with twin spouts.

For forty-five years and during most of these adventures, he had held the post of Trumpeter to the High Sheriff of Yorkshire, and had invariably come to York twice a year for as long as the assizes lasted.

Through a conveniently placed opening in the ruined walls of St Mary's Abbey in the Museum Gardens, the tomb of the York artist and Royal Academician, William Etty, is easily seen in St Olave's churchyard. In appearance, Etty was not everyone's idea of the typical artist. He had a large head with unruly, sandy hair. His face was marked by smallpox scars, his figure was stocky and he had rather large hands and feet. And yet he produced the most exquisite flesh tints, and his nudes had a lushness which must have disturbed the collective subconscious of nineteenth-century society. Many of his works may be seen in the York City Art Gallery in Exhibition Square.

He was born and was to die in houses very near to each other, though he spent much of his life in London where he had a studio in Buckingham Street, off The Strand. Born on 10th March 1787, he was the seventh child of a baker and miller who sold his locally famous gingerbread at the shop attached to his home in Feasegate, York. Sir Thomas Lawrence said Etty's mother, Esther, had "a face for a Madonna" and according to Etty's autobiographical notes it was she who encouraged his artistic bent as a child.

It was in August 1846 that he bought a substantial, two-storey house in Coney Street in readiness for his planned retirement. From the rear windows he had a good view of the River Ouse.

Alterations to the property included the building of a bow window in the painting room overlooking the river. Etty moved there in 1848. In his last years he had the rare experience of seeing his pictures go for high prices. "It was said last week," he wrote, referring to a sale at Christie's, "Etty sells for more than Raphael."

The country's most beautiful public clock is the hallmark of a city church which came through the fire-bomb Baedeker raid of April 1942, to serve today as an oasis of quiet in the heart of busy Coney Street. The rebuilt church of St Martin-le-Grand was re-hallowed in its new form in April 1968. Now a chapel of ease to nearby St Helen's Church, it is also a shrine of remembrance to the citizens of York who lost their lives in the 1914–18 war, to those who died in the air raid which destroyed the church and to those who fell in the 1939–45 war and have no known grave. As an act of reconciliation, the book of remembrance to those who died in the raid—placed in a niche in the north wall—contains the words: "Remembrance is also made to those members of the German Air Force who died in the course of duty in this raid." The contemporary organ, partly hung from the arches of the church, is the gift of the German government and the Evangelical Church of West Germany.

Only the tower and south aisle were restored as a chapel of ease; much of the site has been converted into a garden of rest. The old and the new have been skilfully blended. Medieval glass from the old church fills three windows on the south side, while the east window could best be described as a multi-coloured abstract design suggesting the fury of the fire which destroyed the building.

A new north wall was built with a special five-sided tower to frame the thirty-two-foot-high St Martin Window, one of the finest early fifteenth-century windows in the country. The paved courtyard adjoining the south side of the church was the gift of the Westminster Press Ltd, owners of the *Yorkshire Evening Press*, whose offices adjoin, and the York Civic Trust.

St Martin's is easily identified, for its great clock, mounted at right angles over the street on a huge, elaborate bracket and topped by the figure of an eighteenth-century naval officer using a cross-staff, has been a Coney Street landmark once more since its restoration in May 1966. The clock was first fitted on its bracket in 1668, but was a victim of the fire raid. The "Little Admiral", as the figure is known, survived the fire, and I look at him with affection almost every day, remembering the bleak morning after the raid and my visit to the Minster Clerk of Works yard to see the charred "Admiral" in his new quarters. The gilded head of Father Time overlooking the street from the side of the clock face is a replacement. About twenty-five years after the raid the original head, badly charred, was bought for £1 by a visiting German architect. The clock mechanism is in the church tower seventy feet away and the delicate timing rods run over the roof.

The smallest of the three headstones now resting against the south wall of the church is, very fittingly, a link with the newspaper industry in the city, for the church is flanked on two sides by the offices and works of York's evening paper and general printing department. It is to the memory of Benjamin Lund, who died aged seventy-nine on 23rd March 1808 and was buried four days later in a vault under the vestry. He was not only clerk of the parish for forty-seven years, but he spent his entire working life in the office of the *York Courant*.

He was the foreman in the printing office of this paper (a direct ancestor of the present-day *Yorkshire Evening Press*) which was first published in August or September 1725. The old man's burial in the church he served was one of six there in 1808, and the parish register records the cause of death as "decay of nature". The report of his death in the *Courant* on 28th March that year said he "attended in the office on the day of his death" and that "his integrity was fidelity in the duties of his station, and his zeal for the interest of his employers have rarely, if ever, been equalled".

The *Courant* was first published from an office in Stonegate, near St Helen's Church. Later the office was moved to a site "almost opposite St Martin's Church". When Ann Ward, widow of Caesar Ward, took over the running of the paper she moved to a house next to the George Inn on the other side of Coney Street, which had previously been known as Kidd's Coffee House.

Though not actually part of the present-day street, St Helen's Church is correctly described as being in Stonegate, for until the eighteenth-century Stonegate extended to Coney Street, the modern St Helen's Square being occupied by the graveyard. A near neighbour of the Mansion House and the Guildhall, this is now the only York church dedicated to the Empress Helena, mother of the first Christian Roman emperor, Constantine the Great. St Helen-on-the-Walls and St Helen's Fishergate no longer exist.

First mentioned in 1235, this was the gild church of the York glass painters, and their coat of arms is incorporated in one of the windows. There is a fine early twelfth-century font, and there is fourteenth- and fifteenth-century glass in the west window.

In 1970 an interesting facet of life in eighteenth-century York came to light in the church and was restored at the expense of the York Civic Trust. It is a plaque to the memory of two remarkable York sisters—the Misses Barbara and Elizabeth Davyes. Both lived to the age of 98 and died in 1765 and 1767 respectively. They saw seven monarchs on the throne of England during their lifetimes ... Charles II, James II, William III, Queen Anne, and the first three Georges.

There is an intriguing entry in the York Chamberlains' Account Book for 1602–3 where it is recorded that at the reception for King James I in 1603 a contraption was built up against the tower of St Helen's to produce a fountain of wine.

The whittling away of the churchyard began in October 1729 when the vicar and churchwardens proposed to cut off part of it "so as a coach may drive with greater ease and conveniency". In September 1733 the whole of the churchyard was sold to the city for £90 and St Helen's Square was created.

Part of a twelfth-century church, demolished in the 1880s, still clings to its old site. In its long life, the old church, smaller and simpler than the building which succeeded it, had a pretty rough time. In 1644, during York's Civil War siege, St Lawrence's, standing outside Walmgate Bar on the main road to Hull, was almost destroyed, and stayed in ruins until 1669 when restoration work began. It was a slow process, not being completed until 1817.

Comprising nave, chancel and tower, the original church had good early twelfth-century work at the entrance on the north side. The tower and this medieval doorway—now built into the east wall of the tower—were preserved and may still be seen in St Lawrence's churchyard.

Old St Lawrence's saw a society wedding on 14th January 1719, when the architect-dramatist Sir John Vanbrugh married Henrietta Maria Yarborough of Heslington Hall, an Elizabethan mansion two miles from the city centre which was, in the 1960s, to form the nucleus of York University. Vanbrugh gave his name to one of the colleges.

A "most sweet-natured gentleman", Vanbrugh found great pleasure in life. Early in his career he had been found sketching fortifications at Calais and the resulting eighteen months in a number of French prisons, including the Bastille, did nothing to sour his good nature. When he was not dining and drinking with his gaolers, playing cards or writing a comedy in the style of Wycherley and Congreve, he was studying the architecture of his prison. On release he returned to England in 1692. Attracted to the theatre, which was largely supported by the aristocratic members of society with whom he mingled, he wrote *The Relapse, or Virtue in Danger*, four years later, following it in 1697 with *The Provok'd Wife*. Soon he was a member of the exclusive Kit-Cat Club which met in a tavern in the Strand.

Friendship with Charles Howard, third Earl of Carlisle, developed his interest in architecture. When the Earl decided to replace the old family home, Henderskelfe Castle, with a splendid and fashionable mansion, he could have commissioned Wren, who was then Surveyor of the Works, but the inexperienced Vanbrugh, full of enthusiasm and ideas, was chosen for the task, and in the spring of 1701 the foundation stone of his incomparable Castle Howard, just a few miles north-east of York, was laid. With Nicholas Hawksmoor as his technical assistant, Vanbrugh saw the main part of the house built in less than five years.

Apparently Lord Carlisle had been a little apprehensive about the height and size of the interior, a fear shared by the Duchess of Marlborough later in his career when he designed Blenheim. But he need not have worried: ". . . he finds what I told him to be true," Vanbrugh wrote, "that those Passages would be so far from gathering and drawing wind as he feared, that a Candle wou'd not flare in them. Of this he has lately had the proof, by bitter stormy nights in which not one Candle wanted to be put in a Lanthorn . . . He likewise finds, that all his Rooms, with moderate fires are Ovens."

An amusing account of his stay in Yorkshire in 1710 or 1713 was written by Lady Mary Pierrepont, daughter of the Duke of Kingston, who lived for a time in Minster Yard and made a runaway marriage with Edward Wortley-Montague, English ambassador at Constantinople in 1717–18. She wrote: "I can't forbear entertaining you with our York lovers. Strange monsters you'll think, love being as much forced up here as melons. In the first form of these creatures, is even Mr Vanbrugh. Heaven, no doubt compassionating our dullness, has inspired him with a passion that makes us all ready to die with laughing; 'tis credibly reported that he is endeavouring at the honourable state of matrimony, and vows to lead a sinful life no more . . . but you know Van's taste was always odd; his inclination to ruins has given him a fancy for Mrs Yarborough: he sighs and ogles so, that it would do your heart good to see him, and she is not a little pleased, in so small a proportion of men amongst such a number of women, that a whole man should fall to her share." Lady Mary's insistence that Vanbrugh was interested in Mrs Yarborough rather than Colonel Yarborough's young daughter, Henrietta Maria (who surely could not have been called a "ruin"), points, I think, to her general unreliability as a witness of the

social round. We are left with only two other possibilities: either Vanbrugh was indeed chasing his prospective bride's mother, or Lady Mary's letter refers to some other Mrs Yarborough. However, out of this literary muddle emerged the fact that Vanbrugh married Henrietta when she was in her twenty-sixth year. Bridegroom and father-in-law were the same age . . . fifty-four. Breaking the news to his friend the Duke of Newcastle a few days before the wedding, Vanbrugh wrote: "There has now fallen a Snow up to ones Neck . . . In short, 'tis so bloody Cold, I have almost a mind to Marry to keep myself warm."

"Mark the brief story of a summer's day . . ." These words may be read in St Lawrence's churchyard where they form the first line of a monumental epitaph written by the Sheffield poet James Montgomery in memory of seven young people—six of them members of the same family—who were drowned in the Ouse at York one August afternoon in 1830. White and dove-grey marble stands over their vault, the work of the York mason, Plows, and paid for by young friends of the drowned.

The monument, completed and erected by 15th January 1831, is full of symbolism: carved water and ivy leaves for friendship; classical echoes of the 2,000-year-old tomb of Greek youths at Thysillus. The brief summer day began at 3 pm on 19th August 1830, when three daughters and four sons of John Rigg, a nurseryman of Fishergate, York, Grace Robinson of Ayton, near Scarborough, and Thomas Sellers, son of the landlord of the Falcon Inn, York, set off in a rowing boat. About 100 yards upstream from Acomb Landing their boat was run down by a keel coming down river before the wind under full sail and travelling at eight knots. Thomas Sellers and nine-year-old Jessy Rigg were the only survivors. Six bodies were found at 6.30 pm and laid on the grassy river bank before being moved to a nearby barn. Ninety minutes later the seventh body—that of Mr Rigg's youngest son—was recovered. The behaviour of the public on this day was curiously unrestrained . . . "the conduct of the populace", said a newspaper account, "when the bodies were conveyed into Fishergate was most disgraceful. Utterly regardless of the sorrows of the parents, they rushed into the grounds through the gates and it was with difficulty that anything like order was restored."

The inquest, too, revealed unpleasant aspects of the incident. Little or no help was given by the crew of the keel, and the

7

Monk Bar

rowing-boat party was accused of being drunk, though a woman who saw them set off remarked that she had never seen a party "look more genteel".

Today, all recriminations long forgotten, the draped urn of the Rigg monument, especially when falling leaves drift across the inscription, is a sweetly sad survival of a turning point in time—the beginning of the seven-year hiatus between Georgian and Victorian England.

Sir Nikolaus Pevsner, whose incomparable series *The Buildings of England* has now completed the picture of English architectural heritage, once said that St Michael's, Spurriergate, had the most beautiful church interior in York. With the completion, in 1971, of five years' restoration work at a cost of £25,000 this is truer than ever, but the exterior gives little hint of the richness inside. Major structural alterations both in the early nineteenth century and the mid-twentieth century have given the original church an oddly squat disguise. In 1821 the east wall was set back 7 feet to widen Spurriergate, and at the same time houses along the south wall were removed and the wall rebuilt. In 1967 35 feet were sliced off the tower, the existing parapet being retained. All but one of the bells were removed and the clock—with probably one of the oldest movements in York—was set up on the south wall facing Low Ousegate.

It was this piece of timely amputation which saved the church's life, and it was done on the advice of the eminent church architect, the late Mr George Pace, who spotted a two-inch wide crack in the tower. A survey showed that the tower was in a very precarious state, and that it was on the move in the direction of the river. Mr Pace had spotted the signs just in time. "In the upper storey", he said, "we discovered some fine pieces of medieval jerry-building . . . some external stones were only two inches thick."

During restoration of the interior fine gold lettering was revealed on the painted reredos. Beneath this nineteenth-century lettering was a second layer, probably of the eighteenth century.

It was here in the Middle Ages that offerings were made to St Osyth—affectionately known as St Sith—the patron saint of housewives, and in the early sixteenth century, before the Reformation snuffed them, there are references to the Summer Games Light and the Children's Light. The games were held on Midsummer Day, and the Children's Light may have been maintained by the boys of the choir, often called "the children" in documents of the time.

St Michael's now has the impact of a true city church whose feoffees, by wise administration of the trust funds and properties in their care, were able to support the restoration programme generously, and it could regain its medieval position as one of York's most important churches.

Echoing that of St Mary's on the opposite side of the river, the spire of All Saints', North Street, is a distinctive landmark in a riverside area once wholly industrial but becoming much more attractive now that gardens and a Scandinavian-type hotel—The Viking—have replaced warehouses and derelict sites. Near here is the staith where in the first half of the tenth century ships from Dublin were moored. This landing and the narrow lane leading to it were known as *Dyvylinstanes* . . . Dublin Stones. Restored cottages and a glimpse of half-timbering on the corner of the path leading to the church's north door help to create an eye-catching scene.

The church offers the finest glass in any parish church in the city, set in windows which were dismantled and reassembled in the 1960s. It was a difficult job for the experts, because at some time in the distant past several of the windows collapsed and were put together again by unskilled glaziers in a hurry. The result was a jumble of coloured glass, disembodied heads and hands appearing haphazardly. It was a jigsaw puzzle with only one clue—a seventeenth-century sketch of one of the windows showing the nine orders of angels and found in the Bodleian Library, Oxford.

The fifteen panels of the fourteenth-century Doom window—called the "Pricke of Conscience" and thought to have been inspired by the work of Richard de Hampole, a hermit-poet—shows the sea rising and falling, fishes and monsters appearing, the raising of the dead, stars falling and total destruction by fire. The east window of the chancel shows St John the Baptist, St Ann and St Christopher with figures of two Nicholas Blackburns, the elder and younger, who were merchants and Lord Mayors.

Good examples of fifteenth-century woodwork are to be found in the chancel and chancel aisle roofs, and in 1970 attempts were made to rid the forty carved angels and sixty bosses of their coats of brown Victorian varnish. Under a scheme devised by the rector, £10 was the cost of adopting an angel in need of a wash; bosses came a little cheaper at £5.

Lapped by the tide of open-market shoppers, the church of
St Sampson, closed in 1949, has now found itself a popular centre
for the city's old people, where a thousand cups of tea are served
daily.

4

THE LIMESTONE RIBBON

THE CREAMY limestone ribbon of York's medieval city wall runs for two and a half miles on a green mound splashed in spring with thousands of daffodils. The raised footpath behind the battlemented parapet is a natural 'history trail' across the city, changing mood with every stretch; sometimes high, windy and exposed, often overhung by forest trees in secluded gardens running up to the inner face.

Four great gates, each with its own brooding personality, pierce the defensive circle. Micklegate Bar . . . its topmost point used as a look-out post by security men during the Queen's visit in 1971. Monk Bar . . . the tallest of all, carrying figures in the act of hurling stones down into the street. Bootham Bar . . . on the site of the Roman north-west gate. Walmgate Bar . . . still bearing the cannonball and bullet scars of the seventeenth-century civil war. And in between, the turrets, towers and posterns that go to make up an urban scene unrivalled in this country; a scene which could have been the inspiration for an illuminated manuscript.

Since the sixteenth-century Mure-Masters were given the responsibility of keeping the walls in repair and occasionally clearing them of reeds and rushes, maintenance has been a more or less continuous operation, and today the walls are groomed and restored when necessary by a special task force of craftsmen in the Corporation's ancient monuments department. But in the York of George IV, William IV and Victoria things were different. Stretches of the wall were crumbling, the sharp outlines of the Bars were becoming blurred as the searching wind and frosts took their toll. Even the Multangular Tower, that powerful link with Roman York, had become silted up with earth, like the Sphinx sinking below the sand of the desert.

Things came to a head in July 1822, when an old woman died

after falling off the wall near the North Street Postern. The persuasive Dean Cockburn managed to talk the authorities into making some slight but essential repairs the following year, and in 1825 Archbishop Harcourt promised generous support for any fund that might be opened for the complete repair of the medieval defences. But the public was not very interested. Indifference was so great that some of the Bars were used as billposting stations. After a visit to York on 29th April 1824 Mrs Hughes, wife of the Rev. Dr Hughes, Canon of St Paul's, and grandmother of the author of *Tom Brown's Schooldays*, thought it "foul scorn" to see Micklegate Bar advertising boot blacking, the departure of coaches and the details of cattle sales. It was about this time that the corporation under the banner of 'restoration' began to mutilate the Bars to such an extent that three—Micklegate, Monk and Bootham—lost their barbicans or outer defence works. Only strong public opposition in 1831 saved the barbican at Walmgate Bar where it may still be seen, almost islanded by traffic. Sir Walter Scott is said to have offered to walk from Edinburgh to York if this would induce the corporation to preserve the Micklegate barbican, but it obviously had no effect.

The corporation's most unpopular move came in July 1832 when seven months after pulling down the Bootham barbican they proposed the complete demolition of Bootham Bar, one of the most beautifully sited of the city gates, facing the fountain-cooled Exhibition Square and with the Minster towers as a backcloth. Centre point of the square is held by a statue of the Victorian artist William Etty who was one of the first citizens to protest against the scheme. A public meeting demanding preservation instead of destruction was the crucial event of the year and set the seal on future corporation policy.

Certain portions of the wall were too far gone to be saved, and in 1833-4 the corporation pulled down a stretch of 350 feet between Bootham Bar and the Multangular Tower to make way for a new street, St Leonard's Place which, with an elegantly curved and stuccoed terrace on its western side, gives this part of the city a spa-like air. The wall in this section was so decayed that heavy rain caused some of it to collapse. Meanwhile, since the corporation had stressed that no funds were available for the repair of the walls, a number of residents had formed the York Footpath Association, aiming to raise money by public subscription. By 1833 they had collected £2,410 and spent it all on the repair of the wall between North Street Postern and Skeldergate. During the next few years other stretches were restored.

During this period when official vandalism and conservation seemed to go hand in hand, the corporation made one marked improvement by reopening Fishergate Bar, a truncated gateway which had been bricked up for centuries. The closure followed street fighting in the area in 1489, when the mob burned houses near the Bar. This must have been annoying for William Todd, Lord Mayor in 1487, who had just repaired 60 yards of this stretch of wall at his own expense. The city had to wait until 1827 before the Bar was reopened so that the new George Street could be linked with the cattle market then being built outside the city wall. When the new market opened for business on 4th October 1827, the people who lived on the city's south-east to north-west axis must have been very relieved, as it had been common practice to hold cattle fairs in Walmgate, Fossgate, Colliergate and Petergate. It is more than likely that trading used to spill over into neighbouring streets, as part of George Street was known as Nowtgate Lane, and 'nowt' is an archaic word for cattle.

Human bones were dug up in this area in 1826, 1855 and 1946— reminders of the demolished church of All Saints', Fishergate, which stood about 150 yards outside the Bar. Between 1428 and 1448 the anchoress Lady Isabel German lived in the churchyard, attended by a servant. In 1724 men working for William Hutton, the city Sheriff, found the remains of a large church-like building in a field near here.

Vandalism at an authoritative level had a final fling in 1852 when a consulting engineer suggested pulling down the wall between Fishergate Postern and the Red Tower—the south-eastern sector of the defences—and using the stone to fill in the River Foss. This unsuccessful bid was made in November of that year by J. C. Birkinshaw in a report to the Board of Health. He drew a picture of neglect, decay and falling returns. The locks and other works between York and the head of the navigation were so dilapidated that no vessel could use the whole length of the canalized stretch. The gross annual receipts for the previous three years had averaged £57, not enough to meet day-to-day expenses. Two methods of improving the river remained to be considered: the deepening of the channel or the carrying of the water through a tunnel. It was at this point that the engineer suggested "another improvement"—the removal of the city wall.

"By the removal of these walls simultaneously with the construction of the tunnel", he said, "material might be obtained sufficient
to fill up the Foss to the level of the streets, and also by its use in
other works to effect a reduction on the estimated cost to the
extent of £3,000. I am aware that I shall probably be considered
as wanting in due regard for those relics of antiquity, but I cannot
look upon them in the same light as the walls on the Micklegate
side of the city."

He felt that few people would "on mature consideration"
oppose the demolition. After this startling suggestion Victorian
local government took its languorous course, and possibly it was
"mature consideration" which guaranteed the survival of this
particular stretch of wall. Time passed, and in October 1854 it
was agreed that the city surveyor should be authorized to obtain
rubbish to raise the level of the Foss islands. In the following
April the council was still trying to find "any high ground"
which could be used to fill up this troublesome area.

The stretch of wall running north from Walmgate Bar ends
in the Red Tower, the only structure in the city's defences made
mainly of brick. Probably built at the end of the fifteenth century,
it is a two-storey building on a stone foundation. The walls
are 4 feet thick and the roof has two dormer windows. In the
sixteenth century it actually stood in the water of the King's
Fishpond, created by the damming of the Foss below York
Castle, but the pond was gradually shrinking and filling up, and
by 1645 the Red Tower was high and dry. The gap of a third of
a mile in the city's defences at this point is explained by the belief
that the Fishpond was an adequate barrier.

Now completely drained and crossed by Foss Islands Road,
the Fishpond was mentioned in Domesday Book and the dam
helped to power corn mills built in the eleventh century near the
spot where the Foss joins the Ouse. Mills of a later date stood at
the head of what is now called Foss Basin. Within a short distance
of this point, a water-powered mill from Raindale has been
reconstructed on the bank of the Foss as an outdoor exhibit of
the York Castle Museum.

Decorated with the heads of executed rebels as late as the
mid-eighteenth century, Micklegate Bar is the first of the city
gates seen by most visitors as they arrive from the west along
the tree-shaded Tadcaster Road, past the elegant town houses of
The Mount and through wide and busy Blossom Street.

As the sun glances off the heraldic colours of the royal arms and deepens the texture of the warm stone, past horrors recede. But it is not so very long ago that a direct link with barbaric custom was to be found in the Bar. One cold day, probably in the nineties of the last century, the tenant of the chambers in the Bar looked around for firewood. A bundle of staves, each tipped with a spike, served the purpose. I have heard tales of how, years ago in a Yorkshire village school, a medieval jousting helmet was used as a coal-scuttle, and how priceless documents were made into kites. On the grounds of antiquarian interest, this was an act in the same class. For this was how the poles used for exposing the heads of traitors were casually chopped up and burned.

Shakespeare, in *Henry VI,* makes Queen Margaret exclaim:

> Off with his head and set it on York gates;
> So York may overlook the town of York.

This refers to the execution of Richard, Duke of York, after the battle of Wakefield, fought six days after Christmas in 1460. His head was displayed on Micklegate Bar. Was one of the 'firewood' poles used at that time? It is not very likely, but it is almost certain that they were used in 1746—the last time heads were exposed—following the battle of Culloden.

Many of the captured Jacobites were brought to York for trial and convicted of high treason. Twenty-two were executed at Tyburn in the November. The head of Captain James Hamilton was put in a box and sent to Carlisle, and all but two of the remainder were buried intact behind the castle walls near the Foss. For some reason, the heads of William Conolly and James Mayne were set up on Micklegate Bar, and stayed there for more than seven years until they were stealthily removed on a stormy January night in 1754. On 4th February the Corporation offered a reward of £10 for information leading to the conviction of those who "wilfully and designedly" took down the rebels' heads. The Duke of Newcastle, one of the Secretaries of State, wrote to the Lord Mayor saying that the King wanted the strictest inquiry to be made into this "wicked, traitorous and outrageous proceeding" and the reward was stepped up to more than £100 after the intervention of the Government and the anti-Jacobite Rockingham Club. In July of the same year, William Arundel, a York tailor, was convicted of the offence. He was fined £5, sentenced to two years' imprisonment and faced a further two years unless he could find £200 surety for his good behaviour. Surely a very light sentence in the circumstances.

Though the poles have been destroyed, we know the exact spot at which they were fixed . . . behind the centre battlement of the Bar, one on each side of the stone warrior which stands there and above the gargoyle which once drained the flat roof. The carved man-at-arms is one of three made in the early 1950s during a restoration scheme. As late as 1936 a young architect, writing a thesis on the medieval fortifications of the city, saw the corroded iron fittings which had supported the poles.

Workmen repairing part of the city wall near Micklegate Bar in July 1831 found a cannonball embedded in the stonework. "This was", reported a local newspaper, "doubtless a relic of the war of the great rebellion."

The city's fortifications played an important part in the civil war of the seventeenth century, particularly during the siege by the Parliamentary army in 1644 after the Royalist defeat at Marston Moor, now a tract of farming land just a few miles west of York. Up to six days before raising his standard at Nottingham in August 1642, Charles I, distrusting the loyalty of London, had been staying in York. Orders went to the Earl of Cumberland on 2nd September to put York in a "posture of defence" and the following day cannon were mounted on the Bars.

Deserted remains of the earthworks thrown up during this period of feverish activity were still to be seen in the following century, and Daniel Defoe during his tour of England in 1724–6 recorded: "York is indeed a pleasant and beautiful city and not at all the less beautiful for the works and lines about it being demolished, and the city, as it may be said, being laid open, for the beauty of peace is seen in the rubbish; the lines and bastions and demolished fortifications have a reserved secret pleasantness in them . . ."

The peak of Micklegate Bar's involvement in the war came on the moonlit night of 2nd–3rd July 1644 after the Marston Moor clash. Parliamentarians chased the survivors to the city walls, killed them at the gate and left a three-mile-long trail of bodies behind them. The dejected Prince Rupert arrived in the city about eleven o'clock that night, his surviving officers making their way singly to Micklegate Bar where there was terrible confusion. Those on the inside were attempting to discriminate between those who had been part of the original garrison and those who had just arrived with Rupert. An eye-witness, Sir Henry Slingsby, later wrote in the diary: ". . . at ye barr none was suffer'd to come in but such as were of ye town, so yt ye whole street was throng'd up to ye barr with wound'd and lame people . . ."

Among the wounded Royalists who finally reached the city was John Dolben, a young Oxford scholar who had joined the king's cause. A member of the original York garrison, he later recovered from his serious wounds. After the civil war he entered the church and in 1683, nearly forty years after his experiences in the throng at Micklegate Bar, he was enthroned sixty-seventh Archbishop of York, successor to Archbishop Sterne, great-grandfather of Laurence Sterne, famous in the following century as the author of *Tristram Shandy* and *A Sentimental Journey*. A biography of Dolben published in 1884 records that he joined the Royalist army in 1643 as a student at Christ Church, Oxford, rising to the rank of Ensign. While carrying the colours at Marston Moor he was wounded in the shoulder by a musket ball, and during the siege of York had his thigh broken—a wound which kept him in bed for a year. His bravery earned him promotion to the rank of major, but in 1646, the king's cause lost, he returned to his studies. On his death in 1686 he was buried in York Minster, and his reclining figure is to be seen on a marble monument in the south choir aisle. The long Latin inscription includes the words: "Severely wounded in the defence of York, he consecrated the place with his blood . . ."

Micklegate Bar is mentioned by name in the twelfth century, but it was probably no more than a gate punched through the earth ramparts of the city. It had no superstructure until the fourteenth century after the stone walls had been built. By the time it had been made large enough to provide living quarters, it commanded a higher rent than other Bars. In 1376 it would have cost 13s 4d a year to live there, compared with 10s for Walmgate and 4s for Bootham.

When the historian William Hargrove had a look round in 1818 he found in the lowest room "a sloping wooden frame or soldier's bedstead, nearly the whole length of the room, with a raised part apparently for the head to rest upon".

Hargrove claims the portcullis fell and was destroyed in about 1809–10.

In the seventeenth century a lath and plaster construction was attached to the inner face of the Bar, carrying the arms of Queen Elizabeth and the words "God Save The Queen". This addition, which must have looked very much like the city face of Walmgate Bar as it is today, was demolished and replaced with stonework in 1827. The three archways set about the central arch are comparatively modern, dating from 1826, 1854 and 1863.

After centuries of inactivity, punctuated only by the flurry of occasional restoration schemes and the steadily increasing volume of traffic (a lorry was jammed under the main arch in 1969) history caught up with Micklegate Bar on 28th June 1971 when trumpeters on a specially erected platform on the west face sounded a fanfare of greeting for the Queen and Prince Philip as they drove into the city during the high point in the celebrations to mark the 1900th year of York's foundation. And just at the point where the heads of traitors had once been displayed, was the figure of a security officer, binoculars in hand.

Visitors mounting the wall at the Bar and walking north-westwards see on their left the modern Queen Street and on the right the concrete Hudson House, headquarters of the Eastern Region of British Railways, standing on the site of the ghostly little station that served early Victorian York until the building of the vast curving train-shed further to the west in the 1870s. A 'cathedral' of the industrial revolution, it was the outward symbol of York's supremacy as a rail centre in the nineteenth century. As the network of main lines comes into view the wall turns sharply north-eastwards to run almost to the river where it is crossed by Lendal Bridge, opened in 1863 to replace a ferry which had operated there since the Middle Ages.

This long run down to the Ouse gradually brings into perspective one of the most photographed views in York—the towers of the Minster rising above the huddle of streets north of the river—and reaches a high and wind-swept point opposite the Royal Station Hotel. Here the limestone battlements are smooth and rounded by the elements, like sea-washed pebbles, and the steep grassy rampart holds a daffodil tapestry each spring, a sight to lift the heart of the traveller who arrives by train. The wall, after arching over the modern roads serving the station, ends at Barker Tower under its conical roof. It takes its name from the tanning trade which was established in the inner moat at this point. In the Middle Ages a chain was hung from Barker Tower to St Leonard's Tower on the opposite bank. Similarly a chain was drawn from Davy Tower to Hyngbrig Postern at the end of Skeldergate, downstream from the city centre. The chains prevented ships slipping away after dark without paying their quayage dues.

In the sixteenth century St Leonard's Tower was usually occupied by a ferryman—and sometimes by a ferrywoman. In 1545 Jennet Collynwood held the lease. But in the late seventeenth century it was altered and enlarged to play its part in the city's water supply, housing the various engines which raised the river water with varying degrees of success. Bored elm trunks, which were frequently blocked by sediment from untreated water, were not replaced by iron pipes until about 1810. Lengths of the old wooden pipes are kept at the tower as curios.

From Roman to medieval times, York citizens drew their water from wells which must still exist under modern property. The only alternative was the river, which was used as a general dumping ground. Both sources were suspect, even in easy-going Tudor York, and attempts were made in 1552 to tap pure spring water. The Earl of Shrewsbury, President of the King's Council in the North, offered to help with the expense.

The corporation "searched certain springs" and eventually "spied one nigh St Andrew's" but nothing further was heard of this scheme. Another attempt was made in 1579 when an expert in piping spring water was consulted. In 1593 a "conduit maker" pointed out that York had no springs strong enough to meet the case. At the turn of the fifteenth and sixteenth centuries citizens were canvassed to see how much they would be willing to pay towards pipe-laying, but the response was poor. A few years later plague ravaged the city. In 1677 a London merchant was given a 500-year lease at a peppercorn rent to fit up the tower as a "Waterhouse and Waterwork" and his original pump is said to have been worked at first by a type of windmill and later by two horses. Since 1895 when the undertaking supplying the city's water was renamed the York Waterworks Company, large-scale development has taken place, the number of houses served almost doubling between 1900 and 1936. Post-war expansion included the building of a new, fortress-like water tower on Heslington Hill. Only one aspect has not changed . . . the water still comes from the Ouse.

Bootham Bar, beautifully proportioned and surmounted by three figures, is the point at which the wall is mounted again. The figures were made in 1894 to replace defaced statues, and are the work of the York sculptor, George Walker Milburn, who died in September 1941 at the age of 97. They have a direct reference to an historical event . . . Edward III's directive in 1327 that York should look to its defences under the threat of invasion by the Scots. In Portland stone, each 3 feet high, the figures represent, in the centre, Nicholas Langton, who was Mayor of York at the time, a fourteenth-century mason holding a model of the Bar, and a knight of the period. Langton is robed and carries in his hand a scroll inscribed for posterity . . . "Restored 1894".

In medieval York strong racial discrimination was to be found, the antipathy towards the Scots being stoked by the memories of intermittent wars. In 1419 the Council resolved that no Scotsman, whatever his status, should hold any official rank in the city. In case they overheard secret discussions, Scotsmen were not allowed to set foot in the Common Hall. They were not to be called as jurymen and were not even allowed to hold meetings. In 1501 it was ordered that a great door knocker should be fixed to the oak doors of Bootham Bar and that "Scottish persons who were wishful to enter York should knock first." This attitude, enthusiastically supported by the citizens, began to disappear after the death of Elizabeth.

Bootham Bar's barbican was considered the finest in York, but it did not stop the corporation from pulling it down in 1832. They even thought to improve the entrance to Petergate by destroying the Bar too, but a public meeting in the York Tavern in February 1832 brought the citizens' indignation home to the authorities. During repairs in 1889, the portcullis was saved from mutilation only by the intervention of a lone protester.

The work of restoration is continuous, a major scheme being carried out in 1969–70. During this £25,000 face-lift, 160 holes, 5 inches in diameter, were drilled through the masonry and deep into the ground. Each swallowed about seven hundredweight of grouting material. In addition, sixteen stainless steel tie-bars were used to strengthen the walls. But the most intricate work, carried out by the sixteen-man ancient monument unit at the corporation's Foss Islands depot, was the making of a replacement coat of arms for the Bar. A block of Portland stone, weighing a quarter of a ton was carved into the royal arms of the Stuarts, painted in gold, silver, red and blue, and set at a height of 30 feet on the outer face. The arms, which replaced those of Richard I dating from 1864, presented the masons with a tricky problem . . . the carving of twelve tiny lions measuring 4 inches long by $1\frac{1}{2}$ inches high. It was impossible to chisel away the stone because of the lack of working space, so dentist's drills were used.

There may be some Roman material in Bootham Bar, standing as it does on the site of the gateway to the *via principalis*. The Romans built a double-arched entrance through the centre of their dark gritstone gatehouse, with guard chambers on either side. Fragmentary decorations found on the site include a deity driving a *quadriga* and a triton blowing a conch shell.

Much of this Bar's particular charm is to be found in the contrast between its outer and inner faces. The outer has an open prospect towards Exhibition Square, the Art Gallery and the King's Manor, but the inner, rebuilt in 1719, is jostled, almost undercut by shops and houses of mixed periods in the short High Petergate, a largely underrated street which runs—with a gap at the Minster's west front—from the Bar to the corner of Minster Gates.

From the Bar the wall runs north-east, following the line of Gillygate, a sadly blighted area where the east side of the street, masking the wall, is due for demolition. At the point where the wall (all this time following the Roman fortress wall) turns sharply south-east, stands the northern angle tower, greatly enlarged at the beginning of this century. Its earliest name was the Bawing Tower, and in the fifteenth century it was called the Frost Tower, after William Frost, five times Lord Mayor. In 1622 there is a reference to it as the Robin Hood Tower.

Here begins the most endearing stretch of the city wall, as it forms a boundary to gracious gardens, running through the rustling curtain of mature chestnut trees, giving glimpses of long lawns where sundials chart the slow summer hours. Here is the Minster's protected, unchanging, northern side where the Dean's Park, the white-walled houses of Minster Yard and the ogee gables of Gray's Court and the Treasurer's House dream quietly in this green heart.

Monk Bar breaks this run of wall at the halfway point, its steep, narrow staircase to the street a tourist log-jam in the summer. Ten feet higher than Micklegate Bar, Monk Bar is topped by menacing figures, perhaps dating from the eighteenth century, each clasping a stone. Two cannon were mounted here during the siege of 1644. Few travellers passing through the main arch on their way to the east coast notice the tips of the spikes on the portcullis which hangs in the darkness above their heads. For the first time in living memory, and probably for the first time in three centuries, the portcullis was dropped in the spring of 1914. In an upper storey the windlass was still in position, though the chains had been detached and the great oak gate was supported by wedges. The grooves were clear and the portcullis was lowered by block and tackle capable of holding a ton or more.

There was no Roman gateway at this point, and Monk Bar may owe its position to the presence of a long gap in the north-east Roman defences. Very little of the Roman wall is to be seen between the Bar and the northern angle, but from the eastern angle in the street called Aldwark the fortress defences still stand to a considerable height. Excavation started in this area in 1925–7. When the Normans began to raise their earthen mound along the Roman fortress line they probably found a roadway running from the Danish royal palace in King's Square to the ford over the River Foss, and they bridged it with a stone arch.

As early as 1445 the rooms over the Bar were let at a rent of 4s, but in 1577 the Council decided to turn them into a prison. Eleven years later, there is a record that Robert Walls was committed there for "drawing blood in a fray", and in 1607 insulting words against the Mayor earned a man fourteen days in the Bar. Later the rooms were lived in by the Bar caretaker.

The wall which runs from Monk Bar to the terminal point at Layerthorpe Bridge gives the walker on the parapet a simple overhead view of the archaeological dig which has uncovered the footings of Roman buildings, but as the fortress wall is actually under his feet at this point, it is difficult to see. Recalling his work here in 1925–6, the late Angelo Raine, rector of All Saints' Pavement, and at one time the city's honorary archivist, said: "Here the Roman wall was still standing to the height of 20 feet, and the rampart against the inner face of the wall was intact. This isolated portion of the Roman defences here was about 80 yards long. It seems to have been partly ivy-covered; we found tendrils still clinging to the Roman wall. It must have

Walmgate Bar: inner face
Georgian doorway with torch snuffer, High Petergate
Entrance to King's Manor

been a most impressive sight, this solitary, massive monument of Roman might."

Southwards from here lies the industrial Foss Islands Road which crosses the drained site of the King's Fishpond. The wall starts again at the Red Tower in a once marshy area now dominated by the bulk of a former flour mill, used today as a raw materials store by Rowntree-Mackintosh. But the focal point is the remarkable Walmgate Bar, the only one to retain its barbican, rebuilt in 1648 after damage during the civil war. In the early years of this century it was said that "fragments of inscriptive tombstones" were built into the walls from the ruins of the nearby Church of St Nicholas, also a victim of the seventeenth-century war. It was reported in 1730 that a "great part of its once handsome steeple and of the south wall yet appear" and six years later: "It has been a noble structure, as appears by part of the tower yet standing."

There appears to be no trace of the "inscriptive tombstones" today, but cannonball scars and pock marks left by bullets may be seen on the eastward-facing Bar. A search for these vivid reminders can be hazardous, however, as one of the city's busiest crossroads creates a traffic tangle at the entrance to the barbican. In 1644 the message of danger was carried in the whine of 9-pound shot from a gun platform on Lamel Hill; today it is in the rumble of the passing lorry. Lamel Hill, one of the Parliamentarian batteries, stands 73 feet above ground level and is to be found in the garden of The Retreat, the mental hospital established in 1796 by the Society of Friends. A summerhouse has been built on the site. An iron cannonball found at the foot of the hill at the beginning of the 1939–45 war was used as a doorstop for many years until it passed into a private collection. More relics of the siege, two unexploded bombshells still filled with gunpowder, were found in April 1836, during excavations for a drain near the Bar.

Walmgate Bar still has its portcullis and heavy inner wooden door with wicket. The original outer gate of the barbican was of iron, and the City Chamberlain's Accounts mention new locks and bolts; Richard Lebb was paid 3s 4d in 1588 for a "great lock and an iron slot". The inner face is quite different from those of the other Bars, for in the sixteenth century a two-storey wooden structure with ornamental palisade was added to enlarge the domestic accommodation. The Bar was also a home for

8

Bootham Bar

centuries, an annual lease of 10s being recorded in 1376, and it was not until 1959 that the last family left. Behind the 3-feet-thick walls, which muffled traffic noise, were a sitting-room, kitchen and two large bedrooms, and for nearly fifty years this was the home of the Clark family. "I always think standing here is like being on the bridge of a ship," said a member of the family in 1951. At one time there was even a garden on the roof.

From Walmgate Bar the wall runs past the site of the cattle market (now moved outside the city) where pens for the beasts adjoined the grassy rampart, and ends at the monolithic Fishergate Postern Tower which once stood with its feet in the broad pool of the Foss. A red tile roof was added in 1740 to this rectangular tower which has two rooms, a bricked up fireplace, a spiral stair and the remains of a garderobe.

In 1836 the police began a daily patrol of the entire circuit of the wall at dusk each day, locking the access gates behind them. This custom was unbroken until the night of 31st March 1971, when a policeman turned the keys for the last time. The duty is now in civilian hands.

The wall, at Fishergate Postern, is also relieved of its duty, for the defence of the city lay beyond this point with the castle and the river, dominant features which close the gap. Panels in the Bayeux tapestry show soldiers working to build up the castle mound at Hastings—a scene which must have been repeated at York where, in 1068–9, two castles were raised. One, on the west bank of the Ouse, was sited on a natural ridge about 40 feet above river level. Today the surviving mound, known as the Old Baile, has a very natural look, having been planted with trees in 1726 (it was here more than thirty years ago that I had the rare sight of a red squirrel within yards of one of the city's main traffic bridges). The second castle, known since the sixteenth century as Clifford's Tower, is a roofless stone quatrefoil on a neat green mound, now shorn of the trees which once clung to its steep slope.

The thirteenth-century Clifford's Tower, an outstanding feature of this sector of the city since the dark, high, encircling wall which partially obscured it was demolished in the 1930s, is only there by the skin of its teeth. It cracked from top to bottom in 1360, and despite repairs the damage may still be seen. Then in 1596 a start was made on pulling down the tower to burn its masonry for lime. The corporation, making one of this country's earliest attempts to preserve an ancient monument, had the work stopped, but not before the bridge connecting the tower with the castle yard had been destroyed. The tower was damaged in the siege of 1644, and in 1684 it was wrecked by a magazine explosion. After this it fell into a reverie as a mere piece of background in a citizen's landscaped garden until 1902 when the building was repaired and, thirteen years later, placed in the care of the Ministry of Public Building and Works.

The story of the remaining three buildings in the castle yard, two of which have been put to a remarkable use, properly belongs to an account of eighteenth-century York.

Our medieval ancestors were fond of building houses and shops on their bridges, and the old Ouse Bridge at York was supporting them in 1307. A list of 1376 shows that there were seventeen shops and tenements on the north side and twelve on the south, but there was still room for more. The Ouse Bridge-master's Roll of 1435 lists twenty-three shops and tenements on the north and twenty-nine on the south. Little wonder that it collapsed in 1565, though it must be admitted that overloading was helped by the pressure of broken ice floes after a sudden thaw.

But this was not the first Ouse Bridge to collapse, if a story first put on record in the fourteenth century is to be believed. According to this the wooden bridge across the river in 1154 collapsed under the weight of the crowd which gathered to welcome Archbishop William. No lives were lost, and this was regarded as a miracle, but William died of a fever that summer. The York Chapter successfully sought his canonization and his splendid shrine probably stood behind the Minster's high altar.

With stone from the Tadcaster quarries and from ruinous buildings in the city, the sixteenth-century bridge was rebuilt with a single main arch between April and October 1566, and it is this steeply humped-backed design which may be seen in many engravings and paintings produced before the building of the present bridge in 1810. The incline of this central bow discouraged the building of houses on the crown of the bridge, but about twenty on each side were still to be found throughout the following century.

The principal building on the north side of the bridge was the council chamber under its three-gabled roof. It had survived the 1565 disaster. Furnishing accounts suggest that green was a

popular colour for the upholstery for at least a century, and it is
known that the chamber was heated by a charcoal-burning fire
in the winter. Council meetings were held during the day, but
candles, bread and ale were often provided for special meetings
at night. The city's records were kept in this chamber. A new
leather bag to keep them in was bought for 5d in 1521, but
twenty-one years later a "close presser" was made for the records
at a cost of 36s 8d.

Not far from the council chamber, at the north-west end of the
bridge, was St William's Chapel, demolished in 1810. Fragments
of it are now in the Yorkshire Museum and its distinctive needle
spire and clock appear in many old engravings. A building of
the late twelfth century, it was a civic chapel with three altars,
an Easter sepulchre and offertory boxes to St Barbara and St
Eligius. Fifteenth-century accounts include items for wine, oil,
Paris candles and "leather for hanging clappers on the bells".
The clock, one of the most important in the city, is mentioned
in accounts for 1441. And it was from here that the town bell—
surely the most familiar sound in medieval and Tudor York—was
rung for a quarter of an hour at 4 am each summer day (5 am
in winter) and at 8 pm.

The Mayor and Sheriff each had a prison on the bridge, sometimes known as the Kidcotes. William Hyndley, carver of the
Minster screen, was committed to the Sheriff's prison in 1490,
accused of murder. The prisons were on two levels, the upper
being level with the street. As late as 1729 prisoners were in the
habit of begging food from passers-by. The lower part of the
prison was foul and damp and, according to the records of a
prisoner, there was indeed "darkness at noon" in what was known
as the Black Hall.

The present Ouse Bridge was built between 1810 and 1820
to the design of Peter Atkinson the younger, and is said to have
cost £80,000. The architect was also responsible for the charming
little classical Foss Bridge of 1811–12.

Anyone walking down the riverside steps near Barker Tower,
upstream from Ouse Bridge, before 8th January 1863, would
have been preparing to cross the Ouse by ferry. That was the
date of the opening of Lendal Bridge and the end of John
Leeman's livelihood, for he had been ferryman at this point
since 1851, the last in a line stretching back to the Middle Ages.
But public sympathy was aroused and on 13th May that year

he was presented with a horse and cart, which cost £25, and with £15 in cash.

Victorians held celebration dinners at the drop of a hat (surviving menus give us a glimpse of their staggering appetites) and the opening of Lendal Bridge was a good excuse for one. The Lord Mayor entertained 120 guests at the Mansion House while the men who had worked on the bridge sat down to their dinner in the "outer wool shed" adjoining the cattle market.

But two years earlier things were not running so smoothly. When 600 tons of iron lattice girder bridge fell into the Ouse at York one September day in 1861, the ripples were to be felt as far away as Scarborough on the Yorkshire coast. Since 1849 the seaside town had been dozing over a plan to build a bridge over the Ramsdale Valley to connect the South Cliff with the main shopping areas. The crash at York, just where the final and more elegant Lendal Bridge now spans the river, jolted Scarborough into action. Out of what the *Illustrated London News* described as "an accident of a fearful nature", the town eventually gained its own bridge. It still serves Scarborough today, though it was rebuilt and widened in 1928.

In 1861 photography, though well established since that remarkable picture had been taken at Lacock Abbey in 1835, was still a very slow business, hardly the medium for on-the-spot news pictures. So the illustrated papers of the day relied largely on artists' impressions, and the engraving showing the collapse of the York bridge, published in the *Illustrated London News*, was based on a sketch made by a Mr B. J. Moore.

The lattice bridge was intended to replace the old ferry service. It was of four iron girders, two to support a carriageway and two outer and lighter ones to carry a footpath on each side. The two carriage girders were in place and the smaller girders had been brought to the site. As one was being lowered into position, it fell on the inner girder. This, in turn, fell on the next until the whole mass collapsed into the river, killing five men and seriously injuring others. After this, a design for an arched, cast-iron bridge by Thomas Page, engineer of Westminster Bridge, was adopted and carried out at a cost of £35,500. Tolls were collected until 1894 from the turreted toll-houses now used as shop premises.

Though Lendal was the first road traffic bridge to share the burden with Ouse Bridge, a rail bridge with accommodation for pedestrians had been built in 1844-5 with the opening of the York–Scarborough line. At first the footway was sited—rather hair-raisingly—between the up and down lines, but in 1874 the footbridge was moved to the south side at a lower level.

As York entered the 1870s the need for another major bridge, this time downstream from Ouse Bridge, became apparent. Thomas Page was again the designer, and after five years' wrangling and three years' building Skeldergate Bridge was opened in 1881. The bridge has five spans, three over the water. One of the river spans, on the north-east side, can be raised. There had been a ferry at this point since at least 1541 and in the early seventeenth century a ducking stool was placed nearby.

Generations of discussion ended in 1963 with the opening of Clifton Bridge, the fifth traffic bridge over the Ouse, and a sixth, Bishopthorpe Bridge on the eastern by-pass, was opened in April 1976.

Of York's half-dozen minor bridges, the Blue Bridge over the Foss near its junction with the Ouse dates only from 1929, but has a delicacy and charm which earns it a place in any portrait of York. The first bridge to be built here in 1738 so that St George's Field, the tongue of land between Ouse and Foss, might be connected with the fashionable, elm-shaded New Walk, was of wood painted blue. The name has stuck. The present bridge, the sixth on the site, was until the 1939-45 war flanked by relics which carried memories of the cold wind out of the Russian steppes as it blew over the Crimean peninsula in December 1854. British regiments outside Sebastopol shivered, starved and died of disease. Trenches were awash and thoughts—in between attacks—were centred on food. Four years later two guns which probably fired on those regiments from the parapet of the Great Redan, Sebastopol's strongest outlying earthwork, were to be found overlooking a very different scene. Old habits die hard, and it took the last war to put a stop to the practice of setting up captured enemy artillery in British towns and cities. But in the mid-nineteenth century the arrival of two Russian guns from Sebastopol was the signal for yet another corporation banquet in York Guildhall. Special stone platforms were built for them on either side of the Foss at Blue Bridge and there they stayed until 1941-2 when they were sold as scrap metal for the war effort. Preserved in the archives of the York

Castle Museum, only a pistol shot from this bridge, is a letter written by Arthur Brooksbank, a young British Army officer who served in the trenches before Sebastopol in the winter of 1854. "The other night", he told his family, "I had to keep a party of unfortunates at work during heavy rain and fire from the famous Redan, you may have heard mentioned. The rascals heard us at work and fired grape and round shot at us which, as there was not an inch of cover, was rather unpleasant." So the guns which threatened him helped to win another war nearly a century later.

Virtually unchanged since its building by Peter Atkinson the younger, the Regency Foss Bridge at the south-east end of Fossgate, is best seen from the river itself which, though partly canalized and hemmed in by industrial buildings, has been proved to be host to an astonishing variety of wild life.

The first bridge here, probably of wood, was in existence in the early twelfth century, and was replaced by a stone bridge in 1403. In time it became encrusted with houses, so much so that Camden, writing in 1586, said that a stranger was unable to tell when he was on it. St Anne's Chapel on the north-east side was in use by 1424, but had become a storehouse by 1555. It was robbed of its stone for repair work in 1564–5 and the last remains, including supporting wooden piles, were swept away between 1664 and 1735. A plan of York made in the reign of Charles II shows houses on the south-west side of the bridge only, and none on the side where the chapel had stood. A sea fish market was held on Foss Bridge as early as the thirteenth century, and was opened by the ringing of a bell, known as the "Scayt-bell", from the tower of St Anne's Chapel.

One of the city's most curious discoveries was made near the bridge on 10th August 1829, while workmen were sinking a well in a stonemason's yard. A *Yorkshire Gazette* reporter was there to record that "when they had gone about 11 feet below the surface of the ground, they found part of a horse's skeleton, the head being couched between the foreknees, and the forelegs were bent as if the animal had been in the act of plunging. A little further, a spur, with the skull and some other bones of a man were discovered." Later the jawbone of a dog and a piece of leather, thought to be part of the saddle, were also found.

"The soil at this place", ran the report, "is for two to three feet a strong loam; below that there were found the remains of

Roman tiles and below that a black soil apparently a decomposition of animal and vegetable matter." Past the twenty-foot mark were found a number of mussel shells, some six inches long and still lustrous inside. At twenty-five feet was another spur with a two-inch rowel. The stonemason himself finally struck the natural gravel and on it what he described as a wall of Roman bricks supporting a jetty, regularly formed of beams and piles. The writer of a guide to the city, published in 1838, had an explanation for the finds: "This place at some remote period has evidently been a swamp or morass and it is likely that the unfortunate object of our present curiosity had galloped his horse into it and thus met a premature death."

A classic case for a haunted site. But I feel the chances of meeting a pale horse with a pale rider in Fossgate are pretty small.

5

VENETIAN WINDOWS AND PILLARED DOORWAYS

IN THE eighteenth century many of York's half-timbered houses and shops with over-sailing storeys which the seventeenth-century traveller Celia Fiennes had found so "indifferent" were replaced by bland brick frontages set with Venetian windows and pillared doorways in the Georgian manner. It was an age of rebuilding, giving the city its Assembly Rooms, Mansion House, Assize Courts and many elegant town houses which still add their leaven of sweet reason to streets of mixed styles. Behind some of these rose-brick faces, which seem to store the warmth of the sun, are half-forgotten gardens, remnants of the open spaces which were such a feature of the city centre. John Cossins' map of 1722, decorated with detailed drawings of sixteen houses in Micklegate, Pavement, Lendal, St Saviourgate, King's Staith, Castlegate, Davygate and Skeldergate, shows that open areas accounted for about a quarter of the city within the walls.

The council began to look to the city's amenities and health, planting trees, improving street paving, fighting pollution, establishing the first hospital and safeguarding property. An Act of 1763 provided a simple but effective way of making life pleasanter by insisting that all new properties should have fall-pipes to drain rainwater from the roofs, though this civilized idea may have been anticipated nearly forty years earlier by Thomas Fothergill whose house at 14 St Saviourgate, illustrated in Cossins' map, appears to have two fall-pipes with box-like rainwater heads. The quality of life gradually improved so that in the last forty years of the century baptisms began to outnumber burials.

That this crusty age had social style is seen from Lord Burling-ton's Palladian Assembly Rooms in Blake Street. Built in the 1730s, debased during the war and splendidly restored by 1951, the Rooms have a special place in the heart of the city. The foundation stone was laid on 1st March 1731 and 220 years later a reopening ball was attended by many of the descendants of the original subscribers. Under the lights of the Venetian glass chandeliers the drab years which the Rooms had spent as York's wartime Food Office dropped away. This costume ball—Georgian, of course—was part of the city's first Festival of the Arts, and guests that night came very close to the true flavour of the eighteenth century.

The vaulted cellars of the Assembly Rooms were a meeting place for the sedan chairmen, a rascally lot, no doubt; hot-blooded in their rivalry and prone to overcharge in the dark streets of Hanoverian England. Here they played dice around the big fire, gossiping with the running footmen who had lighted their employers to the assembly with spluttering flambeaux. It was once believed that the walls of the entrance hall were painted black to the height of the doors because these torches, held in the careless hands of waiting servants, discoloured the stonework, but during the restoration and redecoration no trace of this was found.

Was it all sweetness and light in Burlington's great hall with its close-set Corinthian pillars? Judging from his description of a scene there in the *Expedition of Humphrey Clinker*, the novelist Tobias Smollett thought so: ". . . the company on a ball night must look like an assembly of fairies, revelling by moonlight among the columns of a Grecian temple."

Was it really like that—all scented gavottes and minuets? To begin with, it was the custom of the time to dip the candles in oil before placing them in the candelabra, and the smell was not pleasant. Despite the fact that the glass holders were large and cup-shaped, there is little doubt that dropping grease was a hazard of the dance floor. When it came to dancing the company was just as likely to be tearing into local country figures like the York Maggot, Slingsby's Reel, Tringham's Fancy, News From Denmark, Fordyce's Folly, Mrs Cartwright's Delight and Tristram Shandy—named after Laurence Sterne's novel. It all adds up to a scene like that in Hogarth's engraving *The Country Dance* which he produced in 1753. The guests' tricorn hats are piled in one corner of the candlelit room and a dog snaps at the heels of the dancers. Or again, like his *Wedding Dance* in which the moon looks through the window upon a very mixed company, and the feet thumping on the floorboards may almost be heard.

There is a long history of conservation behind the Assembly Rooms, from the underpinning of the foundations before the war to the £30,000 restoration scheme which assured their future. In the dim Food Office days its splendour could easily have been forgotten, but the corporation was obviously in agreement with the late Mr Oliver Sheldon who, as chairman of York Georgian Society, reminded the city more than twenty years ago that "this is no minor public hall; it is not just another place for meetings, dances and parties. It is a superb building, with all the dignity of Georgian design, to be used worthily under the auspices of the city."

Burlington, as Lord Lieutenant of the West Riding, had close connections with York, but John Carr, the other great name in the architectural development of York, was twice Lord Mayor in 1770 and 1785. Though he died in 1807 worth £150,000, there were times in his youth when he had to stay in bed while his trousers were mended. He was never ashamed of having been poor, nor did he hesitate to turn the hand that was to design Harewood House to much humbler commissions in his adopted city.

At the beginning of his career as a fashionable architect, he designed a house for the Pikeing Well in New Walk, a tree-lined avenue beside the Ouse. The corporation should have paid him £88 13s for the work, but deducted £25 after admitting him to the freedom of the city. The Pikeing Well, later known both as Lady Well and Spring Well, is a natural spring which surfaces near the river at the foot of Hartoft Street. "A remarkably fine spring of clear water" was how local historian William Hargrove described it in 1818. "The door", he said, "is frequently opened by a man appointed to take care of it; the water is drunk by many persons, and is also much used as an eye-water. An open receiver in front of the Well House is visited every morning for these purposes when the Well is not open."

As far back as 1749 the corporation appointed Aldermen Skelton and Mayer and a Mr Mathews to look into the building of "an hansom fountain at Pikeing Well and a ha-ha along Foulforth field". They thought it would cost about twenty guineas. During the next three years costs rose until £88 13s was the agreed figure. On 16th May 1757 the York Chamberlain's account book recorded: "Paid to Mr John Carr for erecting the building about Pikeing Well, he having allowed £25 for his freedom, £63 13s." Three years later a city House Book showed that William Wood was to be paid two guineas a year for "keeping clear and opening and shutting up the well".

Born at Horbury, near Wakefield, in 1723, Carr spent most of his life in York. He was the only provincial architect to be invited, in 1791, to become a member of the London Architects' Club. In that year he also rebuilt Horbury Church at his own expense, and bought a house there which he renamed Carr Lodge.

In time he retired to Askham Richard, near York, where he bought a large house and estate. Late in life he made long tours of the country, showing his buildings to his great-nieces.

Two years after the Pikeing Well commission Carr's design was chosen for the grandstand at the racecourse on the Knavesmire. An engraving by Foudrinier shows that it was a two-storey building with a balustraded roof-line. The ground floor had three doors with rusticated surrounds and the central window of the seven lighting the first floor was in the Venetian style. A history of the city, published in 1785, said that at the time of the building of the grandstand "the spirit of horse-racing had pervaded every part of this country" and that the "nobility and gentry" were attracted to the city during the races. There is no doubt that Carr's building brought him to the notice of these influential visitors and launched him on his career.

Carr designed two attractive buildings on the east and west sides of the Eye of Yorkshire, the circular green plot in the centre of the Castle yard. The Assize Courts of 1773-7 face the former Female Prison of 1780, now the principal building of the York Castle Museum. Between them, facing north, is the elegant former Debtors' Prison, of 1705, with two projecting wings and a central turret. This building, containing much of the stone from St Mary's Abbey, is also occupied by the Castle Museum. This prison was regarded as a model of its kind, and in 1736 it was said that "the justices of the peace for the county have of late years taken great care that this gaol shall be as neat and convenient within as it is noble without, by allowing straw for the felons, and raising their beds, which before used to be on the ground. They have likewise caused an infirmary to be built, for the sick to be carried to out of the common prison, and allowed a yearly salary to a surgeon to attend them."

Two famous novelists of the day who visited York on their travels were impressed by the prison. Daniel Defoe, about 1727, described it as "a prison the most stately and complete of any in the whole kingdom, if not in Europe. Strangers who visit the inside of it seldom depart without making a trifling purchase of some of the small manufactures the prisoners work up for subsistence." Forty years later Smollett thought the prison "the best in all respects I ever saw, at home or abroad". John Wesley, writing in 1759, said "I visited two prisons in the Castle, which is I suppose the most commodious prison in Europe." The condemned cell, occupied by John Palmer, alias Dick Turpin, in 1739 before his execution at the York Tyburn, may be seen today, virtually unchanged.

Carr's plans for an asylum were approved in August 1773, and the foundation stone of what is now Bootham Park Hospital was laid in a five-acre field in the following May. It was opened in November 1777.

A York man, Peter Harrison (1716–75), was America's first practising architect, though he started out as a sea captain and trader. In the spring of 1775, on the eve of the American Revolution, an anti-British mob broke into his New Haven, Connecticut, home and destroyed his treasured library, drawings and papers. Miraculously, every building he designed in Colonial America survived the Revolution, and all are standing today. Among them are King's Chapel, Boston; the Redwood Library, Brick Market and Synagogue at Newport, Rhode Island; and Christ Church, Cambridge, Massachusetts. He introduced the Palladian style into America—a style he had seen take shape in York during the building of the Assembly Rooms. Youngest son of a York family of Quakers, he was a gifted man whose brilliant mind illuminated that rather ingrown New England world but because of the mob's blind hatred of anyone in the employment of George III's government (Harrison was a customs collector towards the end of his life) his unparalleled contribution to American culture remained clouded and obscure for generations.

His first building, the Redwood Library in Newport, Rhode Island, was inspired by a Venetian church, a garden temple at Chiswick and small buildings on country estates in Norfolk and Buckinghamshire. Today, surrounded by mature beech trees, it is one of the town's two public libraries and a source of great pride to Newporters.

But for one man—Dr Carl Bridenbaugh, a director of the Institute of Early American History and Culture at Williamsburg, Virginia—Harrison's memory would have been completely wiped out, not only in York, where he lived until he was in his early twenties, but in the New England States which saw the flowering of his genius. Over a long period of years, Dr Bridenbaugh gathered the scanty records of Harrison's life to build up the first biographical essay. There appears to be no record in York of Harrison's birth or of anything connected with his later fame. But the records in the strong-room of the Friends' Meeting House in Clifford Street, contain references to the deaths of his parents, Thomas and Elizabeth, in 1737 and 1753. A member of the York Meeting of the Society of Friends was also able to show me minutes of a meeting in 1719 when fifty-six Friends gave £33 10s towards the cost of a new Meeting House. Among the subscribers was Thomas Harrison, who gave three guineas, the price of a cow and calf in those days. The only public reference to the family seems to have been the wall tablet in memory of Peter's brother, Joseph, recorded in the church of St Mary Bishophill Senior. Joseph returned to England from Rhode Island in 1769 and died in York on 15th January 1789.

When Peter Harrison died of a stroke on 30th April 1775, it took the *Newport Mercury* three weeks to publish a terse notice: "died, at New Haven, suddenly, Peter Harrison, Esq." Hardly had an inventory of his estate been taken than the rebels broke open the Collector's House at New Haven, where the Harrisons led an elegant and well regulated life. Between 600 and 700 volumes, in addition to manuscripts and drawings, were destroyed. Among them was his copy of Francis Drake's folio volume of 1736, *Eboracum*, which contains a detailed description and three engravings of the York Assembly Rooms.

Not far from where the Roman Praetorian Gate once impressed visitors from the west, the city's most attractive Georgian building—the Mansion House—is a major feature of St Helen's Square at the point where it is joined by the busy shopping artery, Coney Street. In summer when hanging baskets of flowers and overflowing window-boxes decorate the pedimented façade painted in its Georgian livery, a blend of gaiety and civic dignity is created. For the Mansion House is truly a home, most Lord Mayors and their families choosing to live in the apartment provided there during the term of office.

The foundation stone was laid in 1725 (the London Mansion House was built 1739–53) and seven years passed before the gilders and carvers put the final touches to the decorations in the elegant State Room. It was about this time that the city's street lighting was improved, ninety-two oil lamps replacing the candle lanterns which had flickered to little purpose on winter evenings.

Before the building of the Mansion House the Mayors and later Lord Mayors of the city entertained citizens on feast days in their own homes, and often had to receive kings and princes with as much ceremonial as they could muster. When Charles I made his second visit to York in 1639 the Lord Mayor, Roger Jaques, welcomed him in the gabled and half-timbered Sir Thomas Herbert's House, which still stands in Pavement. While on a military expedition against the Scots, Oliver Cromwell visited the city briefly on Thursday, 4th July 1650. The next day the Lord Mayor, Alderman William Taylor, entertained the Protector and his party, but it took him six years to persuade the corporation to pay him "some moderate allowance" for his trouble.

Towards the end of the reign of George I there was a general feeling that the dignity of the city would be enhanced by the building of a house for the Lord Mayor. An entry in the Corporation House Book for 21st September 1724 reveals there had been complaints about the Lord Mayor's "frequent absence and retirement into the country, and neglecting to keep but one publick day in the week for the entertainment of citizens". It was decided that a house should be built in Coney Street on the site of houses occupied by James Young, Mrs Days and Mr Allen, at a cost of £1,000. The tenants of the houses were to be given notice to quit at the next Lady Day. A Building Committee was appointed on 9th December 1724. In addition to the £1,000 voted by the Council, they agreed to sell the South Sea stock and annuity belonging to the city, and to begin work on the new house after the Lent Assizes in 1725.

The site was cleared during the spring. One of the demolished houses, a stone building near the entrance to the Guildhall, which lies to the rear of the Mansion House, was known as the City House, and was originally the chapel of the Guild of St Christopher. Later it became a public house with the sign of the Cross Keys. It was well placed for viewing public processions and pageants, and in a lease dated 1591 the privilege was reserved for the Lord Mayor and his party "to stand in the chamber there for hearing plays and seeing showes".

By the end of 1725, though good progress had been made, the original £1,000 had almost been spent, and a further £300 was voted by the Council. By 1726 the work was so far advanced that the Lord Mayor, Alderman Samuel Clarke, was able to hold some of his functions in the building, and on 31st August the first great feast was held there, the Lady Mayoress acting as hostess to what became known as the "Lady's Feast".

Work was held up by lack of funds and unpaid bills so to ease matters the Council, on 24th October 1726, decided that "all the fines for offices and moneys for fredomes" should be used to pay off the £700 owing to the workmen "for which they are very clamorous". Early in the following year two elegant marble chimneypieces were placed in the State Room as the gift of George Errington, a liveryman of the Coachmakers' and Harnessmakers' Guild of the City of London. When the Lord Mayor-elect for 1730, Alderman John Stainforth, made it clear that he intended to occupy the Mansion House during his year of office, work was speeded up.

The names of the master craftsmen who worked on the Mansion House are to be found in the accounts of the City Chamberlains who had charge of municipal finances. Prominent among them is that of William Etty (no relation to the Victorian painter of the same name) who was a draughtsman, designer and carver. Though the building was once thought to be the work of the Earl of Burlington, who designed the Assembly Rooms in the following decade, it is now considered more likely that the designer was Etty.

Painter-stainer William Midgley did the painting and gilding, helped by James Carpenter, son of Samuel Carpenter, a well-known carver. John Terry was responsible for much of the joinery work and William Fleming worked on the bricklaying. Richard Nelthorp did "the plastering in the Great Room". It is known exactly which work was done by the carver Henry Thrisk, as he was paid £3 for four Corinthian capitals at 15s each. Much of the artistic woodwork in the State Room was done by Matthew Rayson, and the bill presented by William Silcock, whitesmith, was probably for the original wrought-iron palisading in front of the house. Trees and shrubs in the garden

King's Square

in Common Hall Yard were supplied and planted by Francis Gainforth.

A number of craftsmen were admitted to freedom of the city in return for services to the Mansion House. The famous clockmaker, Henry Hindley, who came from Manchester in about 1730 and had a shop at the corner of Blake Street and Stonegate, provided a "very good and handsome" eight-day clock and case for the Mansion House and another for the Common Hall in 1731. Nine years later John Stroud, a surgeon's instrument-maker, gained his freedom by supplying a dozen silver-hafted knives and forks to the value of £25. In the same year, 1740, Richard Eggleston, optician and spectacle maker, presented the city with a reflecting telescope "of a modern invention" and a large barometer.

Visitors to the Mansion House today who, by arrangement, are shown the civic plate, will notice in the hall, on the right as they enter, a painting by Nathan Drake of York's "noble terras walk" by the River Ouse as it was in the mid-eighteenth century. The laying out of the New Walk, as it is still known, was one of the signs that the city was beginning to look to its amenities. Historian Francis Drake, writing in 1736, three years after the walk was constructed, commented: "Our streets are clean and lighted with lamps every night in the winter season; and so regular are the inhabitants to their hours of rest, that it is rare to meet any person after ten or eleven at night walking in them," and added "there is no place out of London so polite and elegant to live in as the city of York".

New Walk was a highly valued facet of this elegance; so much so that when, early in the next century, it was proposed to fell forty-one elm trees, there was a public outcry. According to a reader's letter in the *York Chronicle* for 4th April 1816, York's two major attractions were the Minster and the trees in New Walk.

The *York Courant* thought that the destruction of the trees was "repugnant to the feelings of every person possessed of the smallest share of taste" and reported that a memorial was to be signed by "several of the most respectable inhabitants of the city" for presentation to the Lord Mayor and Council. The *York Herald* for 3rd April 1816 said that when the news first became public "a universal panic seized the inhabitants of all ranks, ages and parties . . ." However, the memorial worked

9

St William's College
Bowes Morrell House, Walmgate

and the trees were saved, though a number were blown down in the Whitsun gales of 1860. It is interesting to note that at this time, when citizens panicked at the thought of losing forty-one trees which, after all, could have been replaced, York's priceless medieval walls had been allowed to fall into a ruinous state.

A bearded, weatherworn stone face has looked out over Lendal for more than 250 years. It occupies a key position over the doorway of a house built about 1720 by Dr C. Winteringham; fittingly it is the head of Aesculapius, god of medicine and healing. In 1806 the doctor's house was bought by the county magistrates as a residence for the Judges of Assize. Before this, the judges were lodged in an old house in Coney Street opposite the George Inn (now a department store). A cul-de-sac still bears the name of Judges' Court and a York directory of 1823 gives its name as Judges' Old Lodgings Yard.

In the Middle Ages the church of St Wilfrid (a dedication now held by the Roman Catholic church in Duncombe Place) stood on and behind the site of the Judges' Lodgings. Here was buried Nicholas Fleming, the brave Mayor of York, who, in 1319, led against Scottish invaders what has been described as a nondescript army of 10,000 men, consisting of clergy, monks, farm labourers, artificers and tradesmen. His troops were heavily defeated at Myton-on-Swale, fifteen miles north-west of York, and Fleming was among the dead.

In the summer of 1786 the people of York had the chance to visit "a commodious room within the courtyard of the Judges' Lodgings in Coney Street" where the "philosophic and curious" among them were invited to see the Speaking Figure, one of the automata which reached the peak of their popularity at that time when a number of families of craftsmen dedicated their lives to the making of these intricate and sophisticated 'toys'. The *York Courant* told them that "this agreeable artificial lady is only 22 inches high, is suspended in the air by a riband, will be taken down and held in the hand, and answer all questions that the numerous visitors choose to put to her in the English, French, Spanish, German, Italian and Dutch languages in a correct, judicious and perfect manner. If desired, she will ask the question." Exhibited with her was "that matchless piece of art" the Automaton Writer . . . "this beautiful small figure stands by the side of a common table and is so curiously constructed as to be able to write whatever is proposed to it, with pen and ink, in a bold, free, legible hand, with the utmost ease, correctness and facility." Both were on display from 10 am to 5 pm and admittance was 1s. This was very reasonable, considering that up to half a guinea was charged in London for a sight of automata with much more modest talents.

The most advanced of modern computers would have a struggle to justify the claims made in this Georgian advertisement. It would be nearer the truth to say that the Speaking Figure may have been programmed to wheeze a word or two, and that the Automaton Writer could probably manage a line of writing, but no more. Brilliant as they were, the automata of the eighteenth century were not always above suspicion. Like the celebrated automatic chess player made by Wolfgang von Kempelen in 1778. It is said that Napoleon lost a game of chess to this mechanical master in 1809. Its secret was a well-trained boy concealed in the box on which the figure was mounted, who watched his opponent's moves in a series of mirrors.

Jacques de Vaucanson (1709–82) built a duck so realistic that it digested food. It was lost for many years until in 1840 it was discovered, broken, in Berlin. It was repaired and exhibited in the Place du Palais Royal in Paris four years later. Many of these fascinating creations, made for pleasure on guide-lines which lead directly to present-day industrial automation, have been preserved in museums and private collections. But how many more—their finery tarnished, their clockwork brains seized with rust—are awaiting discovery in the attics of Europe's chateaux and stately homes?

The York automata were typical of the type of travelling entertainment which trundled its way slowly from town to town in the eighteenth century, offering wild animals, tumblers, conjurers. In November 1790 a pelican, cassowary, orangoutang, tiger, wolf, vulture and eagle fought for breathing space in a "commodious caravan" parked in the Pavement, York. And somewhere in the mêlée were two small marmosets. Showmen, as now, believed in the power of advertising, and the pocket menagerie seen in York that year was said in the *York Herald* to have "just arrived from the East". It was so great an attraction that the proprietor invested in an expensive woodcut to illustrate the flower of his flock . . . "the stupendous pelican". Readers were told that "in form, health and beauty there is

not in the kingdom a curiosity offered to the public inspection
equal to the above bird". There was a bit of a mystery about
two of the exhibits, one described simply as "a curious animal
from Botany Bay" and the other cryptically as "the Lion
Monster". Of the Lion Monster, the showman said that it was
"so rare that naturalists cannot treat of it. He was taken out of a
mountain land near Patna in the East Indies, the first of its kind
ever exhibited in this kingdom."

On market days the caravan was moved to the Haymarket,
off Peasholme Green.

If you classed yourself among the "ladies and gentlemen"
admission was 1s, but if you didn't mind passing yourself off
as a tradesman, then it was only 6d to brave the beak of the
cassowary which stood five feet high and weighed 200 pounds.

Much earlier in the century—in December 1728—the Great
Room of Mr Ward's Coffee House at the corner of Spurriergate
was the setting for "the whole surprising mystery and new art
of the dexterity of hand". Not only that, the Royal Sword
Dance was performed by a Mr Clows from Cheshire "with
abundance of curious actions not common, all being worthy
of the greatest judge's observation".

York was visited by a professional giant in August 1743. But
the advertisement failed to say just how tall he was. Readers
of the *York Courant* were told: "Now is the time, or never, to
see the living Colossus or wonderful giant from Sweden who
had the honour to be viewed by his Majesty, the Prince and
Princess of Wales, all the Royal Family, most of the Nobility
and the Royal Society, with the utmost satisfaction." He was
on show at William Forth's Coffee House at Ouse Bridge End
from nine in the morning to eight in the evening. Admission
was 1s.

The Merchant Taylors' Hall in Aldwark was put to odd uses
in the eighteenth century. In January 1748 it saw the staging
of "a variety of rope dancing and tumbling by Mrs Garman,
Mr Pedro and Others". The "others" included Mr Dominique
who, twice a week, Wednesday and Saturday, "beat a drum
upon the stiff rope". Mr Pedro was billed to "perform on the
stiff rope with a wheelbarrow and a child in it" followed by
"a variety of new tumbling by the Russian boy" and a panto-
mime called *The Force of Magick or The Birth of Harlequin*. Pit
seats were 2s, middle gallery 1s and upper gallery 6d. Crude as

they were, such informal amusements probably kept people out of the ale-houses and cockpits.

In an age when a clergyman was known to have bludgeoned his servant for a trivial offence, and a distinguished member of the Archaeological Society kicked his maid when she did not move fast enough about her work, sport was—not surprisingly—cruel. Cockfighting 'mains' were regularly advertised in the newspapers, and county matches sometimes went on for days.

Glancing through the window of a silent, timbered room into the busy street below, and again, standing under an oval, concave roof on the top floor of a tall Georgian house, I tried to imagine the heat and turmoil of the average cockfight. A search, some years ago, for rooms in York where the tradition of the cockpit still lingered, took me to two buildings of widely differing styles on opposite sides of the river. As the last legal main was fought 200 years ago and the rattle of fair silver spurs is now the faintest of echoes, cockpit sites are not easy to find in the twentieth century. Unlike Samuel Pepys on his first visit to a cockfight, I could not be directed by "bills upon the walls" and the Cockpit House in Bootham—an obvious starting point— was pulled down shortly before the Crimean War. The trail of rumour, report and other people's memories led first to a fifteenth-century half-timbered house in Stonegate. Under the eaves lay a small room where the bones of the building were dark against the plastered walls. A window gave a restricted view of the pattern of gable and tile on the other side of the street, but it was the floor which was pointed out as the feature of the room. It was covered by a form of old, cracked concrete. Here on the hard floor, I was told, the birds had surely fought. This was the information passed on—largely by word of mouth— by successive occupants of the house. Evidence? None, except that a concrete floor is far more suitable to receive the savage downward strokes of the birds' spurred legs than a wooden one. Later I was told by an expert that this type of flooring is not unusual. Nearly all the houses in the Shambles at one time had that type of gypsum floor as a form of damp or fire-proofing.

Inquiries on another tack led me west of the river and posed another problem. Could an elegant town house of the early eighteenth century, the home of the then Lord Mayor of York, have been used for cockfights? A room at the top of a pair of

Micklegate houses which appear in the Cossins map of 1722 has a graceful, elliptical, concave ceiling with a heavily moulded cornice bearing the crest of the Thompson family. This, I was told, was traditionally the cockpit room. The concave ceiling was, in fact, the head of the staircase which had been removed at some time, another staircase being built nearby. The stair well-head had then been floored to form the curious room.

Most old prints show that the cockpit was a raised circular stage about twenty feet in diameter, surrounded by a barrier. Mains consisted of fights between an agreed number of cocks, matched singly. Three weeks before the main, the owner handed over their birds to professional trainers known as 'feeders'. When the birds were fighting fit they were kept on top of their form with barley soaked in sherry and 'cockbread' steeped in port. They fought in silver spurs of an agreed length up to two and a half inches.

The *York Courant* carried a number of advertisements for cockfights which could be seen in Bootham, the Royal Cockpit in Blake Street, the Sign of the Cock in Old Work (Aldwark), Coffee Yard, the Grand Pit without Bootham Bar and Micklegate. Fights were held every morning of race week. In the edition of 4th May 1784, there was advertised "Cocking at York Spring Meeting. To be fought at the Cockpit in York, on Wednesday, 12th May . . . a gentlemen's subscription for two guineas a battle." On 14th February 1774 a main was fought at Mrs Scarrot's pit in Coffee Yard, for a grey horse valued at 12 guineas. Sixteen birds fought in "fair round silver spurs, according to the articles of cockfighting".

Cockpit House in Bootham was perhaps the most famous pit in the city. It stood just where the street St Mary's joins the main road today, opposite the entrance to Bootham Park. As well as being a refreshment room for those who came to the mains, it was often let for public assemblies. Drake, the eighteenth-century historian, described it as "a handsome assembly room, by a beautiful bowling green". But it was seen in the following century as "a rather unsightly structure" and was demolished in 1850.

Much of the raw material of the social history of this period is to be found in the pages of the newspapers. The first copy of the *York Mercury* went on sale on 23rd February 1719, and there has been newspaper production on the present site of the

Yorkshire Evening Press offices in Coney Street since 1759. The city's first paper was published by Grace White, who had inherited her husband's printing house in Coffee Yard, off Stonegate. By 1724 the business had passed into the hands of Thomas Gent, and his first issue for the week 16th–23rd November carried the new title of the *Original York Journal or Weekly Courant*. Four years later he renamed it the *Original Mercury, York Journal or Weekly Courant*, and it was published until at least 1739. Gent, who moved his press to Petergate in 1742, had great competition from the *York Courant*, established by John White in 1725. It was in August or September of that year that White, working from an office in Stonegate, near St Helen's Church, issued his first number. In 1734 the business was sold, first to John Gilfillan, then to Alexander Staples, a Londoner, who moved the press to Coney Street, almost opposite St Martin's Church. Staples did not prosper and in 1738 the business passed to Caesar Ward and Richard Chandler. When Ward died in 1759 his widow, Ann, moved to a house next to the George Inn on the opposite side of Coney Street. Part of the frontage of these premises, now occupied by the city's evening and weekly newspapers, is scheduled as being of special architectural and historic interest, and one pillar of the gateway leading to the old Inn Yard still remains. Modern expansion has taken place towards and parallel with the river bank.

In 1788 Ann Ward took George Peacock into partnership, and she died in the following year. During her time the *Courant* had connections in some of the London coffee houses where advertisements were taken. Business was done on her behalf at the Chapter coffee house in Paternoster Row; St Paul's coffee house; the Edinburgh coffee house at the Royal Exchange; the Guildhall coffee house, King Street, Cheapside; St James's coffee house, Ludgate Street; at a stationer's shop in George Street, Cheapside; and at the Fountain in Wych Street, near Temple Bar.

If we wish to know what the people of York in the eighteenth century ate, read and wore, how they amused themselves or what they expected of their servants, then the newspapers will tell us. By human standards a century is time on a vast scale, and the wide tapestry of happenings between William III and George III offers such a complex pattern of everyday life that it is often better to take a 'sample' of the age. The year 1771 was the 1700th anniversary of the city's founding and represents

the 'middling' period when old people could still recall the
last flicker of Caroline England and the upheavals which were
to spread like ripples from the French Revolution lay eighteen
years ahead.

It was a time when scented Venetian soap could be had for
9s a stone . . . when Black Antigua pineapples were grown in
a greenhouse in Bishophill on the west bank of the Ouse . . .
when a liveried servant, able to dress hair, could hope for £12
a year . . . when a seat in a theatre box, lit by the best wax
candles, cost 3s . . . when wallpaper, made in the city, was 6d
a piece.

Life was a mosaic of contrasts, the gap between high and low
life wide and unbridgeable. While hard-worked apprentices ran
away from their masters, often to be swept up by the Press
Gang on their stealthy trips up the Ouse, candle-lighting time
in the gracious houses of Micklegate saw the opening of the
latest three-volume novels. Women shopping for imported silks
and muslins or making their way to dancing lessons in the
upper rooms of taverns, must have passed young men enduring
a three-hour stint in the stocks, perhaps for gambling on a
Sunday. Meanwhile, it was possible to hear a performance of
Handel's *Acis and Galatea* in the Assembly Rooms.

Though cramped and poorly lighted by our standards, the
city's shops met the growing needs of the rising middle class
with a keen eye to business. A typical hardware shop, kept by
a Mr Northrop in Feasegate, would have in stock "a great
variety of plain and open-work china-pattern fenders with sets
of iron and japanned waiters and tea boards; green and white
ivory knives and forks with shagreen cases; plated goods; swing
and pier glasses; and a large quantity of coat and waistcoat
buttons."

Mr Seguin, the confectioner in Minster Yard, sold "all sorts
of wet and dry sweetmeats" including perfumed comfits,
almonds, ginger, cherries, coriander, caraway, cardamom, biscuits, macaroons and cakes . . . also the "true marshmallow
paste for the cough". The contents of James Todd's shop in
Pavement would fetch a high price in today's auction rooms.
He stocked an elegant assortment of perfume and essence pots,
urns, candelabra, vases, tea urns, sugar dishes, toothpick cases,
snuffboxes and ivory toys from London and Nuremburg.

Mr W. Tesseyman, a bookseller, of Minster Yard, was a

versatile trader, selling novels and rat poison side by side. A three-volume novel, *The Old Maid or the History of Miss Ravensworth in a Series of Letters*, by a local author, cost 7s 6d. The rat poison was 2s a box. He also sold a racy publication, *The Town and Country Magazine* which, for 6d, told the tale of *The Amorous Agent and Miss B . . . e* and *Jemmy Twitcher and Miss R . . . y*. Readers were assured that "the characters drawn are all original and real, and may be considered as a just mirror of the times".

Thomas Marshall, a butter factor and chandler, moved from his Micklegate shop in April 1771 "to a house where the late Mr Benson dwelt". In a tight little city like York everyone would know where that was. He offered to his wholesale customers Jamaica rums, French and British brandies, Holland and British Genevas, cinnamon waters, porter bottled or in small casks from 9 to 36 gallons, brown soap at 6s a stone, white at 7s 6d and scented Venetian at 9s.

Some idea of the large range of materials available is given by the list of goods on sale—rather vaguely—at the West End of the Minster. Some are familiar, others have disappeared from modern counters: "Fancy and plain silks, rich brocades, tissues, Peruvians, vilderoys, damasks, flowered sattins, tabbies, armozeens, ducapes, enamelled, striped and plain mantuas, flowered sattins."

In a "commodious room at Mrs Sellers's house in High Jubbergate", Miss Vigna, from Rome, offered to teach singing in the true Italian taste and also the French, Italian and German languages. Proficiency was guaranteed in five months. John Mush was busy making and supplying wallpaper, offering to hang it at 6d a piece. In his Blake Street warehouse, Thomas Haxby was proudly showing off his "new, improved, single harpsichord", recently granted the Royal Letters Patent. Over at the Sycamore Tree in Minster Yard, Mr Rochefort, the dancing master, was teaching the latest steps.

The winter of 1771 was exceptionally mild. In Henry Myres's garden a passion tree flowered in mid-December, bearing "as fine blooms as in the month of August" and a Bishophill hothouse was producing a good crop of pineapples. The owner regularly cut eighty of the fruits each year, and when he decided to sell his greenhouse it was valued at £100.

Entertainment was limited to productions at the Theatre

Royal, music at the Assembly Rooms and the infrequent visits
of showmen. Early in the year, for the benefit of the County
Hospital, the Theatre Royal, "lately ornamented in a most
elegant manner", presented Shakespeare's *Henry IV Part One* with
a trifle called *Thomas And Sally* as a chaser. Patrons were told
that "the boxes will be illuminated all round (both inside and
out) with wax candles and there will be new Arms over the
front of the boxes." Prices were: Box 3s; Pit 2s; First Gallery
1s 6d; Upper Gallery 1s.

One spring evening, just outside Bootham Bar, Christopher
Petero "the celebrated Italian artist" put on a firework display
offering "rockets of various sorts, globes, curious fire-wheels,
a beautiful fire-mill and a palm tree full of roses which will be
discharged by a pigeon upon a cord". In addition, there were
"all sorts of fireworks to be sold at his lodgings at the Punch
Bowl in Stonegate". For one night only, on 10th April, at the
Merchant Taylors' Hall, a talented Mr Pittard, described as
"late comedian at the Theatre Royal, Covent Garden and
formerly of the York theatre", presented *The Temple of Taste or
The Impromptu.*

At the end of July there was a hint that a "most superb and
surprising piece of mechanism" was to visit the city. At that
time it was in Leeds and was to be in York for race week.
When it arrived it turned out to be The Microcosm "now
opened for the inspection of the curious in a commodious room
in the Pavement, directly opposite Crux Church at the lower
end of the Shambles". Those who promoted it were fulsome
in their praise: "The universal applause given to this superb
structure cannot be expressed. If the beauties of art and the
elegancies of architecture, sculpture, painting, music and astronomy can please, and if a vast variety of figures moving in the
most lively manner, where the imagination is ever delighted
and the mind enjoys the unbounded curiosity by an exhibition
of the grand, the uncommon and the beautiful; if these can give
satisfaction, the Microcosm bids fairest for that of any machine
ever exhibited." Behind this verbal jungle was probably some
kind of lantern slide show, with primitive moving pictures. It
was available to parties of five or more at a shilling a head.

The Riding School, which stood behind the Minster, was used
regularly by itinerant showmen and sometimes by balloonists.
It was visited in August 1771, by the Grand Venetian Company

from Sadler's Wells who offered "stiffrope dancing and lofty tumbling". The star of the show, Signor Le Nomora, made a speciality of the Lion's Leap. He guaranteed to surprise all the spectators and "turn round as quick as the Fly of a Jack".

More than one craftsman in the city embroidered in human hair. Among them was S. Boverick, a watchmaker, lodging at Mr Heffey's on the corner of Low Ousegate. Orders for his work were taken at the Golden Tea Kitchen in Spurriergate and the Golden Cup in Coney Street. A miniaturist, he claimed to have carved "the little furniture of a dining room in a cherry stone". Working along similar lines was Ambrose Beckwith, who lived at the Crown and Pearl in Coney Street. He not only embroidered in human hair on silk, but made ivory ships, completely rigged and fitted with brass guns, small enough to be mounted on rings or in lockets.

Servants were in regular demand: "Wanted, in a small family, a grave, sober person to act as housekeeper and cook with a servant under her" . . . "Wanted, in a gentleman's family in the country, sober, grave, elderly servant in the capacity of house-keeper and cook" . . . "Wanted, a steady, sober manservant for a small family. He must be very ready at waiting and write well enough to make a bill. If he can dress hair, the more agreeable" . . . "Wanted, in an Upper Man's Place, a servant that has lived in genteel families and understands dressing hair. He may have it in his choice to wear a livery or his own clothes; if the former, wages £12 a year; if the latter, £20."

Dissatisfied apprentices sometimes took it into their head to make a run for it. In the depth of winter, John Clapham, apprenticed to a miller near Monk Bar, ran away from his master. He was only fourteen, described as "stiff-made, of a fresh complexion, has light brown hair and had on a light-coloured coat and waistcoat, buckskin breeches and grey stockings."

The hardships of army life sometimes proved too much for newly enlisted men. Matthew Ligs, a former weaver, deserted from the 44th Regiment of Foot, recruiting at Malton, about the time that John Clapham went on the run. He was "aged 25 or upwards, 5 feet 9 inches high, is a good deal pitted with the smallpox, has short brown hair that curled a little, grey eyes, thin, sharp nose, is raw-boned and loose-limbed; had on a threadbare brown coat with metal buttons, black waistcoat and

leather breeches." Anyone who found him was offered two
guineas above the reward allowed by law.

This was the year that York was plagued with an influx of
counterfeit halfpennies. Those who knowingly passed them were
warned that first offenders would receive six months' imprisonment. A second offence would be two years' jail, and a third
would be treated as a felony.

At Sutton-on-Forest, a few miles north of the city, two men
and a pair of oxen were bitten by a little black dog. Not knowing
that it was mad, they took him polecat hunting. It is to be hoped
they knew about Mr Brooke, the Fossgate grocer, who sold
"a cure for the bite of a mad dog at 5s 3d per dose", though he
usually addressed himself "to the nobility and gentry".

The State Lottery was doing brisk business through a Mr C.
Etherington, who had an office opposite All Saints', Pavement.
A whole ticket cost £14, but fractions of a ticket down to one
sixty-fourth could be bought at 5s. Prizes ranged from £20,000
to £20.

The year threw up its quota of 'silly season' stories . . . a cat
was discovered mothering a family of young rats in the kitchen
of an unspecified York house, and a foolhardy joiner entered
into a five guinea bet that he could carry a man to Knaresborough
in twelve hours. Before he had covered two of the eighteen
miles he was "obliged to yield to the enormous weight of his rider".

There was a touch of comedy too in the report of the auction
of hardware in a Coney Street shop. The floor gave way and
about sixty people fell ten feet into the cellar which was used
as a smith's forge. But there were no injuries—just a few barked
shins, sooty faces and lost wigs.

Behind their modest frontages, many of York's Georgian
properties retain sumptuous examples of the age of elegance in
which they were built. Though its bricks and timbers have been
dust on the wind for some years now, I shall always remember
an old house in Micklegate for the surprises its interior held.
Seen from the street, it was very plain, and several years of
neglect had not added to its appeal. But its upper floors were
threaded through with the massive medieval timbers of the
original house which had been masked by brick some time in
the eighteenth century. On the ground floor, to the left of what
had once been a butcher's shop, was a curious painted room.
If these things were to be found in one unremarkable house,

what lies behind the exteriors of the city's many buildings listed as being of historical and architectural interest? In the darkness behind a ground floor shop could one have found a seventeenth-century panel painting? Or classical art in an upstairs room where a member of one of England's oldest families must have sat by candlelight after dinner?

The answers are to be found in another house in Micklegate, advertised in 1785 as a "very neat and convenient dwelling house" and used for many years as the headquarters of York Georgian Society. It is now in private possession. Early in the Georgian Society's connection with the house, a natural curiosity about its previous occupants led the late Miss I. P. Pressly, an indefatigable researcher who was then honorary secretary, to go further into the background of the man who had died there at the age of 83 in 1785.

She contended that although many of the large houses in Micklegate were the town houses of county families who came to the city for the August races or the Assize balls, a younger son was likely to live permanently in this fashionable and elegant street. And so the house once occupied by the Society became the home of Matthew Chitty St Quintin, second son of Sir Hugh St Quintin and Catherine Chitty. It had been built in the first half of the eighteenth century by a Robert Bower whose name appears in the deeds, and probably replaced a gabled, medieval building. Compared with the 'town houses' lower down the hill, it was not large. It had three bedrooms or 'lodging rooms', each with a dressing-room, and a panelled room at the back on the first floor. Overlooking the street on the first floor was the drawing-room. Here the chimney-piece has a small bas-relief panel in plaster which, it has been suggested, may represent an incident in the mythological history of the Greek goddess Demeter. The 'speciality of the house' was in a ground floor room—a painting in the overmantel identified as the work of Adam Willaerts, who was born in Antwerp in 1577, but spent most of his life in Utrecht where he settled in 1600. In one corner of the painted panel are the artist's initials and the almost illegible date, 1635. In the foreground are three ships anchored near a quay; the background has been compared in shape with Mont St Michel in Normandy.

Matthew St Quintin had domestic staff, of course. His house-keeper, cook and maids would have lived on the second floor, where the ceilings are noticeably lower. His footman, Thomas Maxon, and postilion, John Stubs, probably lived over the stable in nearby Toft Green.

After St Quintin's death the house was the home of Alderman George Peacock, twice Lord Mayor of York, in 1810 and 1820. He was the son-in-law of the printer, Ann Ward, who produced the first two volumes of Laurence Sterne's *Tristram Shandy*.

Wise men between the ages of 18 and 55 stayed by their firesides on winter nights in 1777. It was not the weather that made them toast their toes, but the arrival in the city of a naval lieutenant and a party of sailors. They had crept up the Ouse in a pinnace and two yawls on the impress service. Their job, according to a contemporary report, was to "beat up for volunteers". To the Press Gang, as they were more commonly known, the interpretation of the word 'volunteer' was pretty liberal. On this occasion—the American War of Independence was at its height—their warrant was backed by the Lord Mayor and aldermen, so the twenty-one men 'impressed' during their visit would have had little chance of making any protest heard. But before the party sailed for Hull, where the men were transferred to a tender serving ships of the line, someone—probably a relative—was driven to desperation. On Sunday 26th January 1777 the Lord Mayor received an anonymous letter, bearing the York postmark, threatening to burn not only his private residence but the Mansion House, if the Press Gang was not withdrawn from the city by the following Tuesday. The corporation offered 100 guineas reward for information leading to the discovery of the sender, but the result is not known.

Legally the Press Gang was supposed to seize only able-bodied seamen and watermen from 18 to 55, provided they were British subjects without a certificate of exemption. Exemption was often claimed on the grounds of age, but the impress men had a way of dealing with this by saying "Prove it" . . . and the simple souls they were talking to didn't know how to start.

With government backing, the Press Gang had a free hand. No one cared how they got the men into the ships. Unwilling 'volunteers' were beaten into submission and once aboard they were virtual prisoners. With a net cast as ruthlessly as this, anyone who happened to be in the wrong place at the wrong time could find himself swept up in it. Many of the new crew members didn't know one end of a ship from the other. The system was so old—it was used by the Anglo-Saxons—that it was accepted as a fact of life. There was a brief period when it was outlawed by the Long Parliament in 1641, but by the Restoration it was in full swing again.

Pepys saw some of the heartbreak it could cause, recording on 1st July 1666: "Lord! how some poor women did cry . . . running to every parcel of men that were brought, one after another, to look for their husbands, and wept over every vessel that went off, thinking they might be there, and looking after the ship as far as they could by moonlight, that it grieved me to the heart to hear them."

The Gang was still on the rampage in the reign of William IV, and only recently a naval historian revealed that the Press Act remained unrepealed as late as 1967.

Built on the site of the cloisters of St Leonard's Hospital in 1744, York's Theatre Royal has seen many structural changes, but none more dynamic than those carried out in 1967 during the city's most exciting architectural project since the war—a story which properly belongs in an account of life in the modern city.

In the early part of the century, after the building of a new market cross or hall in 1705 in Thursday Market (today's St Sampson's Square) plays were sometimes performed in this building's upper room, which was supported on five open arches and topped by a turret with clock and weather vane. Historian Francis Drake described it in 1736 as "a beautiful and useful structure for the shelter of market people in bad weather, which stands on the west side of the square". The upper room, said to be "a spacious apartment", was probably about forty feet long and served various purposes. Imagine candles burning behind the windows of this room at six o'clock on an autumn evening in 1768, and a small group of people sitting by this fitful light to listen to a lecture . . . on electricity! On 4th October that year a Mr W. Cross advertised in the *York Courant*, telling readers that "having fitted up an extensive electrical apparatus" he intended to begin his course of lectures on electricity in the market cross room at six the following evening. He also promised "a large collection of curious experiments, comprehending whatever is most materially useful and entertaining". Everyone in the audience had paid either 3s for the whole course or 1s for each lecture.

Some years after the building of the market hall, a travelling company of actors controlled by Thomas Keregan, gave performances at the Bootham Cockpit House, and were so pleased with their reception that in about 1730 they built a theatre in Minster Yard. Little is known of this theatre after Keregan's death in 1741, but there is no doubt that set as it was in the tennis court of the old Ingram House near the Minster, it proved too small. It was Keregan's widow who leased the medieval cloisters in 1744 and built the city's first permanent theatre.

Inigo Jones's surviving Banqueting Hall gives us no real idea of the size of the vast and now vanished Whitehall Palace. In the same way, the gaunt fragment of St Leonard's Hospital still to be seen adjoining the public library in Museum Street carries no hint of the original extent of this great medieval institution. There was a time, covering a period of about three centuries, when its eastern boundary ran to High Petergate. It is a portion of the vaulted crypt of this building which is still embedded today in the structure of the Theatre Royal, and perhaps it is the 'power-house' of the Grey Lady said to haunt the building. Not even the Bristol Theatre Royal, which claims to be the oldest in the kingdom, can match that. Before the 1967 reorganization this medieval room was chopped up between the stalls bar and other facility rooms, but as it is officially an ancient monument it was destined to play an important part in the redesigned theatre. This historic core is now the Green Room.

In the 1760s extravagant claims were made for the theatre. On 8th January 1765 readers of the local newspaper picked up that day's edition to learn something about the building. Five days previously it had been reopened after extensive alterations, and patrons on the first night had seen performances of *The Provok'd Husband* and *The Lying Valet*. Building operations had been carefully dovetailed so that, according to a contemporary account, the "tail" of the new theatre was being finished while the players were employed in the "head" of the old. "This theatre", reported the newspaper, "is by far the most spacious in Great Britain, Drury Lane and Covent Garden excepted, and for Convenience and Elegance it is thought to be equal, if not superior, to either of them." This enthusiasm is understandable. The theatre, no matter how small and ill-lit we should find it, was preferable to the cockpits.

But how accurate was this picture of York's theatre? The

paper's claims were pretty large, judging by the comments of Tate Wilkinson when he took over the management the following year to find the theatre "in a very declining state, even to the disgrace of the city; dirty scenes, dirty clothes, all dark and dismal".

However, the new theatre was much bigger than the old and had an additional tier. This made three tiers above the pit . . . boxes and first and upper galleries. Usual prices were boxes 2s 6d; pit 2s; first gallery 1s 6d; upper gallery 1s. The auditorium was, of course, square; a lay-out which may still be seen in the charmingly restored Georgian Theatre in Richmond in the North Riding. The building stayed this shape for another fifty-seven years until the interior was entirely remodelled in 1822. In this year the semi-circular plan was introduced, following the line of Smirke's Covent Garden, built in 1808. This shape had been brought from France to Bristol as far back as 1766, and a number of new theatres in London and elsewhere had followed the lead, so York was a little behind the times. Lighting was by wax candles in handsome glass chandeliers and prices had not changed much over the years . . . boxes 4s; pit 2s; gallery 1s. As the century advanced more changes were made. In 1875 the gallery was raised, an upper circle was built and alterations were made to the pit. Five years later the exterior was remodelled. The front arcade of 1835 was removed and placed by its buyer in a suburban garden where it may still be seen, and the present façade took its place. In 1901 the interior was entirely rebuilt.

Tate Wilkinson brought the gift of respectability to the York theatre, spending £500 in 1769 in obtaining a royal patent and making the players "His Majesty's Servants of the Theatre Royal, York". He even taught manners to unruly audiences.

Following the royal patent the theatre attracted actors and actresses of high calibre. Mrs Siddons, who made her first appearance at Drury Lane in 1776, went on a tour of the provinces in 1777 and reached York—where she was to stay for more than a month—on 15th April. Nine years later, as the greatest tragic actress of the English stage, she returned to the Theatre Royal during the August assizes. Her brother, John Philip Kemble, appeared in York on 13th April 1779 in *Zenobia*. Mrs Jordan joined the York company in 1782, leaving for Drury Lane three years later.

Two of the city's leading manufacturers have roots in the

10

eighteenth century, beginning as small family businesses. Mary Tuke opened a grocer's shop in 1725. It passed to her nephew, William, the Quaker philanthropist, in 1752. His son, Henry, joined him in 1785 and from then on the Tukes made cocoa and chocolate at the rear of their shop in Castlegate. In 1862 this business was transferred to Henry Rowntree. In 1767 a confectionery business was established in St Helen's Square, York, later to become Terry and Sons, Ltd. In time they were to send their cakes, biscuits, pickles, anchovies, acid drops, gumballs and Pontefract cakes to all parts of the country. Many of these old-fashioned confections, made from original recipes, have been preserved in a most unusual way as part of the incomparable York Castle Museum, established in 1938.

The rise of Quaker businessmen coincided with an upsurge in the city's nonconformist life, though we must return to the end of the seventeenth century for the building of the Unitarian Chapel in St Saviourgate, accepted as the city's oldest nonconformist place of worship. It was brick-built in 1693 with money provided mainly by Lady Hewley, who founded the almshouses nearby, and a broad seventeenth-century chair, known as Lady Hewley's chair, is now kept in the vestry.

In 1755 the Rev. Newcombe Cappe was chosen as co-pastor with a Mr Hotham, and a year later, on Hotham's death, became sole pastor. In 1792 Mr Cappe's age made it necessary for him to have assistance and in that year the Rev. Charles Wellbeloved settled in York as assistant minister, taking over as pastor in 1800 on the death of Mr Cappe. Wellbeloved, whose reputation as an antiquary was unsurpassed in the city, ministered to the congregation for fifty-eight years, and although at the time of his death in 1858 the churchyards of the city had been closed for four years, the Order in Council forbidding the opening of any burial ground in the city or within two miles of its boundaries, was waived. So today, in a small, secluded, garden-like plot, only a few feet away from the walls of the chapel he had served for the greater part of his life, the grave of Charles Wellbeloved may be seen.

The iron railing and gate which form the frontage to St Saviourgate have stood on the site of the original high boundary wall since 1860 when a number of alterations were made. The old wall was meant to discourage attacks which were often made on Dissenters. The chapel, approached through a well-kept garden, is in the form of a Greek cross, a tower rising above the central intersection. The round-headed windows are late-Georgian insertions of about 1830. The chapel is entered through a porch and under a small singing gallery, the site of the organ given in about 1800 by a Miss Rawden of York. By this gesture she made it the first Dissenting chapel in the city with such an amenity. This chapel, still the heart of a faithful congregation, was one of the 2,418 buildings registered for public worship by the Congregationalists, Baptists and Presbyterians during the years 1689–1700. Most were built of brick and the walls were often whitewashed.

Though the actual form of York's first Quaker meeting house, built near the Castlegate end of what was known as Far Water Lane in 1674, is no longer to be seen, the distinction of being the oldest established nonconformist place of worship in the city belongs to the Friends' Meeting House, a complex range of buildings between Castlegate, Friargate and Clifford Street. At its centre, practically unchanged, is the beautifully plain Large Meeting House of 1816–18, designed by the York architects Watson and Pritchett.

Two small books in the basement strong-room may appear insignificant, but they reveal themselves as incomparable historic records of the Society's early days of persecution. Dating from the eighties and nineties of the seventeenth century, they are receipts for the 'chamber rent' of Quakers imprisoned in York Castle. As far back as 1659 the Friends in York had the support of an "eminent grocer", Edward Nightingale, who allowed them to meet in his High Ousegate house. He continued to give his support for many years despite the fact that in 1670–1 he was heavily fined, suffering distraint of his goods to the value of £57 18s. On five occasions the meetings at Nightingale's house were broken up, either by soldiers or the civic authorities. The grocer also owned land near the present Clifford Street which was used by the Quakers as their first burial ground, and it is possible that members of the Society who died during imprisonment in the Castle were buried there.

Dissenters' chapels built in the eighteenth century had no pretensions to architectural beauty. Town meeting houses were sometimes built of stone, faced with plaster, had a sanded floor, backless forms, a fireplace and a high pulpit with brass candlesticks. There was a gallery on three sides, often reached by ladder. Men sat on the preacher's right hand, the women on the left.

The open-roofed, candlelit chapel built in a court off College Street in about 1749 by the Countess of Huntingdon's Connexion must have been typical of its period. In later years it served both as stable and warehouse until, in the 1890s, it was demolished as an unsafe building. That it represented the bare bones of necessity is evident from a description of the chapel shortly after it had been taken down . . . "The chapel was severely plain, a brick building . . . 26 feet by 19 feet 6 inches, presenting the appearance of a very ordinary, square warehouse. It was open-roofed and plastered up to the span of the roof, having no ceiling. The floor was lime cement, and all the cleaning the place ever got was by whitewashing the plasterwork. The lighting was miserably poor, being effected by two windows in the front wall in the day time and by candles at night. The desk or pulpit was at the Goodramgate end of the building and the seating was by benches without backs, placed so close together that the building would hold 200 people." Traces of the chapel's foundations were found during an archaeological excavation in June 1964.

During a visit to York on 25th April 1751, John Wesley arranged for services to be held in the Countess of Huntingdon's chapel. The following year the services were transferred to a building adjoining the north-west corner of the Minster which some time later was converted into a public house with the sign of the Hole In The Wall. Increasing in numbers, members of the York Methodist Society began to use a building on the corner of Patrick Pool and Newgate, which was entirely rebuilt in 1963 with the exception of a portion of the south-west angle of the ground floor, now carrying a commemorative plaque. John Wesley preached in this building on 9th May 1753, and it is generally referred to as "the room in Pump Yard".

In 1759 the Methodists bought 800 square yards of land at the junction of Aldwark and Peasholme Green, and worked so quickly on this, their first meeting house to be built in the city, that when Wesley came to York again on 19th April that year he was able to preach in the shell of the new building. The completed chapel, opened by Wesley in the July, had a gallery only at one end. Used today as a warehouse, the building was renovated in 1955 when a plaque was erected.

One of the saddest reminders of the early days of nonconformity in York was to be seen on the north-east side of Coffee Yard, between Stonegate and Grape Lane where, masked by a rough fence and a large elder tree, the little six-sided Grape Lane Chapel of 1781 lay roofless to the weather, its floor five feet deep in summer weeds. Demolition work began on 22nd August 1963. The previous day I saw for the last time the rotted remains of the gallery of 1800 which had elegant fielded panels and was supported on six plain pillars. Originally York's first Congregational meeting house, it served the needs of six sects until the mid-nineteenth century when it became a warehouse.

When, as the last in a long line, the Primitive Methodists began their thirty-one-year occupation of the chapel in 1820 the building was dark and depressing with a low ceiling and brick floor. There was no heating and lighting was by candles. The walls were damp and cheerless. To add to the gloom the congregation was subjected to brutal but admittedly ingenious persecution involving open mockery, the fights of starving dogs let loose in the building, the explosions of home-made crackers and the extinguishing of the candles by the wings of frantic sparrows.

This attitude may have been a hangover from the eighteenth century when many believed Wesley to be a Catholic priest raising forces for the Jacobite Pretender.

Winter in York is usually pretty mild—a matter of astonishment to migrants from the south who tend to arrive with all-wool underwear and survival kit. But just occasionally the temperature flexes its muscles and shows it really means business by freezing the Ouse. It is a widely-spaced phenomenon, probably occurring no more than half a dozen times in a century.

One of the longest ice-bound spells fell in the winter of 1740, the year when "Rule Britannia" was composed, when Richardson wrote his novel *Pamela*, when biographer Boswell and typographer Bodoni were born. The ice was so thick that booths were set up on it, and football matches on the frozen Ouse were a common sight. Citizens opening their copies of the *York Courant* on Tuesday 23rd December that year would read: "The frost has been so intensely severe that our river has been frozen over these ten days." But on the previous Sunday night "a prodigious quantity of snow" had fallen, followed by a "thorough thaw" making many roads impassable and holding up the London Mail.

Coach lamps casting soft pools of light on the snow. Frost-nipped travellers bundling their luggage through the lighted doorway of the Black Swan in Coney Street. Horses stamping impatiently, their breath hanging on the winter air. Four days (God willing) on the road to London. A typical scene in the palmy days of coaching, but a little romanticized. Accidents were common. In dusty summer the heat was fierce in the jolting box; in winter the horses struggled painfully through a white world, and merely to be an immobile outside passenger in hard weather could be fatal. The weather was not the only enemy. Highwaymen have been surrounded by a romantic glow, but there was nothing particularly romantic about being hit on the head—or worse—by armed thugs. But travel slowly improved. The time from York to London was cut to about twenty hours and the peak of stage-coach efficiency lay in the next century.

6

ROAD, RAIL, RIVER

NOT WITH a bang, but with a black flag. That's how mail-coaching came to an end in York in 1842, when the Edinburgh Mail ran into the city for the last time, its dark banner streaming behind the driver, Tom Holtby. Yet only four years earlier twenty coaches a day were using the yard of the Black Swan Inn, Coney Street, demolished in the 1950s to make way for a multiple store, though its doorway lives on in the Castle Museum. When the door pillars were being dismantled, it was found that the laminated paint layers, going back about two centuries, had never varied in colour—a light buff. The Black Swan yard which had rung to the arrivals and departures of the Leeds Highflyer and the Harrogate Tally-Ho was just one of many focal points for the coaching trade. Others were the York Tavern in St Helen's Square; the George Inn, Coney Street, where one of the gate pillars and a portion of the yard may still be seen; Etteridge's Hotel, Lendal; the White Horse, Coppergate; the White Swan, Pavement; the Elephant and Castle, Skeldergate; the Commercial, Nessgate; the Robin Hood, Castlegate; the Pack Horse, Micklegate; the Old Sand Hill, Colliergate; and the Golden Lion, near Monk Bar.

Four days was the time allowed between London and York in 1706. Seventy years later it had been cut to a dramatic thirty-six hours, probably as a result of the introduction of turnpike roads and a coach known as the "flying machine". By 1836, the time had dropped to twenty hours. Holtby, the man on the box seat of the last Edinburgh Mail, at the end of its fifty-six years on the road, is buried in the churchyard at Haxby, a North Riding village on the city's fringe. Pride of the country as a coachman, he was described some years after his death in 1863 as "a tall, gentlemanly-looking man of good presence with a smart, showy style of driving and a dash of confident recklessness

which commanded attention and gained for him the name of
Rash Tom."

Born in 1791, he began life as a post-boy at Easingwold
with the Laceys who kept the principal inn there. It was not until
he was twenty-nine that he became a regular coachman, but
he soon reached the top of his profession. A bit of a speculator,
he bought an unproductive brick-yard at Haxby and also
became part-proprietor of a newspaper. Though he lost money
on both ventures, he died worth £3,000. The Edinburgh Mail,
the service that made his name, was put on the road in October
1786, and ran from the Bull and Mouth, London, calling at
Tadcaster, York, Thirsk and Northallerton.

Concentrating more today on the quick lunch trade, the pubs
of York number about 160. But over the past 150 years an
almost equal number seems to have vanished. What happened
to the Whale Fishery? And to the Artichoke? Thinking back
over recent times, the demolition of an inn seems to be a pretty
rare thing, and when it happens people sit up and take notice.
There was quite a stir when the Plumbers' Arms in Skeldergate
came down (though, of course, it was replaced by a new pub
with many reminders of the old) and the destruction of the
Queen's Head in Fossgate did not go unnoticed. In 1971 a pub
in Church Street was taken out like an old tooth and was
succeeded by a neat piece of neo-Georgian work bearing a
name which commemorates the celebration of the city's 1900th
anniversary.

The tracing of an inn's pedigree is not simple, and is often
complicated by the fact that it might have had more than one
name in its lifetime. One of the city's Bay Horses hung out at
least three other signs at one time or another. In the nineteenth
century, 112 inns in York closed their doors for the last time.
Many of them were variations on the usual Horse, Swan, Dog,
Bell and Crown theme, but one or two oddities stand out.
There was the Artichoke in Micklegate; the Boot and Slipper
in Bedern; the Cannon in Lendal; the Cotherstone in Hungate;
the Crispin's Arms in Church Lane; the Jolly Bacchus in Micklegate; the Lottery in Hull Road; the Sawdust Parlour and
Stanhope Press, both in Swinegate; the Steam Hammer and the
Labouring Man in Skeldergate; and the Upholsterers' Arms in
Trinity Lane.

The Whale Fishery was at the corner of Haver Lane in

Hungate. It was given the name by the landlord, Christopher Bean, who had been a harpooner in the polar seas. The sign was a miniature carved whaling boat and a painting of a harpooner. Mr Bean was so attached to the name that when he moved to another licensed house in the same neighbourhood he took the sign with him. The present drill hall in Colliergate stands on the site of the Old Sand Hill which had extensive stabling. At the entrance to the yard there was a 'tap'—presumably alcoholic—for the use of stablemen and ostlers.

In the past, odd things have happened at inns. A back room at the Blue Boar in Castlegate was a resting place for Dick Turpin's corpse after his execution, and at Etteridge's Hotel actors on a provincial tour were nearly arrested as body-snatchers. They had carried a life-size dummy used in a melodramatic sketch, in a potato sack which left the head exposed. In 1814 a Roman tessellated pavement was found at the Jolly Bacchus near Micklegate Bar, but it was ruined by unchecked souvenir hunters. Fragments were removed by the corporation in 1837, but what was left probably still lies under the city wall. The inn was taken down in 1873.

Two of York's most popular public houses in the first half of the last century must have been the Golden Fleece in Pavement and Stonegate's long-vanished White Hart; that is, if a landlord with an interesting tale to tell is any attraction. Matthew Todd, who was landlord successively of these houses, had made the Grand Tour of Europe as a gentleman's gentleman during the dramatic years 1814–20, the years of Napoleon's escape from Elba, the period of Waterloo and the aftermath of the long war. What stories did he tell his drinking friends during the years when the old Georgian ways were gradually erased by the new queen's influence?

Perhaps he had told them of the ghosts he encountered both at Grimston Lodge on the Hull road out of York (raps on a cupboard door) and at the lonely village of Saltmarshe, on a bend of the Ouse near Goole (a white figure in the garden). Or of the Yorkshirewoman who sold snuff in the "beautiful clean town" of Brussels . . . the rigours of the white marble bathroom on a very cold day in Genoa . . . the day he and his employer decided to visit the captive Napoleon on Elba, only to be told at the bank that he had escaped. There was the time too when he sat down to eat oranges on top of Mount Vesuvius and followed them with "bread toasted by the burning mountain". Todd, the country boy who became something of a curiosity—a travelled and literate servant—provided a tantalizing taste of England and the Continent before the full tide of the industrial revolution. His journal—published in 1968—is simple and charming, like the furniture, utensils and houses of his youth. For the ageing Figaro in his York inn, it must have been a passport to lost pleasures.

From the end of the eighteenth century onwards, swinging inn-signs were increasingly joined in the city streets by trade emblems. It all started, I suppose, with that famous bush. The bush that good wine never needed. Shopkeepers began to realize the value of an eye-catching trade-sign. There followed a flood of larger-than-life boots, kettles, brushes, jugs, guns and cigar-holding Indians, all doing a first-class public relations job. York, like other cities, bristled with these signs. For the illiterate they were a picture book; for everyone, they gave a sparkle to the workaday streets.

Today two genuine signs survive . . . a wooden figure of a snuff-taking Napoleon outside a tobacconist's shop in Lendal, and a little 'cigar store Indian' of the kind made between 1790 and 1820, which stands on a bracket outside a restored medieval shop in Low Petergate. On the left door lintel of this shop is another link with the past . . . a small metal horse's head. Its nostrils used to flare with gas jets for the convenience of the passing smoker.

Many of the old trade signs have found a new home in York Castle Museum. Saved from destruction and preserved in the museum's timeless setting are the huge padlock which advertised a hardware shop in Parliament Street; a large broomhead from a Petergate brush shop; a clogger's sign; a long whip from the saddler's which stood on the corner of St Saviourgate; a gold-beater's sign in the form of a gilded hand holding a hammer; an outsize riding boot which hung outside a shoemaker's shop; two Scottish Highlanders and an Indian from tobacconists' shops; a barber's pole with bleeding bowl attached; an apothecary's pestle and mortar sign; and a ten-gallon blue and white patterned jug which signified a china shop.

The public house signboard attracted the talents of famous artists in the past. A number were painted by Holbein, Hogarth, Morland, Crome and Millais. But York's most dramatic inn sign—that of the Olde Starre in Stonegate—calls for no more than the art of a competent letterer. The strength of its appeal lies in the fact that it spans the street and has done since 1733, though it has been renewed from time to time. Standing in its own courtyard, the Starre is one of the oldest inns in the city; a pamphlet dated 1644 was printed "over against the Starre".

When York's first railway station opened in 1841, mail coaches were of course still making the journey north from London. For many years to come, railway stations had the air of inn yards, and flintlock pistols were fired to warn platelayers of approaching trains.

But before that date trains ran from a temporary station in Queen Street. If you were a director you stepped into a first-class carriage. Second class was for "respectable persons". And if you were neither you ran beside the train for as long as you could keep pace. That is how society's ranks were kept closed on an April day in 1839 when an experimental trip was made on the York and North Midland line. Though the train did not go any further than a mile beyond Copmanthorpe, a contemporary report said: "The depot of this railway presented a scene of considerable animation", reminding us that the word 'depot' in this context was still an English term. The engine chosen for the occasion had a name—*Lowther*—and was "greatly admired for its beautiful proportions and workmanship". It had been built by the Stephensons of Newcastle, and carried all the latest improvements. The first class carriage held eighteen directors and their friends and was "fitted up in a style of elegance far exceeding anything we ever before observed in any public carriage".

Holgate Bridge was crowded with spectators and "a great number of lads had up to this place contrived to keep pace with the train, but on clearing the bridge the speed gradually increased until it attained a rate of probably 15 or 20 miles an hour. Horses grazing in adjoining fields capered about at a most fearful rate . . ." After a lineside stroll by the directors, the return trip from the Tadcaster bridge to the engine house, a distance of about two and a half miles, was covered in less than six minutes.

Railway development moved ahead at an ambitious clip and by the end of May 1839 York had been connected to the Leeds and Selby line at Milford Junction.

Bells, flags, booming cannon . . . York was festive for the opening of this line. The *Yorkshire Gazette* rhapsodized: "A finer day for the general holiday than shone on Wednesday could not be imagined. A cloudless sky of an azure more deep than is often seen above our misty atmosphere and a sun of intense brightness and warmth might have belonged to a southern clime". That Victorian speciality, the public breakfast, was held at the Guildhall where the decorative plants had come from the conservatory of George Hudson, the city's "railway king" and first chairman of the York and North Midland. Hudson dominated local politics from 1837 until in 1849 he was publicly exposed for irregular conduct in railway business. It was, as a contemporary cartoonist illustrated, the "wreck of the Royal George" and even his portrait was removed from the Mansion House in the November of that year. It was later restored, and well over a century later there were moves to rehabilitate him in the history of the city. The new headquarters of the Eastern Region of British Rail was named Hudson House and Railway Street was renamed George Hudson Street.

Scattered among the private carriages in the procession to the station were "new omnibuses", one of them drawn by six black horses and trimmed with flowers, garlands and branches of royal oak. The train was made up of nineteen carriages and two engines—*Lowther* and *The Leeds And York*. Mr D. Hardman's "band of brass instruments" travelled in a third-class carriage.

"Preliminary notice of the start", ran a contemporary account, "was given by the ringing of the bell and, at the moment of creeping into motion, by the piercing whistle of each engine. The huge, snake-like body was soon making its way with an imperceptibly accelerated speed and, stealing away under the broad arch of Holgate Lane bridge, was soon lost to the sight of the crowds who thronged the station, the adjacent bar walls and ramparts, while the gay travellers experienced the exciting sensation of the gradually increased swiftness till they were borne along with the speed of a racehorse." The speed was slower on the return journey to allow passengers to see different parts of the line and—curious phrase—to "view the moving landscape".

Dinner, with George Stephenson sitting on the Lord Mayor's right, followed in the Guildhall which was brilliantly lit by gas after dusk (George Hudson was a director of the York Union

Gas Light Company). The railway company kept the champagne flowing "till the cloth was drawn" and a grand ball at the Mansion House lasted until 4 am.

On a winter's day in 1966 the first demolition hammer was swung against the iron and glass railway station of 1841 which, tucked away behind the city wall, had been superseded by the present station, built outside the wall in 1877. The track and the only survivor of eight early-Victorian turntables had disappeared during the summer. This was the station used by a rather disgruntled Queen Victoria (there was criticism of the expense of entertaining her) when she visited York briefly with Prince Albert and five of their children on 13th September 1854. It was also familiar to Charles Dickens who was often in York, either to visit his brother or to give his famous readings.

Charles Dickens spent the last twelve years of his life fulfilling an old ambition—to be an actor—by giving public readings from his works. In that period he visited York twice (a third visit was cancelled rather abruptly) giving his readings in the Festival Concert Rooms. For his first visit on 9th September 1858 he chose *A Christmas Carol*, perhaps the greatest crowd-puller of them all. "Last evening", recorded the *Yorkshire Gazette*, "Charles Dickens read his ghostly little book before a most fashionable and numerous audience. His reception was most enthusiastic and he proceeded, amidst repeated marks of applause, to dilate upon the foibles of his hero, Scrooge. The tale itself, as all who have read it—and who has not?—is excellent, but its interest is increased tenfold by the exquisite and powerful reading of the author . . ."

Dickens was pleased with the city's reception and said in a letter that it had been "a most magnificent audience and might have filled the place for a week. I think the audience possessed a better knowledge of character than any I have seen." And it was in York that he had warming evidence of his popularity. "I was brought very near to what I sometimes dream may be my fame, when a lady, whose face I had never seen, stopped me yesterday in the street and said to me 'Mr Dickens, will you let me touch the hand that has filled my house with many friends?' "

He was to have returned on 25th October to read *The Poor Traveller, Boots At The Holly Tree Inn* and *Mrs. Gamp*, but this reading was cancelled at short notice, and word got round that Dickens felt the ticket sales had not gone well enough. The *York Herald* was critical: "If every gentleman who itinerates the country for his pecuniary benefit were to imitate the example thus afforded, there would soon be an end, and deservedly so, to all public confidence and support."

The truth was that Dickens was in poor health, having caught a severe chill from what he described as "a great draught up some stone steps near me." His reading in York on 11th March 1869 was billed as "the last Mr Dickens will ever give in York". About this time Dickens received news of the death of his old friend, Sir J. Emerson Tennent, to whom he had dedicated his latest book, *Our Mutual Friend*, but remembering the disappointment in the city eleven years earlier, decided not to cancel the reading. In order to catch the 9.45 train to London that night he had to make certain alterations to his programme. He gave his usual full-blooded performance, but instead of taking a break between each reading, merely had a glass of champagne and returned to the stage. Dickens always stayed at the old Station Hotel in Toft Green, and the proprietor had a supper placed in the carriage to be used by his party. A few of the author's friends met on the platform to see him off, and the train pulled out on time.

Until recently the home of the small exhibits section of the York Railway Museum, the former first class refreshment room is the least changed building of the 1841 station complex, designed by the York architect, G. T. Andrews. It is an elegant and well-proportioned room with decoration in the Regency style. The entrance to the bar at the south-west end of the room, though blocked, retains the simple pilasters and entablature surrounding the original opening. The bar led to the still room, the second-class refreshment room, the first and second-class ladies' waiting rooms and the footpans workshop, where the hot-water footwarmers to be found in most carriages were prepared. At the opposite end were the waiters' pantry and the glass and plate rooms.

In the late eighteenth century the site of the old station was described as "a spacious garden". For many years an Alderman Telford had bred forest trees there and persuaded the local gentry to use them as ornamental plantings in their gardens. By the beginning of the nineteenth century the ground, known as Friars' Gardens, was occupied by nurserymen. In 1838 the

House of Correction in Toft Green was demolished, and its site and that of the gardens was sold by York Corporation to the York and North Midland Railway.

Before the building of Andrews' station, which opened for business on 4th January 1841, York's first railway station was a two-roomed wooden hut with a staff of two—the company secretary and the booking clerk. The successor to this humble shack was a surprisingly large and well-designed layout. The novel idea of building the central train shed in iron and glass caused considerable delay. The main front, facing Tanner Row, was 250 feet long and built in the Italian style of polished stone. Though there have been alterations and in-fillings, its general lines may be seen today. This was one of the earliest stations in the world to provide access between the platforms across the head of the tracks, and the train shed, 300 feet by 100 feet was of an advanced design.

York's first station was forward-looking; those were the days when many railway buildings took their inspiration from the past. Richmond station was all buttresses, pointed arches, octagonal chimney stacks and mullioned windows, while the Gawksholme Viaduct and Bridge on the Manchester and Leeds Railway had, in 1845, romantic battlements. These were examples of how, early in the railway age, art and industry sometimes combined, though there can have been little that was poetic in the dangerous tunnel workings manned by near-slave labour.

Primarily it was the world of the real Victorian hero—the engineer. But if you wish to see a contemporary view of the romance of the railway as it was, say, in the 1860s, there is no better example than the bustling painting *The Railway Station* by W. P. Frith, born in 1819 in the tiny village of Aldfield, near the West Riding city of Ripon. Basically a portrait of Paddington Station, it is also a fascinating cross-section of Victorian bourgeois society, addicted as it was to comfort and respectability. But, just for good measure, there is, in the right-hand corner, a curious group of three. An Inverness-caped young man is being arrested by top-hatted plainclothes policemen. One, with a satisfied smile, is toying with a pair of handcuffs. Today all this romance of the rail is distilled in one of York's most valuable assets—the National Railway Museum. The decision to base this museum at York was announced by Viscount Eccles, then Minister for the Arts, in May 1971. It was opened by

the Duke of Edinburgh in the autumn of 1975 and attracted
nearly three-quarters of a million visitors in the first few months
of its life.

Despite the use of extra platforms beyond Holgate Bridge in
the 1860s, the old station could not cope with the increasing
traffic, and a decision was taken in 1865 to build an entirely
new station a short distance away to the west, outside the city
wall. I have heard it said that the view into the train shed from
Platform 8 South is the finest in York. Whether we agree with
this or not, there is no doubt that its prefabricated strength, its
railway heraldry and its dynamic curve make it a cathedral of
civil engineering. The design of the roof creates a diminishing
cone of pearly light, subtly changing with every angle of the
sun, every passing cloud.

Keeping pace with the station development were the carriage
and wagon works, which started in a small way in Queen
Street in 1839, moving later to the Holgate area. By the middle
of this century they covered sixty-two acres.

Visitors arriving by train have one of the finest welcomes
any city can offer—the medieval wall on its green rampart—and
turning towards the Minster towers they find themselves in
Station Road and Station Avenue, perhaps a little puzzled by
the gravestones standing in a neat plot in the middle of the
traffic. They are a reminder that in the decade when railway
technology gathered momentum, a kind of plague was running
through the city. This extra-mural burial ground holds victims
of the cholera epidemic of 1832.

Hagworm's Nest was never a very good address in York.
But in the fateful summer of that year this court off Skeldergate
was just about the last place in the city anyone would wish
to be. The court itself has gone, but the headstones near the
station are a reminder of what came out of it. For it was in a
house in Hagworm's Nest that a drunken and near-destitute
ferry boatman called Thomas Hughes fell ill on 2nd June . . .
he had contracted what was known as the 'blue plague' or Indian
cholera. Twenty-one-year-old Thomas, who inaugurated York's
share of four great epidemics which, until 1866, were to kill
nearly a quarter of a million people in Britain, had been ferrying
visitors from Selby, Hull and other infected places only two
days before. He survived the attack, but the disease spread,
first to his brother and father, and then, on 5th June, to his

Mansion House

neighbour, John Graves. Such was the ravaging power of cholera that Graves, taken ill at 3 am was dead by 4 pm.

That year there were 185 deaths from the blue plague in York, and it was estimated that one in every fifty-six of the population (then 25,357) had suffered from the disease. Victims were buried in St George's churchyard and in the new burial ground made specially for the purpose in Thief Lane (now Station Road). This first epidemic gave impetus to drainage plans in the city and by 1837 about three and a half miles of brick-lined sewers had been laid.

In 1833 Mr J. P. Needham, a member of the Royal College of Surgeons, published a report on the York outbreak, proving that much preventive work was done in the poorer parts of the city where "every source of filth was as completely destroyed as possible". York had ample warning from other infected centres, and this wholesale clean-up was done well in advance of the actual appearance of the disease. This probably did much to keep the death roll low.

Competent man of science though he was, Mr Needham, at one stage in his report, betrays a curious naïveté: "when at last it did appear in its undoubted character, it was not ushered in by any extraordinary conflict of the elements; by meteors, hailstorms or hurricanes; but suddenly and insidiously, almost before the expiration of a week of more than ordinary joyousness and merriment; in short, it appeared just after our races, and was beyond all doubt introduced by some of the ragged and beggarly 'gentlefolk' who had come to be present at our 'festivity'."

Needham's report, a Board of Health broadside dealing with the disposal of the dead and a form of service of thanksgiving for deliverance from cholera are sad pointers to the other side of the progressive nineteenth-century coin.

From the gardens of the Royal Station Hotel, opened a year after the new station, in 1878, there is a view across the river to the rare trees of the Museum Gardens, the old Manor Shore. Perhaps the most historic ten acres in the north of England, they contain not only the ruins of St Mary's Abbey, and the Roman Multangular Tower, but the classical Yorkshire Museum of 1827–30 and the site of a public swimming bath opened in the reign of William IV.

The driving force behind the museum, designed by William

Guildhall
Lendal Water Tower and Bridge

Wilkins, was the Yorkshire Philosophical Society, established in January 1823, two years after the discovery of prehistoric animal bones in a cave at Kirkdale in the North Riding had stirred interest in scientific research. The society began life in rooms in Low Ousegate, but in 1827 obtained from the Crown a grant of the grounds of St Mary's Abbey, including the ruins of the abbey itself. The museum was opened in February 1830, and largely as a result of this pioneer work the city was chosen as the meeting place for the first assembly of the British Association, held in September 1831.

In 1833 a small observatory, now screened by trees, was built on the lawn which slopes down to the river, and three years later a swimming bath was opened. It was to have a life of almost a century. This was the first bath of any size and permanence in the city and its disuse in the 1920s coincided with the demolition in an alley off Coney Street of a much earlier establishment . . . the Bagnio of 1691. With its segmental pediments over the doors and elliptical bull's-eye windows, it was a typical William and Mary building and was first mentioned by being given publicity in the *London Gazette* of 19th October 1691, a generation before York had a newspaper of its own. A bath there cost 5s.

The museum, and its annexe in the half-timbered Hospitium of the abbey, houses fine geological, archaeological and natural history collections, though the display of larger exhibits—like the Roman tessellated pavement of the Four Seasons—is hampered by a building which, though intrinsically attractive, is inadequate for the museum's purposes. The Hospitium is too close to the river and is sometimes lapped by flood water; another argument for a building, perhaps in the Roman style, in which all the Romano-British exhibits may be seen together. Meanwhile, much has been done in the museum—allegedly haunted in the 1950s by the shade of a rather prosaic alderman—to display the smaller exhibits in an eye-catching way.

Some meetings of the Yorkshire Architectural and York Archaeological Society are also held in the museum—now administered by York Corporation. This society originated as the Yorkshire Architectural Society in 1842, and added "York Archaeological" to its title in the 1901 annual report.

What was York like in the 1840s? In fact, what was it like on 29th July 1845? It was the day William Henry Fox Talbot, one of the 'fathers' of photography, set up his camera in the city streets, followed by an interested crowd. In 1970 the Science Museum in London produced a set of prints from Talbot's negatives, the earliest known photographic records of the streets and monuments of York.

The streets are deceptively quiet; no hint of the curious crowd behind the lens. Buildings stand out sharply as if etched in acid. An ashen light falls on half-drawn blinds, shuttered windows and humble shops.

Talbot, in a letter to a member of his family, written on that summer day, said: "We took twelve views of York today, most of them good. Crowds of admiring spectators surrounded the camera wherever we planted it." He also mentioned a dash of excitement at York station when the luggage on the roof of the carriage caught fire. Apparently a passenger had four pounds of gunpowder in his portmanteau.

The photographs of the Minster, St Mary's Abbey and the Multangular Tower show no signs of change in the overall scene (though there is a clock over the Minster's south door) and these views depend on human intrusion for their interest. In one or two there is a glimpse of early Victorian male fashion; the Minster forms the background to what appears to be a phantom coach. But the interest quickens when Talbot turns his lens on to the streets of the city. Here the changes are remarkable . . . the handsome, cupola-topped tower of St Crux Church in Pavement, demolished in 1887; the narrow Lop Lane, forerunner of Duncombe Place; a gabled, medieval house on King's Staith; the old Harker's Hotel in St Helen's Square; an ancient building standing on the corner of Nunnery Lane.

Talbot is best known for the photographs he took in and around his thirteenth-century home at Lacock Abbey in Wiltshire, where, on the terraces and in the cloisters, he persuaded his family and friends to help record forever the golden afternoons of the privileged class in the first half of the nineteenth century.

A few eyebrows were raised in the late 1960s when the latest list of buildings of special historic or architectural interest, compiled by the Ministry then responsible, turned out to be unashamedly Victorian in emphasis, for York is not especially Victorian in character. It is not like Bradford or Leeds or any of the smaller West Riding towns where the mills, lying in the Pennine valleys like lighted ships at night, are Italianate in style and are, no doubt, already scheduled. York still has at the heart of its tree-like growth the vital and very broad rings labelled Roman, Tudor and Georgian, and in such a city the claims of the Victorians tend to be elbowed aside. But it is a long time now since it was considered unusual—if not eccentric—to find any interest in Victorian buildings. The writings of Sir John Betjeman helped many over the wall of prejudice, and the Victorian Society is well established, with a thriving northern branch. The charms of the Regency were widely recognized only forty years ago, so the day of the Victorians was bound to come sooner or later. The long years of odium are over, and today it is even possible to buy a recording of the noises made by Victorian sewage-pumping machinery.

Three nineteenth-century schools were included in the list. One, on its curiously open site in an inner suburb, looks uncannily like St Michael's Mount when seen at dusk through half-closed eyes. All three were tipped as favourites as far back as the mid-1950s when a local expert said that, aesthetically, they were "amongst the most precious of York's heritage of all ages".

York's examples of the age tend to be isolated from each other. They do not agglomerate into what is popularly supposed to be the Victorian scene . . . the intricate dark network of pubs, chapels, churches, canals and viaducts which, seen subjectively at the right time, can be as moving as a Lowry painting. Living in this kind of muddle is, of course, a different matter. On behalf of those who have to do so, I should not like to think that Government lists of this kind might in time be seen as a licence to sanctify buildings which, though technically interesting, are visually hideous.

My choice as the city's finest Victorian building—one which is seen to advantage by citizen and tourist—is G. T. Andrews's Yorkshire Insurance Company office of 1847. It gazes down Coney Street from its site in St Helen's Square like a little Italian Renaissance palace. Perhaps the Farnese? This, of course, found a place in the Ministry list, as did my runner-up, J. P. Pritchett's mortuary chapel of 1837 which could exchange the overhanging trees of York cemetery for the thyme-scented scrub around Athens without stretching credulity too far. A charming piece of Greek Revival, it is built of soft Roche

Abbey stone. At the time of its building the land was divided equally between the Church of England and Dissenters, and the dividing line ran down the centre of the chapel; each denomination kept to its own half.

The York County Savings Bank, on the corner of Blake Street and St Helen's Square, carries echoes in its details of a vanished York chapel. Decorative features of its roof-line are very like those of the old Salem Chapel, demolished in 1963-4. Both buildings were designed by Pritchett, though ten years separated them in time, the bank of 1829 being the earlier building.

A child baptized in York's simple brick Roman Catholic chapel in 1828 grew up to design the elaborate stone church which replaced it. George Goldie, architect of St Wilfrid's Church—an essay in the French Gothic style in Duncombe Place—was the son of Dr Goldie, a prominent parishioner. The tympanum over the west door carries some of the most intricate Victorian carving in the city. The foundation stone of the £10,000 church was laid by Bishop Cornthwaite and the building was opened for worship by Cardinal Wiseman in June 1864. This is now a scheduled building.

The inclusion of an hotel in the Ministry list gave recognition to the appeal of *art nouveau*. Elm Bank in Mount Vale was decorated in 1897-8 when it was the home of the miller, Sidney Leetham, by George Walton, a Glasgow bank clerk who set up in business as a designer and interior decorator. During his gradual expansion southwards to London, where he eventually went to live, he opened a shop in Stonegate, York. Though the chimney-pieces, staircases and massive gallery of W. G. and A. J. Penty, the York architects, still largely fix the personality of the house, the charms of Walton's *art nouveau* have become less noticeable over the years. Gone are the ochre and black lions from the walls of the entrance hall, but the Smoking Room—now the Walton Bar in honour of the designer—is very much as it was. Here there is a repeated motif of opaque, coloured glass set in a frame almost like a hand-mirror, against a background of elongated flowers of a tulip style. A fresco above the dining-room fireplace is a romantically-treated study of a medieval couple flanked by a round bay tree and clinging, climbing roses. The former drawing-room has a pastoral scene in glass mosaic.

One of the chapels chosen by the Ministry was Centenary in St Saviourgate, not far from the Unitarian Chapel of 1693. Though it was planned as a "cathedral of Methodism" there were those who said at the time of its building in 1839–40 that it would prove "a waste and howling wilderness", but its healthy survival in an area now largely commercial underlines the affection in which this elegant building is held. The nine pillars supporting the gallery have elongated Corinthian capitals in gilt. The ceiling is almost entirely coffered, the deep panels set with elaborate acanthus leaf bosses, and the frieze is a running floral pattern in blue and white. At gallery level the marginal lights of the windows have ruby, orange and blue flashed glass.

The city's Art Gallery, also listed, is perhaps one of the cosiest in the north of England, with deep, dark carpeting and wall coverings to suit the paintings—brown fabric for the sixteenth and seventeenth centuries and a rich Victorian drawing-room red for the works of William Etty. The gallery is a permanent reminder of the 1879 Fine Art and Industrial Exhibition, though its roots go a little deeper than that. The Victorian Gothic Revival had an off-shoot in what can only be described as the 'Swiss chalet style', which is to be found in places as far apart as Darjeeling and the Isle of Wight. It came to roost in York, for a brief period, more than a century ago, for this was the style chosen for the temporary building in the grounds of Bootham Park Hospital which housed the city's Fine Art and Industrial Exhibition of 1866. The Great Exhibition of 1851 put the country in an 'exhibition' mood. A meeting called by the Lord Mayor in November 1865 agreed to the staging of the exhibition, and by the following March a guarantee fund of more than £6,000 had been subscribed.

Archbishop Thomson opened the exhibition on 24th July in the huge 'Swiss Chalet' which covered one and a half acres. It was a prosperous season. When the show closed on 31st October there was a cash surplus of £1,900, a sum which was earmarked for the building of a permanent exhibition hall in the city. The money stayed in the bank for thirteen years, and the outcome of this prudence was the Art Gallery, a £25,000 project opened on 7th May 1879. Archbishop Thomson again performed the opening ceremony and the city fluttered with bunting and rang with bells.

In the high summers of the Victorian age, anything up to
300 acres of delicate blue flowers covered the fields on the
north-eastern fringes of York. Fully expanded in the morning
sun, the blossoms were sometimes two inches across. Someone
who once saw them said: "Few things in the natural world
are more beautiful than the chicory flower." By the turn of
the century the twelve drying and roasting kilns which clustered
around the nearby village of Dunnington were decaying, for
the processing of the root had been moved to York. But almost
every farmer in the village still had his patch of chicory, grown
for luck. In 1902 the largest of the kilns was described as "a
picturesque brick building, strong as a castle, with its 18 inch
square beams, 20 feet long". A flight of stone steps led to the
main door, and at that time the flues still remained and the
drying floor was in good condition. Children's school teas were
sometimes held there, and at least one observer thought that this
neglected building was the ideal place for "a rustic barn, granary
or kiln dance".

The chicory industry, introduced into Yorkshire in 1839, took
a hard knock in 1863 when Gladstone, then Chancellor of the
Exchequer, levied a heavy duty on the product. A deputation
of Yorkshire chicory manufacturers was raised but, as often
happens in these cases, only one man was left to confront the
Chancellor . . . Thomas Smith of Layerthorpe, York. He must
have put up a good defence of home industry, for the duty
was appreciably lowered. The Ordnance Survey maps of 1892
and 1909 show Smith's chicory works both in Layerthorpe and
at the corner of Orchard Street and Foss Bank. The second
site was cleared for use as an off-street car park in the summer
of 1967. The firm's traditions carried it forward for almost
another half-century, as Thomas Smith and Son are listed in the
city directory as chicory merchants up to 1949-50.

Digging the parsnip-like chicory root led to the development
and forging by Dunnington blacksmiths of two or three varieties
of tool. The main implement was described as being like a
chisel on a spade shaft, with a tread on one side. After many
years of use it became as slim as a bayonet. The roots were
washed in a large wooden trough in the field, carted off to York
and tipped in Chicory Yard, Layerthorpe. Sliced, dried, roasted
and crushed, they ended up as grains the size of gunpowder.
Roasting was in cylinders revolving over gas jets. It was said

that the blue fumes were chokingly dense on a foggy winter's day and that after ten minutes spent among them, the aroma clung to one's clothes for a week. Few Dunnington farmers would consider digging chicory until All Saints' Day (1st November), not because of superstition but because the chicory and potato harvests clashed. In the last century, hundreds of itinerant labourers made their way to the village for this dual harvest.

It used to be woad, wine and wax. Today it's more likely to be cocoa beans and cordials. York's river traffic has been on the decline for the past two centuries until now an average of only two laden craft a day pass through Naburn Locks into the city where it is possible to accommodate vessels up to 230 tons. But if the activity has declined, the sites have altered little. King's Staith, Queen's Staith and Skeldergate—the old haunt of wharfingers—still have a scent of commerce in the air, and the warehousing, particularly on the right bank, is impressive. Wilkie Collins, novelist and friend of Dickens, chose Skeldergate as a setting in his little-known book, *No Name*. "The few old houses left in the street", wrote Collins, "are disguised in melancholy modern costume of whitewash and cement. Shops of smaller and poorer order, intermixed here and there with dingy warehouses and joyless private residences of red brick, comprise the present aspect of Skeldergate." But architectural experts have taken a more cheerful view of the area recently, describing some of the warehouses as "outstandingly handsome". These are the two former Bonded Warehouses, put up in 1873 and 1874. Both have interesting roof-line ornament, but the larger is particularly elaborate on the river frontage. They are used today by Rowntree Mackintosh for the storage of ingredients, many of which come by water from Hull. The site chosen for these warehouses had been the centre of the city's river commerce in the Middle Ages, being next to the Old Crane Wharf. The "old crane" was augmented by a new one in the 1770s.

Charges for using the Old Crane appear regularly in the city's accounts in the fifteenth century, and give a good idea of the wide range of goods moving along the river . . . wine, woad, madder, alum, spices, grain, salt, wax, steel, iron, linen, sea-coal and lead. Upstream cargoes today are fuel oil, coal, gum, straw-bond, wood pulp, paper, cocoa beans, cocoa butter, grain, soya beans, concentrated cordials, refined sugar and fruit pulp.

Quite a crowd gathered on York's riverside New Walk on 25th April 1816. They were awaiting the arrival of the first steamboat seen on the Ouse . . . the *Waterloo*, named after the battle which was still fresh in everyone's mind. Only four years previously, Europe's first steamboat, the 30-ton *Comet*, had begun to operate between Glasgow and Greenock, so York was not slow to learn. In time, the passenger steamer, linked with train services, became as familiar as the long-distance bus of today.

By 1836 the river steamer service was big business. In that year the York–London mail coach still had six more years of life, and the prospect of a 33-hour journey by water to the capital was quite acceptable. The *Arrow*, the *Ebor* and the *Old Ebor* sailed regularly from the crane wharves in York, connecting not only with the early railway system but with the southbound steamers *Vivid*, *Wilberforce* and *Waterwitch*, plying from Hull's Custom House Quay. Contemporary advertisements claimed that cabins were "fitted up with every regard to comfort". From timetables and advertisements in *Bradshaw's Railway Guide*, it can be safely assumed that the service to London was still running twenty years later. The charge was 11s. for a saloon or 7s a fore-cabin.

But the end was not far off. In the early days, the railway system with its devious routes was no great threat to the steamers, but the opening of the York–Doncaster line in 1871 was quite a blow, putting Selby only half an hour's run from York. By 1875 the passenger steamboat service had gone. In the early 'eighties a more restricted pleasure steamer service between York and its neighbouring riverside villages was begun. The *White Rose*, the *May Queen*, the *Waterlily* and the *Celia* (a paddler) were all owned by John Hobson, a familiar figure on King's Staith. After his death, Edward Grace carried on the service with the *River King*.

Local historian Francis Drake, writing in 1736, commented: "Except for some few wine merchants, the export of butter and some small trifles not worth mentioning, there is no other trade carried on in the city of York at this day." A century later the city was equipped with its basic industries, all of them, happily, of an inoffensive nature . . . confectionery, glass, optical instruments. These, together with the later railway carriage works, were to carry York into the twentieth century.

Now established in a factory covering four acres two miles north of the city, Vickers Instruments (formerly known as Cooke, Troughton and Simms Ltd) had its origins in a small shop "under the dial of St Dunstan's Church" in Fleet Street in 1688. Edward Troughton and William Simms joined forces in 1826, when Troughton, described as both blunt and slovenly, destroyed all the papers relating to his earlier business. He retired in 1831 and it was said that "towards the last, he was seldom seen absent from his dingy back parlour at 136 Fleet Street where he sat with a huge ear trumpet at hand, wearing clothes stained with snuff, and a soiled wig".

The merger with the York firm of T. Cooke and Sons Ltd came in 1922. Son of a shoemaker, Thomas Cooke was born at Allerthorpe in the East Riding in 1807 and taught himself astronomy and navigation. In 1837 he set himself up at 50 Stonegate, York, as a maker of telescopes and a wide range of instruments from electrical machines to sundials. He was a resourceful man, for he not only managed to create a telescope lens from the base of a tumbler, but also invented a steam car which he exhibited in the city in 1866. It could carry fifteen passengers, travel at fifteen miles per hour and climb a hill of 1 in 9. But the Road Act prohibiting vehicles that travelled over four miles an hour resulted in the engine being transferred to a river launch. In Cooke's Buckingham Works, built on an historic site in Bishophill in the 1850s, fines were imposed for smoking, drinking and "for reading a book or newspaper in the working hours, wasting time in unnecessary conversation or otherwise, or whistling".

Part of the works of Redfearn National Glass Ltd in Fishergate is built on the site of St Andrew's Priory, founded in 1202 by Hugh Murdac. A human skull, with a sinister hole in one side, and a gold ring were discovered during excavations for additions to the glasshouse buildings. John Prince, a York jeweller, established the Fishergate Glass Works in 1794, building his factory on pastureland known as Scutt's Close. A new company was formed in 1835 by Joseph Spence who, with the aid of model furnaces, a gas-heated crucible and a glassworker, gave public demonstrations of the craft. A catalogue and price list of about 1840 illustrates the highly decorative chemists' jars produced by the factory. Bearing elaborate coats of arms, they were labelled romantically as Peruvian bark, hartshorn and colocynth; or plainly as magnesia, arrowroot and tartaric acid. Other products of this period included alembics, aromatic vinegars, bee-hive glasses, beetle and wasp traps, bird fountains, cake shades, cruets, cupping glasses, Daffy's Elixir glasses, drawer knobs in crystal, sapphire, blue, jet or canary yellow topaz. Railway lamp lenses were made in all colours.

Now operating on the rural fringe of the city, Cravens of York preserve memories of Mary Ann Craven who in 1862 was left a widow at thirty-three with three young children and two confectionery businesses under her wing. Her father, Joseph Hick, had a confectionery business dating back to the beginning of the nineteenth century, and her husband, Thomas Craven, died at the age of forty-five, leaving his Coppergate confectionery business to her. She managed her inheritance alone until her son, Joseph William, was old enough to become a partner in 1881. She died in 1902, remembered by old employees as a "real homely old lady, who made us all feel one of the family".

Founded in 1767, J. Terry and Sons Ltd have had their 'front shop' in St Helen's Square in the heart of the city since 1824. Their products are made in the neo-Georgian factory of 1924–30 beside the country road leading to Bishopthorpe. Though now one of a group of companies, the firm is the creation of the Terry family over five generations. Joseph Terry, farmer's son and apothecary, joined the confectioners Bayldon and Berry at their premises near Bootham Bar in the 1820s and was eventually in sole charge of the business. By 1840 he was selling his products—jujubes, candied citron, mint cakes, coltsfoot rock, anchovies, acidulated drops, gum balls, Nelson balls, Pomfrit cakes, squill, camphor and horehound lozenges—to seventy-five towns in England. After his death in 1850, his son, Joseph (later Sir Joseph), leased a riverside site at Clementhorpe, a little downstream from the present site of Skeldergate Bridge, and moved his factory there from St Helen's Square. Sugar, cocoa, glucose, orange and lemon rinds in brine, and coal for the steam plant were brought by a twice-weekly steam packet. A chocolate factory was developed there in 1886.

Rowntree and Co. Ltd (now known as Rowntree Mackintosh) date back to 1725 when Mary Tuke opened an unlicensed grocery shop and fought a long but successful battle against the once-powerful Court of the York Merchant Adventurers' Company. The business passed to her nephew, William Tuke, in 1752, and the manufacture of cocoa and chocolate—including milk chocolate—probably began when William's son, Henry, joined him about 1785.

Henry Isaac Rowntree appeared in 1862 when he took over the manufacture of cocoa, chocolate and chicory from Tuke and Co. His main product continued to be Tuke's Rock Cocoa, though in a very small way; the total amount of cocoa sold there in the mid-nineteenth century was probably not more than twelve hundredweights a week.

But with a shrewd eye to the future, H. I. Rowntree—who was to be joined by his brother, Joseph, in 1869—took over an old foundry in Tanner's Moat, a site between the city wall and the river which was to be operative until 1908. The six-storey building had no lifts and was remembered grimly for its endless flights of stairs; many of the workrooms were badly shaped and poorly lighted. Seebohm Rowntree, one of Joseph's sons, said in his old age that "Tanner's Moat was Hell".

Towards the end of the century, twenty-four acres of land were bought on the northern edge of the city, between the Haxby and Wigginton Roads. The nucleus of today's complex began to take shape, purpose-built, electrically powered. In 1896 weekly working hours were reduced to forty-eight. The twentieth century was just around the corner; it was to see a bold social experiment just a little further up the road from where the new buildings were adding their contribution to the modern city.

7

ALL'S WELL WITHIN THE WALL

A SATURDAY night in the summer of 1900. The city's gas-lamps flowered in the dusk. In the distant suburbs ribboned maids drew curtains against the fading light. Down in the Hungate slums the landlord of a public house—its grimy parlour could hold ten drinkers—had spent the day serving 550 customers drawn from a hundred insanitary courtyards where Sunday morning's warming sun would prod a dusty finger into unpaved corners, stirring up the scent of poverty.

The customers were counted over a period of seventeen hours that day by investigators who provided statistics for Seebohm Rowntree's book on poverty in the city. Hungate and areas like it were the outcome of the nineteenth-century population explosion which produced 77,793 inhabitants in 1901 where there had been only 16,846 in 1801. The hungry 'forties brought immigrants from famine-struck Ireland—more than a million by 1844, with 50,000 still coming every year. Though the majority settled in the industrial cities, some came to York, probably to find work in the chicory industry. Rowntree observed that on summer evenings it was a common sight to see the women in the Irish quarter sitting on the kerbstones outside their cottages, smoking clay pipes. The opening of the railway brought workers from other parts of the country, and the confectionery trade gradually expanded until by the beginning of this century between 2,000 and 3,000 were employed in the works.

During their vigil in Hungate, Rowntree's investigators (how did they pass themselves off successfully in such a tightly knit community?) saw 258 men, 179 women and 113 children enter the public house which opened its doors at 7.40 in the morning. Between 10 and 11 am several of the women residents returned with bundles of all sizes and shapes, presumably from the pawnshop. Taking up their posts about noon one Sunday later in the month, they found all the small shops open and doing brisk business, especially fried fish shops. Women stood gossiping in the streets while dirty and badly clothed children swarmed around them. In the evening there were several slanging matches between women neighbours when, reported the observers, the language was "very bad". Three men tried to hold a gospel meeting, but gave up after singing a hymn and giving a short address.

Photographs taken at this period exude a grey hopelessness etched on walls and faces. The city's health, though about the same as that of the thirty-three largest towns in England and Wales, was worse than the average, and also below the average for other centres of about the same size. Until 1900 there was no full-time Medical Officer of Health, the post being filled by a doctor with a private practice. Rowntree thought the high death-rate was due to the "insanitary conditions which have for too long been allowed to continue in many of the poorer districts of the city". In 1901 2,229 houses—15 per cent of the total—were without a separate water supply, and of 105 courts shared by the houses built around them, more than half were entirely unpaved. Caught up in this urban tangle were ninety-four private slaughterhouses; none was built in accordance with the local by-laws.

But on a site three miles to the north of York, not far from the new Rowntree factory, times were changing. Under the guidance of the Joseph Rowntree Village Trust, New Earswick, taking its name from the much older village of Earswick lying a short distance to the north-east, began to take shape in the early years of the century. Houses were well spaced and the best use was made of both existing and newly planted trees. Each house was planned so that the main rooms received the most sunlight. In time the Folk Hall became the centre of village life, as it is today, when many of the original houses still hold their own, architecturally, with the best of the inter-war designs. New Earswick is in no sense 'tied'. It was an important principle of the founder that people from all types of employment in the community should be able to make a home there without any feeling of dependence on charitable funds or paternalism in administration. But it differs from its neighbouring villages in one respect . . . there is no public house.

Though there was a sharp increase in population during the first third of this century, the number of licensed premises fell, and it has been estimated that between 1900 and 1936 the average working-class expenditure on drink dropped from 16·6 per cent to about 10 per cent. Higher incomes and shorter working hours created a demand for recreation, and there to fill the gap was the first flicker of the cinema. The first performance in York of 'moving pictures' in the cinematographic sense as opposed to the earlier panoramas and dioramas, was probably given by a Captain Pain who had a booth in the market place about 1900. He was the forerunner of many travelling showmen with the new attraction, and also made the first film in York itself, photographing railwaymen leaving the Leeman Road depot.

Later the shows moved out of the market into the Opera House, the Festival Concert Rooms, the Exhibition Buildings, the Victoria Hall, the New Street Wesleyan Chapel and even the Theatre Royal, home of the live drama for so long and where one would have supposed the film show would be regarded as an unworthy rival. Some time after it closed for worship in 1908, the New Street chapel, a charming building built in the year of Trafalgar and now replaced by a shopping arcade, was taken over by the Yorkshire Bioscope Company and saddled with the name Hippodrome. In 1920 it became the Tower Cinema. Known for a while as the National Picture Theatre, the Victoria Hall in Goodramgate was converted to a dance hall in 1924 and later demolished. The original façade—like a huge proscenium arch overhanging the street—of the first purpose-built cinema in the city may still be seen in Fossgate, though the interior has been a furniture shop since 1957. It was opened as the Electric in 1911 and re-named the Scala in 1951. It was one of eight cinemas which sank into oblivion after the 1939–45 war, leaving only two survivors in the city.

In the days when a motor-car was about as rare as an orchid in the dusty byways, and when horse-power was still taken literally, a small York engineering firm was turning out elegantly furnished steam-driven cars which travelled smoothly and silently with only a slight hiss from the burner. A 1902 catalogue published by the firm—the Gardner-Serpollet Company—reveals how much care was lavished on the hangings, fringes and awnings of these lovingly produced machines. Many were painted in personal liveries, like the carriages of the nobility, and their coachwork design owed much to the phaeton, landau and barouche. Some years ago a 1904 Gardner-Serpollet, in process of being restored, was sent to a coach-painting firm with instructions for it to be repainted in "Dutch pink".

It was explained that this was the traditional Victorian name for carriage livery in one-inch wide dark green and black vertical stripes. The original black leather hood was treated with pints of neatsfoot oil and then polished with three tins of black boot polish to a patent leather shine. Though the Gardner-Serpollet had its drawbacks—notably high fuel and water consumption—its advantages were summed up by an owner who brought one to York for the 1960 rally of the north-eastern section of the Veteran Car Club of Great Britain. "To drive in fine weather in a beautiful steam carriage such as this, in smoothness, silence and comfort, is to experience the supreme satisfaction and pleasure of veteran motoring. By comparison, and with all due respect, the veteran petrol car is noisy, rough and uninteresting."

The British rights for the Gardner-Serpollet patent were acquired by the British Power Traction and Lighting Co. Ltd of Hull Road, York. Potential customers were told that their cars could be turned in the same space as any horse-drawn carriage and were "instantly responsive to the will of the driver". As silent in running as an electrically propelled vehicle, the cars would take "reasonable hills" at full speed and long, difficult hills at 12 miles per hour. "The fuel", they announced, "is common petroleum (not petrol) or ordinary paraffin lamp oil which can be readily procured in any town or village." Extras included a detachable waterproof front canopy with bevelled plate glass windguard and side curtains at 25 guineas; side lamps for electric light at 13 guineas; a family crest with motto at one guinea and a coat of arms at 3 guineas.

Supplied free with each car were a complete set of tools, two oil cans, six spare springs, three dozen joint rings, two spare steam valves, two spare pump valves, one tyre inflator, one water filter funnel, one methylated spirit can, one signalling horn and two gallons of special cylinder oil.

For a variety of reasons, the York company did not prosper, and in 1903 a winding-up order was made against them. The company had been promoted in 1900 with a capital of £52,000 and although it had interests in Halifax, Bradford and London,

it concentrated its business on the Hull Road factory. Among the difficulties the company had to face were failure to have the cars ready for delivery, training workmen in what was then a new industry, and lack of capital. It might be fair to add that, in the steam car, they had also backed the wrong horse.

Two small incidents in York in the years 1902–3 may give some idea of the public's attitude to motoring. One September afternoon in 1902, ex-Superintendent Dove, who had recently retired from the North Riding police, was driving his horse and trap in Goodramgate. The next moment his horse shied, lost its footing, overturned the trap and threw Mr Dove into the road. This accident, the local newspaper reported rather indignantly, was caused by "the passage of a swift-travelling motor-car". Prejudice against this new form of transport also crept into local politics. Some people objected to voters being taken to the polls by car. A horse-drawn vehicle was admissible, but a car ride, they said, was "equivalent to offering a voter half a pint of beer or a couple of shillings".

Seebohm Rowntree's York has gone now, with the slaughter-houses and the crowded courts. The city is spruce but traffic-bound; flower-hung but fume-choked. If only the steam car had prospered. An example of the breed is still to be found in a little Edwardian garage where the walls carry plates advertising forgotten products of the days when petrol was supplied either by the tin or was hand-cranked from one of the new-style pumps. It is to be found in Half Moon Court, a pedestrian precinct *par excellence* which no traffic has ever invaded, nor ever will, for it is one of the period streets reconstructed in the York Castle Museum.

Alderman's Walk, Kirkgate, Princess Mary Court and Half Moon Court, their vacuum-cleaned cobbles and flagstones trodden by more than 700,000 visitors a year, are just as much a part of York's streetscape as Stonegate and Petergate. The museum now occupies two of the three elegant eighteenth-century buildings which flank the Eye of Yorkshire, a grass circle in the castle yard which has been everything from a jousting ground in Plantagenet times to a vegetable garden during the 1939–45 war. But the nucleus opened on St George's Day, 1938, to provide the country with an enchanting interpretation of the concept 'museum' and a lasting crystallization of the principles

12

The dramatic curve of York Station

laid down by a Pickering doctor. Everything sprang from the
brain of Dr John Kirk who, in the 'thirties, advertised for the
disposal of "bygones" which he had collected over many years
from the district around his home. At about that time York
Corporation bought the derelict Female Prison and Debtors'
Prison from the County Committee, and the Female Prison
was to form the new home for the doctor's unusual collection.

Between 1933 and 1938 the donor planned the layout of
Alderman's Walk and Kirkgate, gathering the shop fronts which
were to be re-erected, and working closely with the late Dr
J. B. Morrell who was mainly responsible for the creation of
the museum. The names of the streets (Dr Morrell was then a
city alderman) commemorate the two men. Dr Kirk is further
remembered by the erection of his brass plate outside a Georgian
door in the far corner of the street, and a bronze plaque put up
after his death in 1940.

The museum is planned so that the visitor's first glimpse of
Kirkgate is through a Georgian bow window at first floor level,
an inspired introduction to the collection's vital heart. On grey
winter afternoons when the lights in the shop windows are as
warm as childhood memories, or in summer when sunlight falls
through the diffusing screen of the glass ceiling to make dark
shadows across the uneven cobbles, the scene is one of endless
fascination. Its beauty lies in correctness and sincerity; the lily
has not been over-gilded. There are no mistakes here, in the
living past.

This viewpoint is reached by way of four period rooms—
Jacobean, Georgian, Moorland Cottage and Victorian—all carefully re-created in fine detail. In the parlour of the 1850s aspi-
distras droop, the caged bird in the window is frozen in full
song and a gilt cobweb clings to the shaft of the ornate chandelier.
The Berlin needlework, the wax fruit, the fretwork-fronted
piano and the brooding daguerreotypes dream of a world where
it took a great deal to disturb the rooks in the rectory elms.
When the brass cylinder of the musical box revolves, the room
is filled with gaslight ghosts.

Socially, the parlour has its counterpart in Half Moon Court,
created from the old Unshackling Yard of the Debtors' Prison.
Here, with the Edwardian garage as a near neighbour, is the
King William IV, a public house in the brass and glass style
of the last century which was transferred from its original site

in Walmgate, saved from the tide of progress. During the rebuilding of this pub the museum's curator, Robert Patterson, insisted on the ceiling's being stained the correct shade of tobacco-smoked brown. Over the door is the name of the licensee—Barbara Kelly. A nice touch, for the television star, a confirmed York-lover, opened the new street in 1963, and I have affectionate memories of that day when the bat's-wing gas jets flared and the beer flowed in the crowded bar of the King William.

Across in Princess Mary Court the right-hand window of Joseph Terry's sweet shop once looked out on to a Doncaster street, but it is quite at home in its present surroundings for the shop to which it originally belonged specialized in mint humbugs. The appeal of the sweets, all made to the old recipes, is simple and direct. They contribute to the delicate and haunting aroma inside the shop where curious "conversation lozenges" offer their urgent messages and gentle reproofs.

The door of Peter Pickering's apothecary's shop has not been opened for many years. No bell could tinkle into life the days when doctors were top-hatted and moist leeches were found in every surgery. But his twin bow windows at the junction of Kirkgate and Alderman's Walk still fascinate. The barbaric dental instruments (a glass of brandy was the anaesthetic), the puce and gold leech jar and the elaborate blood-letting apparatus are matched by stoppered phials of cordial well over a century old but, on analysis, found to be still quite wholesome.

Dimly lit, the Agricultural Gallery is charged with atmosphere. The rough stone walls, heavy beams and horn lanterns form a perfect replica of an old barn, a link with the sweet, half-forgotten scent of the stored fruits of the earth. In this section one may not only see the countryman's heritage but hear the speech which has been handed down to him, homespun and forthright. A touch of a button brings tape-recordings of dialect examples from the three Ridings.

To represent the large military section in the Debtors' Prison I choose one of the most romantic tales ever to emerge from a campaign. On the eve of a war which was to lay its dead hand on an established way of life, there died a Yorkshireman who remembered the thunder of cavalry and the sun's flash on the sword blade. When he died in his eighty-first year on 16th October 1913, Sir George Orby Wombwell, Bt, of Newburgh

Priory, was the last surviving officer of the Light Brigade's famous charge at Balaclava on 25th October 1854. He could not know, when he left for the Crimea as a 20-year-old senior lieutenant of the 17th Lancers, that he would one day be High Sheriff of his county and be affectionately known as "The Grand Old Man of Yorkshire". Nor could he foresee the day when his uniform, portrait and mementos would find an honourable place in a York museum, twenty miles from his Coxwold home. His experiences in the charge are best told in his own words:

"My horse was shot under me, in what place I know not, but down he came. I, luckily, soon caught a trooper which had lost its rider and got on his back and joined the second line." But this horse at first refused to move. "I at last got him into a slow walk, and was congratulating myself on having passed unseen two squadrons of Russian lancers, when suddenly a horrid yell arose and I was surrounded by a lot of them brandishing their swords and lances and desiring me to throw down my sword which, seeing resistance was useless, I did. They then seized my pistols and my holsters and helped me, in a very rough way, off my wounded trooper, and marched me off a prisoner on foot between two of them, with three more behind. I, of course, walked quietly with them, but seeing the 11th Hussars coming back at a gallop, when they got near I made a rush forward and luckily got another trooper on which I jumped and joined the 11th and rode back with them."

He was, of course, Coxwold's hero. I recall visiting a cottage in the village some years ago to find the walls crowded with photographs of Sir George in his old age and engravings of him in his elaborate lancer's uniform. He is buried in Coxwold churchyard, not far from the spot where, in 1969, the bones of Laurence Sterne, the clerical wit and novelist, were re-interred after having been taken from the cemetery of St George's, Hanover Square, where they had lain since 1768. Well known in York, Sterne was the great-grandson of Richard Sterne, Archbishop in 1664–83, and became the incumbent at Coxwold about the time his two-volume *Tristram Shandy* was printed and published in the city. The novelist's old home, his "peaceful cottage", is Shandy Hall, opposite Coxwold church, and now restored for use as a centre for students of Sterne's life and work.

There is a refreshing lack of smugness in a museum which never stands still. Even now, plans are going ahead to extend the range of exhibits into the 'twenties. But the curator and his staff will face their biggest challenge when the green light is given for the creation of a folk park, an outdoor version of the Castle Museum concept, but concentrating on rural life.

Folk parks are a century old. In 1872 Dr Arthur Hazelius— Sweden's equivalent of Dr Kirk—began to collect objects rooted in his country's pre-industrial past, then turned his attention to entire buildings. Houses saved from demolition were gradually re-erected in Stockholm's Royal Deer Park to form the heart of the now world-famous Skansen folk park with its craft workshops, farmsteads, country mansions and windmills.

Britain's first folk museum was established on the island of Iona in 1936, and Wales produced the first national museum of this type just after the 1939-45 war when the Earl of Plymouth offered St Fagan's Castle with its eighteen acres of grounds to the National Museum of Wales. The rocky, wooded grounds are now a setting for typical buildings from all parts of the Principality, including not only farms and cottages but a Unitarian chapel.

Although it is no longer possible for York to be first in the field, it must ensure that it produces one of the most representative parks on a site large enough to give it the necessary scale. Established folk parks vary in size from 25 to 200 acres with 20 to 200 re-erected buildings. York's, covering perhaps 12 acres in its early years, should be capable of being expanded to 40 or 50 acres.

Before his retirement, the Castle Museum curator, Mr Robert Patterson, visualized a folk park of Yorkshire life including a village green with its pond, maypole, village hall, yeomen's cottages, smithy, wheelwright, pub, store, stocks, ducking stool and everything associated with village life.

Beyond would be found a boat-builder's yard and ropewalk, a gipsy encampment and a farmhouse with its cluster of byres and barns. The highest point would be reserved for a windmill, and a secluded corner for a Troy Town maze, just like Skansen's Trojeborg Maze which has been copied from the example at Visby in Gotland. A similar maze is to be seen at the roadside near Dalby in North Yorkshire. This is the county's only surviving evidence of an ancient game, mentioned by Shakespeare in *A Midsummer Night's Dream*. In various parts of the country the mazes are known as Julian Bower, Robin Hood's Race, Shepherd's Ring, Walls of Troy or City of Troy. Dalby's has always been known as City of Troy, proof of the early association between Yorkshire and Scandinavia.

The buildings would be correctly furnished in their period and wherever possible it would be the aim to have the work-shops actually in use with a craftsman performing the old handcrafts.

There should have been a place in the projected museum for an unusual Dutch-style drawbridge which spanned the river Derwent at Wheldrake, near York. Now destroyed by fire, the bridge closely resembled the drawbridge at Arles, painted by Vincent Van Gogh in 1888. This style of bridge was probably introduced in East Yorkshire by Dutch and Flemish settlers who followed Cornelius Vermuyden, the Dutch engineer, when he came to Yorkshire in the early seventeenth century to cut the Dutch River from the Don to Goole.

Mr Patterson believes that the ideal site for the folk park is as close as possible to a recognized source of visitor attraction, and that it would be difficult to imagine a more admirable centre than York. There should be water on the site, either in the form of a pond, or preferably a river. A river frontage would open up the possibility of transport by waterbus from the Castle Museum which backs on to the River Foss, an Ouse tributary.

Such a park would be the Castle Museum's open-air com-plement—and a necessary one, bearing in mind that country life is not fully represented under cover, and that soon there will be no more space for expansion. Major schemes at the museum came to an end with the building of the joint entrance block between the two buildings, though the roofing of the exercise yard at the rear of the Debtors' Prison may be considered.

At present York is preoccupied with the benefits—or evils—of ring roads, but I feel that the first priority after the unravelling of this knot is the establishment of the folk park without further delay. After all, the city has nailed its colours to the mast as a leading tourist centre, appointed a Director of Tourism and spent a great deal of money on the year-long 1900th anniversary celebrations with their side benefits of extended publicity. The folk park is as important to York as the establishment of some major industry would be in other centres. There is no reason why the attendance figure at the museum and park should not be boosted to the million mark.

One of the most protracted North–South battles to be fought in recent years was over the siting of the new National Railway Museum. York, already the home of one of the country's three railway museums, won the day, surviving brickbats and a change of government. The city's member of parliament campaigned ceaselessly and the Ombudsman backed York's claim. Against York were ranged Prince Philip, Lord Montagu of Beaulieu, *The Times*, the Transport Trust, the London Boroughs' Association and the Victorian Society. Formidable opposition, but it was only common sense to place this great museum in the North where the railways began in 1825.

It was in 1925, during the centenary celebrations of the opening of the Stockton–Darlington line (Locomotion No 1 was the first engine to pull a passenger train on the first run from Shildon to Stockton on 27th September 1825) that the directors of the old North Eastern Railway Company became conscious of the need to preserve relics of the early days. Three years later the York Railway Museum began to exercise its peculiar fascination, an attraction underlined by Lord Montagu in 1967 when he said, during a Lords debate, "I have found that British people are more interested in transport relics than Van Dycks, lions or even nudist colonies."

No national museum has ever been sited outside the capital, so the precedent of the National Railway Museum was watched with wide interest—and southern distress. There was a rowdy scene in the Commons in July 1969 as Miss Jennie Lee, then Minister for the Arts, defended the decision to move the museum from Clapham to York. "We have got to be a little careful," she said, "when men are trying to reach the moon, of assuming that to go to Oxford or Cambridge or York is a journey beyond the capacity of those with specialist interests." In the September, though it was said with confidence that work would start on the York museum within a year, the southern factions continued to put out smoke. Lord Montagu, still battling, said that certain people in Yorkshire and newspapers in the county showed an almost paranoid tendency whenever keeping the museum in London was discussed. Those who put forward the view that it should be retained in the capital were called "metropolitan maniacs", and Lord Montagu deeply resented this charge. It was unrealistic, he said, to expect tourists coming to Britain for only a few days to travel to York.

Plans for the new two-storey museum with café on the Leeman Road site were approved by the city's Development and Planning Committee in February 1970. The main part of the museum is housed in an existing engine shed, refronted and with an extension block added on land that has been cleared of old buildings.

Barriers give access to the refreshment room, lecture room, studios, book store and viewing gallery overlooking the main exhibition area occupied by two wheel-type formations centred on engine turntables, each providing exhibition bays running from the turntable like wheel spokes. The larger has twenty-two bays, the smaller twenty.

There was an agonizing pause with a change of government when Lord Eccles, Paymaster-General, reconsidered the whole question. He visited the site in October 1970 and admitted that it would be extremely difficult to match it in London. At the Guildhall he was presented with a petition carrying nearly 90,000 signatures, by a man who had organized a procession of traction engines, vintage cars and veteran cycles from the Leeman Road site. The signed copies of the petition were carried in a coffin on a trailer pulled by one of the traction engines.

But in May 1971 Lord Eccles announced that it was full steam ahead for the York museum, which would be run by the Science Museum. Historic rail records would be kept in London, eventually at the new Public Record Office at Kew. Responsibility for the building of the new museum would be undertaken by the British Transport Board.

In the "ticking over" period, before the making of this important decision, the York Railway Museum was very capably run by a skeleton staff of retired railwaymen who, I felt, were stopping rail history from seeping away through the cracks in time. All were in their seventies; except an 81-year-old who did a four-hour daily stint of duty. Some of the exhibits are awesome; their suppressed power, one feels, is only just contained within the museum walls. But others are ephemeral, like the name-board of that fifty-two-letter Anglesey station known familiarly, and conveniently, as "Llanfair PG". Outsize platform tickets for this station were also on sale. Asked to pronounce it, one attendant always said "Manchester".

Railway architecture in this country has such a quality of 'belonging' that its origins now seem curiously remote, so that it is hard to believe that in less than 150 years it has done more to change the shape and feel of our towns than any other single influence. It was the architecture of revolution, transferring to train shed, concourse and platform some of the mystique of cathedral building. Away from the dynamics of iron and glass, it had its odd moments when individualism ran riot; when station buildings took on the coy guise of Tudor cottages or eighteenth-century orangeries. But in the main it became the symbol of industrial power, backed by new skills devised by the engineer. So, in 1967, the release of detailed plans for the new British Rail Eastern Region headquarters was of more than ordinary interest.

The regional architect responsible lived in the York area and was fully aware of the challenge facing him when he was called upon to build within a stone's throw of the city's medieval walls. By using blocks of differing heights—two of six storeys and two of four—staggering their positions to form an internal court and making the whole concept subordinate to the headquarters building of 1904—a version of Norman Shaw's Queen Anne style—he showed sympathy for a very touchy area of the city. Semi-mature trees and urban floorscaping complement the shape, colour and texture of the new buildings, and the walls have not suffered from their presence, as there is something inherently 'fortified' in their appearance. The whole complex was given the name Hudson House, first step in the rehabilitation of the railway financier, George Hudson.

York's ability to assimilate new buildings has been seriously questioned in the years since the war, and not all ventures have been as successful as the BR buildings. The Baedeker raid on the city in April 1942 did not cause widespread destruction, so there was no peace-time call for radical redevelopment. But in the early 1950s the eastern end of Pavement was demolished to create a new road, The Stonebow, to link up with Peasholme Green and to allow the buses to dodge the dangerously narrow St Saviourgate. One of the first buildings on the site—the new telephone exchange—was highly praised, but the subsequent in-filling has been of a very pedestrian type. That is, until the early 'sixties when Stonebow House began to rise on the north-western side of the street.

This curving building, constructed of slotted concrete beams, and carrying a tower block, perhaps erred in the other direction—it was too brutal for its near neighbours, the Centenary Chapel of 1839–40, the Unitarian Chapel of 1693 and the redundant but still attractive St Saviour's Church. However, it is on the fringe of the medieval core and not too intrusive, unlike a pale brick office block of the 'seventies which, though quite innocuous in isolation, now appears to diminish Fishergate Postern, the castle wall, the clock tower of the Debtors' Prison and the Castle Museum in a most disturbing way.

In 1965, at a cost of more than £600,000 a club and Tattersalls grandstand was built on the Knavesmire racecourse, centre of the sport in York since the early years of the reign of George II. Its seven floors are linked by a lift and escalators, and its purely functional style caused little comment. But in the heart of the city there have been one or two developments which have raised the dust of controversy, notably in King's Square and Goodramgate. With properties dating from the fourteenth century to the eighteenth, King's Square provides an attractive approach to the top of the Shambles, best known of the city's medieval streets. In the 'sixties a run-down Georgian house and other small buildings were demolished on the west side of the square and replaced by an office block which attempts the marriage of both medieval gables and the Georgian colonnade. I have always felt that the model for this type of development is St Werburgh's Row in Chester. The Goodramgate development, which provides a common frontage for a super-market, restaurant and small shops, is basically not very large, but it is seriously at odds with the charmingly unplanned character of the street, which includes some of the country's oldest houses, and its shallow arches of shuttered concrete stamp it as an interloper.

Three major developments of the last few years have been connected with leisure and pleasure—the Viking Hotel in riverside North Street, the Theatre Royal extension in St Leonard's Place and the Post House Motor Hotel in the western suburb of Dringhouses.

The Viking Hotel, designed on Scandinavian lines, replaced dingy warehouses in a rather neglected street running from

Ouse Bridge to Lendal Bridge. Its builders, in co-operation with the department store which lies between it and Ouse Bridge, created the first stretch of a corporation-inspired riverside walk. The hotel's eight storeys now form a brick exclamation mark in an area occupied by an attractive mixture of commercial premises, cottages, a half-timbered corner house, small formal gardens and All Saints' Church. The Post House Motor Hotel, opened in 1971, was built in the garden of a demolished manor and retains, as a central feature, a 200-year-old Lebanon cedar.

The theatre extension, though miniature in scale compared with these new hotels, is exciting and dramatic. Glass, light, space, cool shades of green and the constant interplay of life and art . . . it was a real-life transformation scene in the heart of the city. The crowning point of four years' planning was reached in December 1967 with the reopening of the revitalized building after only seven months' closure.

The theatre façade was sandblasted to reveal something unsuspected—a creamy sandstone building of High Victorian charm which complements the elegance of the curving 1835 terrace on the opposite side of the street. The building now has dramatic texture. Its medallion heads are seen properly for the first time in generations and skilful adaptation of the old entrance has given the frontage that greatest of all architectural assets, a colonnade.

But it is on the building's north side that a small miracle has been worked. Soaring from the garden there, and following the flowing lines of the mature trees close by, is the glass and concrete foyer wing, designed by London architect Patrick Gwynne. It is as light as a newly blown bubble, hardly seeming to touch the ground at all. It might have landed a minute ago on the slender stalks of its hexagonal supports. It is here that the interchange of outer and inner life between the city and the theatre takes place. Passers-by see clearly the movement of the theatre's social life on different levels. From the inside it seems possible to reach out and touch the day-to-day bustle of the street. The large trees outside are so close to the glass that in winter their black tracery seems part of the décor. In summer, the leaves filter sunlight through the airy, dynamic spaces. The tree motif is followed through in the curving cantilever staircase, supported on branch-like arms, and rising to a blue ceiling set with circular illuminated openings.

The foyer wing is the most exciting and satisfying of York's post-war architectural developments. The architect's achievement affects not only the theatre; it reaches out and enhances the whole area. Doubts about the 'marrying' of the foyer and the old theatre are dispelled by walking up the new staircase and watching the changing textures of what was once an outside wall. New wing and old building are immediately 'right' together in the same way that a Victorian oil lamp, all brass and engraved glass, is at home in the most modern room.

Trees, grass, water . . . between them they also work a quiet miracle, giving instant permanence to the newest buildings. Of the three, water is the most effective softener. Helped by islands, fountains and a winding course, it can break down stone, concrete and brick into the stuff of life. Nowhere in the York area is its effect so dramatically unfolded as on the University of York's 200 acres in the East Riding village of Heslington, only two miles south-east of the city centre. As the University expands (the sixth college will be completed by October 1972) a new landscape is neatly moved into place in the wake of the contractors. Landscape gardeners of the past did not see their work in its maturity, but today there is a head start on time by the use of large trees, like the thirty-foot chestnut transplanted from Castle Howard and now flourishing at the corner of one of the colleges.

But it is in its wildlife that Heslington takes the lead over the average campus. The grounds are filled with an astonishing variety of birds, which find perfect shelter in the topiary garden of Heslington Hall, a restored Elizabethan mansion now serving as the administrative headquarters. But this is only the fortuitous wildlife section. The planned bird life—exotic ducks and geese—has become an essential part of the great fifteen-acre, plastic-lined lake, the original top pond and the islands. The ducks, including the normally shy mallard, respond to twice-a-day feeding, and an increasing interest in them is taken by students, academic staff and the gardeners . . . one ensures that the ice is broken for them early on winter mornings. The basic ingredient of the whole plan is the natural stream which runs through woods to the north of the village, dives under one of the colleges and breaks surface in the guise of the sophisticated Water Court. Given a bit of luck, there is no reason why the progeny of these mallards, pintails, mandarins, coots and shovellers should not be bobbing about the mature landscape of York University centuries from now. After all, the descendants of Charles II's ducks still live on the lake in St James's Park.

The University of York is collegiate, so that students may have a centre of loyalty smaller than the whole university. Every student, and every member of the staff belongs to a college, each having about 390 undergraduate, 100 graduate and 45 academic staff members.

The first five colleges, Alcuin, Derwent, Goodricke, Langwith and Vanbrugh, together with biology, chemistry and physics laboratories, the library, the language centre, the computer building, the concert hall, the central hall, the sports centre and the boathouse are in use. The development plan provides for the phased construction of further colleges and extensions to those already existing. In the city itself, the University occupies the King's Manor, used principally by the Institute of Advanced Architectural Studies; the Borthwick Institute of Historical Research, housed in a medieval guildhall in Peasholme Green; and two handsome Georgian houses in Micklegate. The University-based York Film Theatre, with 1,500 members, has done much to draw town and gown together.

York petitioned for the establishment of a university in 1641, but it was not until 1947 that a planning committee was set up, to be taken over as an academic development committee of the York Civic Trust in 1949. By 1953 the Borthwick and Architectural Institutes had been established. Three years later the academic development committee separated from the Civic Trust to become the York Academic Trust. In 1959 the Trust made an informal approach to the University Grants Committee and in the November of that year the York University Promotion Committee was formed. The creation of the University was officially approved in April 1960. A public appeal for funds was launched in May 1962 and about £1,750,000 has been given or promised towards the target of £2,000,000.

Before the creation of the University, York already held a prime position in the educational field, offering for boys St Peter's School (Guy Fawkes was a pupil); Bootham School, founded by the Society of Friends; Archbishop Holgate's School, established in the sixteenth century; and Nunthorpe Grammar School, opened in 1920. On the south side of the Minster is a very special school—the York Minster Song School, where lessons are punctuated by choir practices and services and whose pupils never fail to lift their red caps to waiting motorists on each side of the busy zebra crossing which leads to the Minster's south door. For girls there are The Mount, another leading Quaker school; York College for Girls; Queen Anne Grammar School, founded in the early years of this century; and Mill Mount Grammar School, dating from 1920. York's reorganized secondary education system, however, proposed the end of two single-sex schools. It was decided that Archbishop Holgate's and Queen Anne Grammar School would take both sexes.*

Primary and secondary modern school accommodation has increased considerably since the war, and the scattered departments of the former York Technical College have been regrouped as the York College of Arts and Technology and housed in new buildings near the city's western boundary.

The removal of Archbishop Holgate's School to new premises on the Hull Road allowed for the expansion of its neighbour in Lord Mayor's Walk, St John's College, opened in May 1841 as a residential teacher training school for the diocese of York. The building in Lord Mayor's Walk was provided four years later at a cost of £12,000. It has since developed into a substantial college of education, the College of Ripon and York St John, with annexes in the suburb of Heworth and a History Department superbly sited in Gray's Court.

Perhaps in an attempt to get away from the car and the television set which have been the main sources of recreation in recent years, more than 3,000 York citizens are now involved in four evening class centres. About 2,000 attend the 150 classes offered at three secondary modern schools, and the remainder sign on at the Marygate Centre of Further Education. Add to this the more academically inclined York Educational Settlement and the School of Art, and it will be seen that the city is experiencing something of a boom in leisure-time learning. The reason for the largely non-vocational aspect of the courses is to be found in the start of the day-release system through which young people were given time off work by law; the old image of 'night school' has faded. In time, it is hoped, a number of schools scattered around the city will have something to offer the whole family between 9 am and 9 pm.

* In May 1976 the North Yorkshire County Council Education Committee voted in favour of a middle-school comprehensive system for York.

In the light of the present-day popularity of the city's central library and its branches, and of the extent of the reference library with its incomparable local history collection, it is hard to believe that it took forty years for the ratepayers to back the corporation in its adoption of the Public Libraries Act of 1850. It was not until 1893 that a public library was opened in a building in Clifford Street formerly occupied by the Institute of Popular Science and Literature, two years after the third, and final, citizens' poll on the question had given the go-ahead. In 1917 the York Subscription Library, founded in 1794, was merged with the public library.

In 1924 the corporation decided to accept an offer of £13,000 by the Carnegie Trustees and to start building a new library in Museum Street on a site near the ruined chapel of St Leonard's Hospital and overlooking the Museum Gardens and the interior of the 1,600-year-old Multangular Tower. Though extensions have been made over the years, the library is still pressed for space; the only direction for expansion is upwards.

The local history collection includes not only volumes but files of prints, photographs and slides, and the source of raw social history—bound copies of the local newspapers dating back to 27th August 1722. Much of the drudgery of newspaper research has been removed by the gradual building up, through the painstaking work of the reference library staff, of a newspaper index, cataloguing the minutiae of everyday life in the city over 250 years; a self-perpetuating task of inestimable value. The newspapers of the eighteenth century, printed on hand-made paper, are in near-perfect condition, but deterioration sets in as the centuries advance and newsprint becomes fragile with age. To counteract this, many volumes have been transferred to microfilm. Complementary to the reference library, the information bureau was set up in 1949 and after a spell in the nearby ruined chapel, finally settled in a ground floor wing of the main building.

York's evening and weekly newspapers, now part of the large Westminster Press group, met their greatest challenge in April 1942 when fire-bombs dropped in the Baedeker raid partly destroyed the offices and works. The brass titles were snatched from the flames and publication was continued for a time from the offices of the now defunct *Yorkshire Evening News* in Leeds under a reciprocal arrangement.

The *Evening Press*, which celebrates its centenary in 1982, did much to present the full impact of the most important document ever to concern the city—Viscount Esher's report to the Minister of Housing and Local Government and York City Council on the conservation of the historic core. The paper published an illustrated digest of the £7 report at a twentieth of the price.

Produced in 1968, this was one of four reports on the historic towns of Bath, Chester, Chichester and York, commissioned jointly by the Minister of Housing and Local Government and the city and county councils concerned, the purpose being to discover how to reconcile our old towns with the twentieth century without actually knocking them down. The problem facing Lord Esher was how to preserve and enhance York's architectural heritage and at the same time ensure that the heart of the city remains alive and able to compete on level terms with its neighbours. It was believed that the environment should be so improved by the elimination of decay, congestion and noise that the centre will become highly attractive as a place to live in for families, students, single persons and the retired. Land uses which conflict with these purposes should be progressively removed from the walled city, and the historic character of York should be so enhanced and the best of its buildings of all ages so secured that they become automatically self-conserving.

York City Council can claim, with some justification, to have spent more money on the conservation and restoration of its heritage than any city of comparable size in the United Kingdom. Between the end of the war and the publication of the report more than £200,000 had been spent on such major projects as the restoration of the walls and the four medieval bars, the refurbishing of the Georgian Assembly Rooms and the reconstruction of the Shambles.

The report acknowledges that learned and voluntary societies have led the way in helping to preserve historic buildings, and mentions the Yorkshire Philosophical Society, the Yorkshire Architectural and York Archaeological Society, the York Georgian Society, the York Civic Trust and the Archbishop's Commission on Redundant Churches. But there was a word of warning. Though from the street York looked cleaner and neater than it had done for over a century, the state of its fabric

Castle Museum
Folk Hall, New Earswick

was precarious, despite devoted work by the corporation and private initiative. The critical state of the Minster, at the time the report was published, was representative of the state of medieval and Georgian York as a whole.

Five courses of immediate action were recommended: Legislation giving local authorities special powers within conservation areas; the creation of a new close south of the Minster, traffic-free, with lawns and paved areas; the designation of Aldwark and Swinegate as action areas, with a phased programme for their clearance and redevelopment; site acquisition and construction of the first of four multi-storey car parks.

The city walls, said the report, identified the historic core as effectively as the walls of a room. Once inside them, there was an unmistakable change of atmosphere which cast certain types of buildings, vehicles and noises in the role of intruders.

It is true, as the report points out, that the Minster is not helped by its topography. In spite of its size, it does not dominate the historic core. The secular city, one of the richest and most complex townscapes in the world, was seen by the Esher team to provide the visual wealth of York. They saw that its materials were dark and rich, its streets narrow and bent, closing all vistas and leading the walker around corners. Wide and straight streets seemed alien in this context.

One of the problems of creating an inner ring road in such a city is that the scale of a four-lane carriageway with its necessary roundabouts and junctions, would dwarf the city walls and bars which depend on the contrasting scale of small buildings for their impressiveness. However, subsequent arguments have centred not so much on the walls and bars but on late-Georgian property in The Mount, an elegant approach road to the west of Micklegate Bar, which would be affected by a large roundabout system. Many local architects consider the whole concept of an inner ring road to be faulty, but at its December meeting in 1971 the City Council, after a two-hour debate, came out twenty-five to eleven in favour of a fully off-set junction scheme, costing an extra £750,000 and involving the loss of an additional twenty houses. The off-set junction would divert traffic from the Leeds–Scarborough road to a new road parallel with The Mount and running about eighty-five yards to the east. However, following a public inquiry, the scheme was shelved.

13

The Central Hall, York University
York Racecourse: the Grandstand

Since the publication of the Esher Report, one small positive action has been taken, and plans for a more ambitious step have been put in motion.

Stonegate, described in the report as one of the prettiest luxury shopping streets in the world, became the city's first experimental 'foot street' on 19th January 1971. Its future was toasted in white wine at one of the most unusual celebration meals ever seen in York when, at 1 pm, Mrs Barbara Hutton, hon. secretary of York Georgian Society, and Dr Patrick Nuttgens, a former director of York University's Institute of Advanced Architectural Studies and now chairman of the Georgian Society, sat down to a meal of steak and chips in the middle of the street. Dr Nuttgens, director of Leeds Polytechnic, but still devoted to the humanizing of York's city centre, commented: "The fact that we can sit and eat in the middle of the street in the peace and quiet shows what a step forward this is." This romantic gesture opened a series of trial periods leading to the street's permanent designation as a 'foot street' in December 1971. The introduction of limited traffic access between 5 am and 10.30 am was followed by a plan to pave the street from side to side—like London Street in Norwich—and later to extend this treatment to other streets.

The rather forlorn Aldwark area of the city may soon be transformed. It has islands of good buildings—the Merchant Taylors' Hall, St Anthony's Hall, a splendid Georgian terrace in St Saviourgate and a handsome period house in the street of Aldwark itself, recently converted to flats by the York Civic Trust.

Lord Esher's plan here was to get together sites for residential development which would attract high-standard private enterprise; to remove activities which conflicted with residential amenities; to cut out heavy transport and traffic not having business in the area; to enhance the setting of the historic buildings; to provide reasonable space for the shops which fringed the area, so that their prosperity was not handicapped.

Although an offer by York Civic Trust to pay Lord Esher's £25,000 fees for an Aldwark pilot scheme was politely refused by the authorities, the city council nevertheless asked Lord Esher to re-plan this area, and his £3,367,000 vision was published in December 1971. The architect described it as an attempt to restore "snug, friendly, cosy environment" for city-centre living. People, he hoped, would choose to return to the heart of the city, reversing the trend of the past 150 years. Twenty family houses and 231 flats and maisonettes were proposed, accommodating about 760 people. In addition, Aldwark's fascinating jumble of old buildings would be preserved. Even buildings falling to pieces would be taken apart and rebuilt.

The civic trust's offer to get the Aldwark scheme off the ground was the latest in a series of altruistic gestures which have typified the trust's activities since its formation in 1946.

The wide range of its interests is phenomenal, from the nurturing of a university to the gilding of a gas-lamp. In 1971 Exhibition Square was turned into a piazza by the trust's provision of the city's first ornamental fountains, turned on by the Duchess of Kent who, as Miss Katharine Worsley of the North Riding village of Hovingham, was married in the Minster in 1961. The trust has paid for the erection of a 30-foot Roman pillar discovered under the Minster's south transept. On its site opposite the south door, it is a permanent memorial to the year which saw the celebration of the city's 1900th birthday. Floodlighting of monuments, the painting of public coats of arms, the tidying of hidden courtyards, the choice of lettering for the street name-plates, the planting of 1,900 white rose trees, help towards the cost of laying Minster Yard with York stone, the saving of a Jacobean staircase, offering to pay for the restoration of the civic plate, swords and mace, the provision of informative bronze plaques in historic streets, the £20,000 renovation of the unique timber-framed Bowes Morrell House in Walmgate, the recolouring of the twenty or so original firemarks still *in situ* in the city, the bringing back to life of one of the city's most notable Georgian houses—Peasholme House— whose elegant frontage had been hidden for many years by an ugly lean-to building . . . the list is far from complete. In addition, its crusading chairman, Mr John Shannon, who sells York as hard as he can wherever he goes, does not hesitate to lash out at what he considers to be lapses in style and taste.

Where does the trust find the money? Commenting recently on the £25,000 offer in connection with Aldwark, Mr Shannon explained that, as in the case of most of their funds, the money was subscribed by those who, having a great love for the life, form and character of the city but wishing to remain anonymous, saw the trust as a body through which they could best express their concern and regard in a practical way.

The Esher Report, he believes, brought home to the people of York that time was running out. There was a rapid change of climate as they woke up to the fact that York as they knew it could disappear.

Men like John Shannon realize that York's natural tangle needs loving care. The city's jumbled roof-lines, dog-leg alley-ways and sudden courtyards are often inspiring, always entertaining. They may be the mongrel offspring of the un-planned ages, but they have the charm of the unexpected. There have been many heart-cries for visually lively cities, for friendly townscapes made by man for man, but behind the rhetoric there must be action. Someone, somewhere must look after these architectural quirks which make cities like York a con-stantly changing aesthetic adventure. The York Civic Trust has taken over this responsibility gladly.

It is ironical that although the city has the air of a provincial capital, and certainly a county town, no county council has ever sat within its walls. The division of Yorkshire into the Anglo-Saxon thridings—or thirds—ensured that government at county level was dispersed. Since the constitution of the county councils under the Local Government Act of 1888, the centre of the huge and diverse West Riding had been at Wakefield, that of the North Riding at Northallerton, and that of the East Riding at Beverley. The city of York was a county in itself, separate from all three Ridings.

Great changes have been made since April 1974 when the proposed local government reforms took place and a ripple of distress, if not horror, ran through the entire county on learning that this age-old pattern was to be drastically altered.

Under the old boundary system, the West Riding alone was the country's largest county, bigger than Northumberland, or Devon, or Norfolk. The North Riding was bigger than Lanca-shire, and the little East Riding bigger than either Staffordshire or Cheshire. Under the new system, York is surrounded by a county stretching from Settle to Scarborough and from Pickering to Selby. It includes bits of all three Ridings, taking in a remote Pennine area near the Westmorland border, Ripon (Yorkshire's smallest city), Sedbergh and the rural districts of Skipton. York should have become the administrative centre of this new area, 135 miles wide by 50 miles deep.

A month after the proposals were announced, the city council was told that York people would have to fight hard to retain their independence. Anyone who believed in conservation and therefore in the great value of the Esher Report, would need to join in the battle.

In a report issued in May 1971 the council viewed the reorganization plans with dismay because they were unsuited to the needs of the city, unresponsive to the wishes of the citizens and thus undemocratic. There were three main objections. It was claimed that the adoption of the proposals would remove from the city council's control responsibility for education, social services, highways, traffic control and important features of town planning. These and other functions would be handed over to a county council serving a mainly rural area of more than 2,500 square miles on which the city of York at best would have less than a quarter of the seats. The city, which for most of its 1,900 years of existence had provided its own local government services, would be left in a district council area with control of not more than 15 per cent of its total budget.

The large new county council of which York would become a part would be primarily interested in rural matters at a time when York's urban problems in regard to traffic and conservation had never been greater. It was seen as significant that the North Riding County Council's main criticism of the proposals concerned the control of the National Parks, probably the local government problem which least concerned the citizens of York.

It was pointed out that many of those who lived in the area had no links with the city of York, and if the proposals were adopted democratic local government in the city would be weakened and unnecessary tensions would develop between York and its rural associates. The council firmly believed that the implementation of the proposals in their present form would be a disaster for great urban communities such as York. It disturbed the Council to learn that elected representatives of a considerable number of local authorities within the proposed area had already publicly made it clear that they regarded Northallerton, with its population of 8,960, as the natural centre of administration. This effectively demonstrated how little community of interest such areas felt they had with the

city of York. Though there were a number of strategic services
which needed to be provided or planned over a large area, it
was preposterous that the new council should try to provide for
the highly urban community of York almost all its major local
government services.

In the great renaming shuffle York found itself in the new
County of North Yorkshire. Much of the old East Riding was
absorbed by Humberside, while West Yorkshire included districts
based on Bradford, Leeds, Halifax, Dewsbury, Huddersfield and
Wakefield. The dropping of the Anglo-Saxon 'Riding'—an
emotive word for all Yorkshiremen—put paid to any hope that
there might emerge the legendary South Riding which provided
the title for Winifred Holtby's celebrated regional novel of the
'thirties, a book which opens with an accurate description of the
press gallery at County Hall, Beverley. Nevertheless, the new
metropolitan county based on Sheffield and Doncaster was given
the name South Yorkshire.

Despite its pockets of poverty and a reputation for depressed
wage levels, York has an air of prosperity and good living. In
the last twenty years it has built up restaurant and hotel amenities
unrivalled by its giant industrial neighbours, given tourism a
triennial boost with the Festival of the Arts and the Mystery
Plays and won for itself such world-wide publicity during
the 1900th 'birthday party' that about $2\frac{1}{2}$ million visitors came
to the city in 1972 for the twin celebrations—the completion
of the Minister's five-year programme of restoration and
the 500th anniversary of the completion of the present Gothic
building.

For those who remember the spreading flames after the fire-
bomb raid, or broken windows in derelict medieval houses in
the grey post-war years, it is a city transformed, vital, uplifted,
confident. And this is the paradox. In what visitors regard as
the most unchanged of England's cities, all is change. But it
is of a special kind, designed to clear the city's clogged arteries,
step up its heart-beat and to keep intact the charm it has inherited
from the slow centuries.

Fresh with flowers in spring, enlivened by colourful summer
crowds, tinted by the spinning bronze leaves of autumn, turned
into a drypoint etching by the first cool touch of winter, York
is a city for all seasons. Though, in the coming years, the scene-
shifters will be at work and at times the stage management

may show a little, the city will continue to offer its greatest gift—continuity. As the change-ringers' solemn call to evensong falls like a blessing on street and square, all's well within the wall.

INDEX

Acomb Landing, 97
Actors, travelling, 66
Agricola, 18
Alan, Count of Brittany, 54, 90
Albert, Prince, 157
Andrews, G. T., 158, 164
Anglo-Saxon Chronicle, The, 90
Anne, Queen, 58, 83
Apprentices, 139
Archbishop's Palace, ruins of former, 46
Archbishop's Prison, 47
Archbishop's Working Party, 69, 70, 74
Atkinson, Peter, the younger, 116, 119
Automata, 130–1

Baedeker raid (1942) 65, 67, 92, 185, 191
Bagnio, 162
Balaclava, battle of, 180
Banners, guild, 60
Barbican, 87, 102, 113
Barker Tower, 108, 109, 116
Bath-house, Roman, 20, 29
Bawing Tower, 111
Bayldon and Berry, confectioners, 171
Bellfounders, 43
Bishophill, 77, 78, 80, 136, 137, 170
Bishopthorpe, 171
Bishopthorpe Palace, 44
Black Death, 54
Black Hall, 116
Blue Bridge, 118

Bootham Bar, 25, 34, 56, 66, 77, 101, 102, 107, 110, 111, 138, 171
Bootham Park Hospital, 125, 166
Boothe, Abbot Thomas, 57
Boundary reforms, 196–8
Bowes Morrell House, 195
Brigantes, 15
Brigantia, 16
British Power Traction and Lighting Co. Ltd., 176
British Rail, Eastern Region, 108, 156, 185
British Transport Board, 184
Browne, E. Martin, 53
——, John, 37, 87
Buckingham, Duke of, 85
Buckingham Works, 170
Burlington, Earl of, 57, 121, 123, 128

Cappe, the Rev. Newcombe, 146
Caracalla, 15
Carr, John, 123, 124
Castle Howard, 41, 85, 96, 188
Cattle market, 103, 114, 117
Celebrations, 1900th, 13, 22, 30, 60
Centenary Chapel, 166, 186
Cerialis, Q. Petillius, 15, 16, 18
Charles I, King, 45, 46, 62, 82, 106, 127
Charles II, King, 82, 119
Chicken, Richard, 79, 80
Chicory, 167, 168, 173
Cholera, 160, 161
Churches
    All Hallows, 72
    All Saints', Fishergate, 103